Language Impairment and Psychopathology in Infants, Children, and Adolescents

Developmental Clinical Psychology and Psychiatry Series

Series Editor: Alan E. Kazdin, Yale Univdersity

Recent volumes in this series . . .

Language Impairment and Psychopathology in Infants, Children, and Adolescents

Nancy J. Cohen

Volume 45
Developmental Clinical Psychology and Psychiatry

Sage Publications
International Educational and Professional Publisher
Thousand Oaks ▪ London ▪ New Delhi

BS

For information:

Sage Publications, Inc.
2455 Teller Road
Thousand Oaks, California 91320
E-mail: order@sagepub.com

Sage Publications Ltd.
6 Bonhill Street
London EC2A 4PU
United Kingdom

Sage Publications India Pvt. Ltd.
M-32 Market
Greater Kailash I
New Delhi 110 048 India

Printed in the United States of America

Library of Congress Cataloging-in-Publication Data

Cohen, Nancy J. 1941–
Language impairment and psychopathology in infants, children, and adolescents / by Nancy J. Cohen.
    p. cm. — (Developmental clinical psychology and psychiatry ; v. 45)
Includes bibliographical references and index.
ISBN 0-7619-2024-2 (cloth: acid-free paper)
ISBN 0-7619-2025-0 (pbk.: acid-free paper)
    1. Language disorders in children.   2. Language disorders in children—Complications.   3. Child psychopathology.   4. Child psychopathology—Complications.   5. Comorbidity.   I. Title.   II. Series.
    RJ496.L35 C64 2001
    618.92´855—dc21   00-013244

This book is printed on acid-free paper.

01   02   03   04   05   06   07   7   6   5   4   3   2   1

Acquisition Editor: Jim Brace-Thompson
Editorial Assistant: Karen Ehrmann
Production Editor: Sanford Robinson
Editorial Assistant: Cindy Bear
Typesetter: Tina Hill
Indexer: Molly Hall

2/11/04

CONTENTS

SERIES EDITOR'S INTRODUCTION

Interest in child development and adjustment is by no means new. Yet only recently has the study of children benefited from advances in both clinical and scientific research. Advances in the social and biological sciences; the emergence of disciplines and subdisciplines that focus exclusively on childhood and adolescence; and greater appreciation of the impact of such influences as the family, peers, and school have helped accelerate research on developmental psychopathology. Apart from interest in the study of child development and adjustment for its own sake, the need to address clinical problems of adulthood naturally draws one to investigate precursors in childhood and adolescence.

In a relatively brief period, the study of psychopathology among children and adolescents has proliferated considerably. Several different professional journals, annual book series, and handbooks devoted entirely to the study of children and adolescents and their adjustment document the proliferation of work in the field. Nevertheless, there is a paucity of resource material that presents information in an authoritative, systematic, and disseminable fashion. There is a need in the field to convey the latest developments and to represent different disciplines, approaches, and conceptual views to the topics of childhood and adolescent adjustment and maladjustment.

The Sage Series **Developmental Clinical Psychology and Psychiatry** is designed to serve uniquely several needs of the field. The Series encompasses individual monographs prepared by experts in the fields of clinical child psychology, child psychiatry, child development, and related disciplines. The primary focus is on developmental psychopathology, which refers broadly here to the diagnosis, assessment, treatment, and prevention of problems that arise in the period from infancy through adolescence. A working assumption of the Series is that understanding, identifying, and treating problems of youths must draw on multiple disciplines and diverse views within a given discipline.

The task for individual contributors is to present the latest theory and research on various topics, including specific types of dysfunction, diagnostic and treatment approaches, and special problem areas that affect adjustment. Core topics in clinical work are addressed by the Series. Authors are asked to bridge potential theory, research, and clinical practice and to outline the current status and future directions. The goals of the Series and the tasks presented to individual contributors are demanding. We have been extremely fortunate in recruiting leaders in the fields who have been able to translate their recognized scholarship and expertise into highly readable works on contemporary topics.

In this book, Dr. Nancy Cohen examines language and communication impairment and its relation to psychopathology over the course of development. This is an enormously important topic. Perhaps the most significant and unrecognized aspect is that impairment in language and communication is highly related to social and emotional functioning. There have been advances in theory, research, and clinical application pertaining to language and communication, and these have remarkable implications for diagnosis, assessment, and intervention with psychiatric disorders as well as with child development more generally. Dr. Cohen provides an authoritative account of the types and range of language and communication impairments and of how language and communication relate to neurological functioning, attachment patterns, emotional regulation, academic achievement, and cognitive development. In addition, the interface of language problems with specific psychiatric diagnoses (e.g., Attention Deficit Hyperactivity Disorder) is well covered. Assessment of language problems over the course of development is nicely detailed. Interventions are covered as well to convey precisely what can be done at different points in development. The advances outlined in this book convey the remarkable progress and critical implications for understanding child functioning. Dr. Cohen has contributed many of the major advances presented in this book. We are quite fortunate to have her evaluation of progress and critical issues.

—ALAN E. KAZDIN, PhD

PREFACE

I came to study the interface between language impairment and psychopathology in the late 1980s. Like those of many researchers, my ideas emerged from observation and clinical practice coupled with reading a pertinent article at a particular moment in time. This turning point occurred while I was carrying out research on the outcome of treatment in a preschool day treatment program. All of the children who attended this program had to have a behavioral or emotional problem to be admitted. For some of the children, language, cognitive, or motor delays were among the reasons for referral. Other children were thought to be developing normally, but when observed by teachers in the intensive 5-day-per-week program, some of these children seemed to have difficulties communicating. Having the luxury of a speech-language pathologist on staff meant that an assessment could be done rapidly. If a language problem was identified, then both remedial help and an alteration in the classroom programming were initiated. Around the same time, a colleague working with adolescents in another intensive program also observed that after routine assessment many youths exhibited a high rate of language impairments and language learning disabilities that often had not been previously identified in the public schools.

Our conversations were stimulated further by an article written by Gualtieri and colleagues (Gualtieri, Koriath, Van Bourgondien, & Saleeby, 1983), who found that when systematically examined, 50% of children in an inpatient unit had a language impairment that had not been identified until the research assessment was done. Many of these children had severe psychiatric problems, and some had subnormal intelligence. Therefore it seemed that 50% might be a high figure. Nevertheless, the article described exactly what my colleague and I had observed in both of the day treatment programs, and the idea of doing a pilot study emerged. We chose as the sample for our study children attending mental health clinics as outpatients because they represent the majority of children for whom such services are sought. That small pilot study showed that 33% of children referred *solely* for a social-emotional disorder had a language impairment that had not been suspected or identified previously (Cohen, Davine, & Meloche-Kelly, 1989). When combined with children whose language impairments had been identified, 50% of children aged 4 to 12 years were language impaired or had a language-related learning disability. This figure was the same as the one reported by Gualtieri et al. (1983) even though the children in our outpatient setting were not so severely disturbed. Since then, we have confirmed these general findings with larger samples (Cohen, Barwick, Horodezky, Vallance, & Im, 1998; Cohen, Davine, Horodezky, Lipsett, & Isaacson, 1993) as have other investigators in the field (Camarata, Hughes, & Ruhl, 1988; Kotsopoulos & Boodoosingh, 1987; Warr-Leeper, Wright, & Mack, 1994), and we have moved downward developmentally to look at preverbal communicative development in infants (Barwick, Cohen, Horodezky, & Lojkasek, 2000).

The same period in the 1980s in which our research program began also witnessed a rapid growth in the understanding of language development, greater awareness of the high prevalence of language impairments in the population, and an increased availability of standardized tools to measure language development and disability. Speech-language pathologists became actively involved in research and clinical work in developmental language impairments and took a broader view of language to include communication disorders (Gallagher, 1999). Just as we had found that children referred for mental health services had problems with language, we also found that they had communication impairments represented by problems with pragmatic language skills and conversational discourse (Vallance, Im, & Cohen, 1999).

Finding that many children in a mental health setting had unsuspected language and communication impairments was unsettling. For instance, at the time our research began in the 1980s, children with co-occurring language impairments and social-emotional problems, and especially children with behavioral problems, were routinely refused service by speech-language pathologists until their behavior problems had been corrected by a mental health practitioner. Similarly, in schools, when a multidisciplinary assessment revealed problems in language and learning that were coupled with behavioral problems, the decision often was made to place the child in a behavioral classroom rather than in a program for children with language-related difficulties. In cases where children were placed in specialized classrooms for language-related learning problems, mental health practitioners breathed a sigh of relief, believing that the language and learning problems were "taken care of." They did not consider that the same difficulties in processing academic information were likely to apply to social and emotional information and therefore to influence therapy. That's history. Over the past decade, there has been increasing awareness that a large proportion of children who are attending speech-language clinics and who are enrolled in classrooms for children with communication and learning disabilities have social-emotional problems. Conversely, there is awareness that a large proportion of children who are referred for mental health services or who are enrolled in classrooms for children with social-emotional disorders have language impairments. The different routes to identification are, to some extent, determined by the vagaries and chance events that lead to any referral to one system or another. A clear direction for referral may be particularly uncertain in this case because it can be difficult to discern what is due to a social-emotional problem from what is due to a problem with language or communication. Therefore there is still cause for concern about the availability of much-needed integrated services. Clinicians and researchers are still struggling to determine how best to treat these co-occurring conditions, and genuine collaborations around service delivery are still rare. This book aims to bridge theory, research, and clinical practice for children in the period of infancy through adolescence. It is not intended to be a blueprint for assessing and treating children with language or communication impairments and social-emotional disorders but, rather, to provide the information that will assist professionals to take a thoughtful, analytical, and critical approach to service delivery. I hope that it will also stimulate further research. The focus is on children who do not have a diagnosis of general developmental delay or significant structural brain injury, autism, or pervasive developmental disorder. Moreover, the focus is on oral language rather than written text, although the latter will be discussed occasionally.

Chapter 1 familiarizes the reader with the terminology of language and communication impairment and social-emotional disorder. An overview of the conditions associated with language impairment is provided in Chapter 2. The way in which language and communication impairments impact on adjustment depends on the developmental tasks with which a child is struggling at any particular point in time. Consequently, in Chapters 3 and 4 a developmental framework is used to examine the relationship between language impairment and psychopathology and associated conditions in relation to normative developmental tasks, first during infancy (Chapter 3) and then in the preschool period, middle childhood, and adolescence (Chapter 4). Possible links between language impairment and psychopathology are examined from a transactional perspective, with the assumption that there is an interplay between language and social-emotional disturbance and the environmental contexts in which children grow up, such that even a relatively mild language impairment can result in serious sequelae. Chapter 5 provides guidelines and measures for identification and assessment of children with co-occurring language impairment and social-emotional disorder. Finally, in Chapter 6, interventions and adaptations of interventions for children with co-occurring language impairment and social-emotional disorder are reviewed. The assumption is made that research and treatment of infants, children, and youths must draw on a developmental knowledge base and that professionals of different disciplines must work together collaboratively. Throughout, case studies illustrate the contribution of language and communication impairments to transactions, adaptations, and maladaptations that can occur during development.

ACKNOWLEDGMENTS

Both individuals and institutions made important contributions to the work reported in this book. In particular, I would like to express appreciation to my collaborators Melanie Barwick, Naomi Horodezky, Nancie Im-Bolter, Lila Isaacson, Mirek Lojkasek, Rosanne Menna, Elisabeth Muir, and Denise Vallance. Each made a unique and important contribution to our research efforts and to the joy of good teamwork. Special thanks to Naomi Horodezky and Melanie Barwick, who read earlier versions of this book. I also want to express appreciation to Health Canada National Health and Research Development Program, the Ontario Mental Health Foundation, and the Social Sciences and Humanities Research Council of Canada for funding the research described in this book. Some of the grants were awarded to my collaborators Melanie Barwick and Denise Vallance. Deep gratitude also needs to be expressed to the families for their participation and to the Hincks-Dellcrest Centre and the George Hull Centre for their institutional support. Finally, at a more personal level, I want to thank Robert Escoe for his patience, his ear, and his unflagging support.

Language tethers us to the world;
without it we spin like atoms.

(Penelope Lively, *Moon Tiger,* 1987)

1

LANGUAGE AND COMMUNICATION IMPAIRMENTS AND CHILD PSYCHOPATHOLOGY

Description and Terminology

The specifically human capacity for language enables children to provide for auxiliary tools in solution of difficult tasks, to overcome impulsive action, to plan a solution to a problem prior to its execution, and to master their own behavior.
(Vygotsky, 1978, p. 28)

It is a wondrous moment when sometime around the age of one year a word
emerges from an infant's mouth. Ordinary in the course of most children's
development, it is a time when learning and social communication shift dra-
matically. The human capacity to understand and use language opens the
doors to thinking, learning, and social relationships. When language development goes awry, it can affect the quality of life across the age span, and
many children with language impairments will suffer lifelong consequences in their social, emotional, academic, and vocational well-being
(Cohen, in press). When children have difficulty understanding others and
expressing themselves, it is not surprising that problems with social and
emotional adjustment often ensue. The ability of children to communicate
and understand language colors their experience in the family, in school,
and in therapy. Because improved communication is a goal of mental health
intervention, understanding language and communicative development is
essential for clinical practice.

Language impairment has been called a "marginal" or "invisible" handicap (Lipsky, 1985; Willmer & Crane, 1979). It is often subtle and cannot be determined without a thorough assessment. Moreover, there is evidence that adults overestimate children's comprehension of language (receptive language) (Sattler, Feldman, & Bohanan, 1985). What is a parent, teacher, or clinician to make of children who do not answer when asked a question or whose attention wanders in the classroom? Sometimes these symptoms may be related to problems in producing and understanding language but appear to adults as noncompliance, inattentiveness, or social withdrawal (Howlin & Rutter, 1987). This is highly relevant in light of studies of children with oppositional and conduct disorders, most of which do not measure language comprehension.

Case Example

Kevin, aged 7 years, 10 months, was referred to a mental health clinic because of his destructive, angry, inattentive, and disruptive behaviors. Because he was physically violent and verbally abusive to peers, he had few friends. Kevin's parents had been separated for 5 years and he rarely saw his father. Kevin's mother described him as a difficult baby who cried a lot and was irritable and overactive, but she reported no delays in development. She felt that Kevin did not have friends because he had a "bad attitude." Kevin's teacher reported that he was performing at grade level with the exception of spelling. The teacher attributed Kevin's problems to his not listening, his mother's inconsistency in discipline, family dysfunction, emotional problems, and social problems with other children. Testing showed that Kevin had difficulties understanding language and expressing himself. He had trouble remembering information and said that he often "got lost" trying to explain things. Even though Kevin's teacher reported that he was performing at grade level, he also exhibited problems with reading and arithmetic. When asked how he would go about resolving a hypothetical conflict between two friends, Kevin could not identify the social problem, label the feelings of the friends, or realize when the problem was solved. It was concluded that unsuspected expressive and receptive language difficulties were a source of frustration to Kevin. These difficulties extended to memory and social reasoning and interfered with his achievement and social relationships. Feedback led to placement in a class for children with specific learning disabilities, where Kevin learned strategies to compensate for language weaknesses. Kevin's mother was relieved that his difficulties were not all her fault, and she was given strategies to help him. Family problems still required attention, but the feedback helped Kevin's mother and his therapist distinguish family problems from Kevin's language-related problems.

Intense examination of the interface between language impairment and child psychopathology is actually relatively new and has emerged from a convergence of observations and shifts in the fields of language and communication and social-emotional development and disorder. Because research and clinical work in these areas have evolved along separate paths, we need to consider how language impairment and social-emotional disorder are associated and the implications for identification, assessment, and treatment of children with these co-occurring conditions. Increasingly, the intimate overlap between language and communication impairments and social-emotional disorders, and how they might be confused for or interact with one another, has come to be appreciated (Audet & Ripich, 1994; Baltaxe & Simmons, 1990; Gallagher, 1999). Of particular interest in this book is that, on average, approximately 50% of children seen in mental health facilities and in special classrooms for children with emotional and behavioral problems have a language impairment, with estimates as high as 70% (Camarata et al., 1988). Similarly, on average, half of the children referred to speech-language pathologists or to special education classrooms for children with learning disabilities have a behavioral or emotional problem (Cantwell & Baker, 1991). Moreover, there appears to be a relationship between the severity and type of language impairment and intensity of services. For instance, teachers of children in a day program rated children's conversational skills higher than teachers of children in a residential program (Griffith, Rogers-Adkinson, & Cusick, 1997).

Despite the high rate of language and communication impairments observed in studies of children attending mental health clinics, language and communication problems often are not considered as a possible contributor to psychopathology (Cohen, 1996). Children are frequently referred for mental health services because of problems in their social interactions such as inappropriate or delayed responding, poor turn-taking skills, and difficulties formulating and expressing their thoughts so that they sound coherent. A common perception among mental health professionals is that these struggles to communicate coherently are related to the symptoms that are thought to be causing the social-emotional disturbance (e.g., anxiety, depression, attention deficit). These same behaviors, from the perspective of communication specialists, could just as well be seen as difficulties with pragmatic competence and discourse. Communication problems can be subtle, and even experienced speech-language pathologists frequently are unable to discern language impairment unless a systematic assessment is done. Professionals working with children with language and communication impairments also may not suspect a social-emotional disorder because here too the symptoms can be subtle or misattributed. This might be the case, for instance, when children who are depressed and withdrawn are simply thought to be shy. Similarly, in children whose communication is disorganized and lacks coherence, a rare disorder such as childhood schizophrenia may not be considered because under stressful conditions the language of an anxious child can become highly disorganized.

It must be acknowledged that it would be inaccurate and irresponsible to suggest that all child psychopathology is due to underlying language impairment. The point being made here is that impaired language and communicative processes are often overlooked as contributing to social-emotional disturbance. Without attention to these, assessment and treatment will be inadequate for many children.

It is presumed that readers come to this book from a range of backgrounds and experience. Some are familiar with the terminology of both language and communication impairment and social-emotional or psychiatric disorder and some familiar with one or the other. It is also expected that others are new to these topics. Therefore, before beginning, it is necessary to review the terminology used to describe the range of communicative impairments and the social-emotional problems discussed throughout the book as potential causes and contributors to language and communication impairment. In the process, examples of the ways in which language and communicative impairment and social-emotional functioning might be confused with one another are given. This is not intended to minimize or ignore either the basic underpinnings or diagnostic approaches of various professions but to encourage flexible thinking when assessing and treating children.

SPEECH, LANGUAGE, AND COMMUNICATION: ETIOLOGY, TERMINOLOGY, AND DEFINITIONS

Although there are speculations about the causes of language impairment, in most cases the origin is unknown. Historically, labels such as *childhood aphasia* or *developmental dysphasia* were applied, under the assumption that there is a neurological basis for language impairment. These designations actually were misleading because they implied that damage to the brain had occurred (Bishop, 1994). Subsequently, a division was made between *language delay* and *language disorder.* The implication here was that children with language delay were simply slower to develop in their language and that they would progress, albeit at a slower pace, and catch up to peers once there was a developmental growth spurt. Essentially, these children's language was expected to look like that of younger normal children. Children with language disorders, in contrast, were not expected to follow a normal path but to differ from the norm in severity, course, and pattern of language functioning and the presence of associated conditions. Although the distinction between delay and disorder seems logical, children in these groups have proved difficult to differentiate in both research and clinical practice. For instance, longitudinal studies have shown that even children whose language problems seem to resolve by 5½ years may have residual problems with literacy skills that are apparent only when the demands on language increase in adolescence (Snowling, Bishop, & Stothard, 2000; Stothard, Snowling, Bishop, Chipchase, & Kaplan, 1998).

In the past decade, research has examined both biological and environmental contributions and currently it is believed that both are important contributors to the development of language impairment. The evidence has emerged on a number of fronts. First, there has been tremendous rapid growth in understanding the genetic contribution to language development. There are genetic syndromes associated with language impairment such as Down syndrome, which is characterized by deficits in phonology and pragmatics, and Fragile X syndrome, which is associated with deficits in expressive language, speech, and pragmatics. As well, family and twin studies provide evidence of familial aggregation of speech and language impairment (Bishop, North, & Donlan, 1995; Hohnen & Stevenson, 1999). Molecular genetic studies have also begun to localize specific chromosomes responsible for aspects of language development (Grigorenko et al., 1997). Second, nongenetic biological factors also have been shown to exert an influence on language development, such as premature birth (Siegel, 1982), temperament (Slomkowski, Nelson, Dunn, & Plomin, 1992), and pathogenic processes such as exposure to alcohol in the prenatal period (Jung, 1987). Third, conceptualizations of brain development and functioning have changed considerably from the earlier part of the 20th century so that the role of both biological and experiential factors on brain development are taken into account. As noted above, because acquired brain injury was associated with loss of language functions, in the past it was assumed that language impairment was caused by alterations in brain function, even when evidence was lacking. Although earlier work on acquired brain injury suggested that the brain is plastic in the sense that among children with injuries unaffected parts of the brain were able to take over functions (Rapin, 1996), the new neurodevelopmental work postulates that plasticity is a basic property of the developing brain (Johnson, 2000; Nowakowski & Hayes, 1999; Steinberg & Avenevoli, 2000). This view opens the way for experiences to exert an impact through alteration of brain chemistry, structure, and function associated with language competence throughout development. A corollary of this is that abnormalities can initially be subtle yet have an impact on future development. This view also presumes that brain functioning can be altered for the better as well as for the worse. Influential experiences can be of various kinds and include environmental factors such as growing up in a low socioeconomic status household (Hart & Risley, 1995), maternal depression (Murray, 1992), and child abuse and neglect (Cicchetti & Beeghly, 1987). In all these circumstances, there is evidence of limitations in the amount and quality of verbal interaction between parents and children, which is discussed at greater length in Chapter 3. Of course, some children are dually at risk because of both their genetic makeup and the environment in which they were raised. Although the findings of this research help understand the cause of language impairments, they also raise new questions. The current terminology therefore is relatively neutral with respect to etiology and the terms *specific language impairment* (SLI) or *language impairment* (LI) are most commonly used to refer to problems in the acquisition and use of language. The term specific language impairment is used to refer to problems in the acquisition and use of language in the context of normal development (Bishop, 1997). Because the latter criterion is being debated (see Chapter 5), the term *LI* is used here.

Language and communication impairments are most likely to be associated with social-emotional disturbance and are of primary interest here. There is, however, a slightly elevated risk for psychopathology associated with speech impairments, and therefore these are described briefly.

Speech Impairment

Speech problems are distinct from language problems. Simply put, language concerns message formulation whereas speech concerns message transmission. In the past, speech-language pathologists primarily treated children with speech problems. Only in a minority of cases do developmental speech impairments reflect problems with language. Speech problems arise from difficulties coordinating oral-motor musculature needed to produce speech sounds, resulting in difficulties articulating speech sounds, fluency, or voice. By far, the most common speech impairment is *articulation disorder,* which occurs when a child distorts or is unable to produce certain sounds or combinations of sounds. Common articulation errors are substitutions of one sound for another (e.g., "wabbit" for "rabbit") and omissions of sounds (e.g., "boo" for "blue"). Although children with speech problems are at somewhat elevated risk for developing a social-emotional disorder, the risk is small compared to children with LI (Cantwell & Baker, 1991). When, however, children's articulation disorder is sufficiently severe as to affect intelligibility, they may experience frustration and embarrassment. Fortunately, articulation problems are highly responsive to remediation. *Voice disorders* include problems with voice quality (e.g., breathiness or stridency), resonance (e.g., a nasal voice that sounds like having a cold), pitch (too high or too low), and intensity (too loud or too soft). Although often caused by physical problems, overuse, or misuse, problems with voice quality may be related to anxiety.

Fluency disorder, more often called stuttering, involves an interruption in the forward flow of speech. Dysfluency becomes stuttering when disruptions in speech occur along with awareness, anxiety, or compensatory behaviors (Cantwell & Baker, 1987). Another kind of fluency problem, cluttering, is a disorder of speech rate and intelligibility. Clutterers speak rapidly, sometimes in short bursts, and may slur their speech so that others find it difficult to understand them (Bishop, 1997).

Language Impairment

Language is formally defined as a system of symbols and rules used to convey meanings (Bloom & Lahey, 1978). Language is not just about producing and understanding words, sounds, and sentences but also about linking sentences into coherent narratives and using and understanding gestures and social and cultural rules for communication. To this end, both structural language and communication skills must be considered (see Table 1.1 for a summary).

Structural Language

Traditionally, structural language has been broken into discrete entities subsumed under the broad headings of receptive language (comprehension) and expressive language. A finer-grained way to divide up structural language is into six subsystems of expressive and receptive language, namely, receptive and expressive phonology, semantics, and syntax. Auditory verbal memory and processing also must be assessed. Although these subsystems are described separately, it is important to keep in mind that in daily language use they are not really distinct, as illustrated shortly.

TABLE 1.1   Components of Language and Communication

Component Skill	Elements of Component Skill	Examples of Impairment
Phonology	Detects, combines, and discriminates sounds and sound sequences Segments words into elements	Mispronounces words Misunderstands sounds Difficulty associating sound with letter symbol (reading)
Semantics	Vocabulary	Small vocabulary Word finding problems Difficulty with figurative language
Morphology	Using correct word endings to indicate verb tense Inflectional markers Prefixes and suffixes Prepositions Articles Auxiliary verbs	Omitted or incorrect verb tense markers Errors in plurals Inaccurate use or misunderstanding of prepositions (e.g., in, under) Incorrect agreement of auxiliary verbs ("She were gone.")
Syntax	Rules of word order Rules of word combinations	Short sentences Difficulty responding to questions Difficulty understanding subordinate clauses Difficulty interpreting passive tenses Poor grammar Poor knowledge of irregular verbs
Auditory Verbal Processing/ Listening Skills	Recall verbal information Analyze verbal information to derive meaning	Long response time Inaccurate or incomplete memory for verbal material Failure to carry out directions
Narrative/ Narrative Discourse	Linking events and ideas Directing, explaining Telling stories Conversation	Difficulty producing and understanding complex sentences Listing events without linking them Limited use of conjunctions Nonspecific or inaccurate pronoun reference
Pragmatics	Rules governing appropriate use of language for communication	Poor flow of information (e.g, repetition, fillers) Poor eye contact Failure to take conversational turn Standing too close or too far Failure to repair miscommunications

The *phonological system* provides the rules for combining and selecting the speech sounds of a language and refers to children's awareness of speech sounds in terms of how they are used to convey meaning. Thus children must learn to detect sounds, to discriminate between sounds (e.g., *got* and *dot*) and sound combinations (e.g., *share* and *chair*), to segment words into elements (e.g., *buckwheat* into *buck* and *wheat*), and to classify sounds, and they must be able to do so quickly and precisely (Bishop, 1997). Each language has some invariant sound or sound combinations, that is, phonological rules. For instance, in English, words can end with the letters "ng" but they cannot begin with these letters, although in Swahili they can (e.g., Ngorongoro Crater). Children need to extract rules for the purpose of organizing sounds in words not only in terms of the sounds themselves but also in terms of individual sound sequences (phonemes) and syllabic units that facilitate learning new words. Phonological awareness or processing (receptive phonology) is recognized as an important predictor of reading ability (e.g., Stanovich, 1988).

Infants are born with the phonological capacity to learn any language (Kuhl, 1980). For instance, infants from English-speaking homes can discriminate between recordings of the same unfamiliar woman speaking English and speaking Italian (Mehler, Jusczuyk, Lambert, Halsted, Bertoncini, & Amiel-Tison, 1988). By 10 months, infants lose some of their ability to discriminate phonetic material that is not part of what they hear because it is not relevant (Werker & Pegg, 1992). Thus, with input from their environment, sounds and sound combinations characteristic of the child's language environment become prepotent. Development of phonological awareness moves from early awareness of rhymes, alliteration, and sound play in the preschool years to awareness of the individual sound segments that make up words. It is this latter skill, the ability to segment words into individual phonemes, that is most closely related to reading competence.

The *semantic* or *lexical* aspect of language concerns the meaning of words or vocabulary. Whereas the basic tasks for development of phonology and syntax are completed in childhood, vocabulary is unique in that it continues to expand into adulthood. The spoken and written language of children with a good vocabulary is enriched by the availability of synonyms and antonyms. A large vocabulary facilitates both literacy skills and social communication. With a limited vocabulary, children are likely to have problems expressing themselves and understanding the language of others. Children with LI may have impoverished expressive and receptive vocabularies and difficulty learning new words. This is likely related, at least in part, to problems in phonological awareness. If a child cannot reliably identify and remember phonological rules and sequences in words, it will be more difficult for the child to learn the word. When there is no pattern on which to rely in word learning, each word is an independent entity that has to be learned on its own. Children with LI also commonly have word finding problems. These are reflected in difficulties finding words in the first place, choosing an alternative word when misunderstood, or injecting variety in expression. In their struggle to find the right word to express themselves, their language is often imprecise, and children with LI use circumlocutions to arrive at their message. For example, a hamburger might become "that meat thing in a bun." Moreover, older children and adolescents with LI use less figurative and inferential language, which limits reading comprehension as well as participation in social banter with peers. In therapy, at home, or in the classroom, children with poor vocabulary, word finding problems, and difficulties understanding and using figurative language may be perceived as resistant, as refusing to speak, or as reluctant to answer rather than as having real difficulties doing so.

Case Example

Examiner: Describe this picture of a playground so that someone not present can see it.

Child (slumps in his chair, looks glum, and speaks in a monotone): This person is going down the slide having fun. This person is going on a ride I don't know what it is called. This person is on a thing and he's about to fall off. This guy already fell off.

Syntax and *morphology* refer to the grammatical aspects of language, which provide the rules for organizing meaningful units into words and words into sentences. Morphemes are the smallest units in language that can either stand on their own or contribute to the specificity of verbs (e.g., use of the *ed* ending indicates tense). Morphemes also may include noun and verb inflections, prepositions, articles, and auxiliary verbs. Syntax (grammar) refers to the organizational rules for generating and interpreting sentence structures. Grammatical rules also support learning vocabulary because syntactic information can be used to help a child deduce the meaning of new words from context. Children with LI use shorter sentences and have difficulties producing and understanding syntactically complex sentences with elaborated verb phrases, pronouns, adjectives, and auxiliaries (Leonard, 1997). Understanding and expressing correct grammatical constructions is important for children to appreciate the context of communication and to place events in relation to person, time, and place. Errors in verb tense or plurals, unclear pronoun referents, and incorrect use of irregular verbs may confuse or provide inadequate information to the conversational partner.

Case Example

Child (in response to a picture on a projective test): He's dreaming he's getting cutten open or something or his brother had an operation and he got it cut out.

All these kinds of errors make it difficult for children to explain what they are thinking and feeling, which interferes with social relationships, education, and therapy. They also make it difficult for children to understand complex concepts and multistep directions or explanations presented by a teacher or peer.

Auditory verbal processing, also important for competent language performance, can be divided into two components: (a) *auditory verbal memory,* which refers to recall of utterances that contain verbal meaning; and (b) *auditory* (or *language) processing* or *listening skills,* which refers to the ability to analyze verbal input to derive meaning. Even for individuals with normal language, some sentences take longer to analyze (i.e., process). For instance, while reading the next sentence visualize the action in your mind: "The girl is eating an ice cream cone." Now visualize this sentence: "She shows the girl the boy." For most people, it takes longer to process the meaning of the second sentence, which is more syntactically complex. For children with LI, processing such complex sentences is even more taxing.

Children with LI often process information more slowly or inaccurately than children with normally developing language. Some children can only process small chunks of information and consequently have difficulty remembering multistep oral directions. When children fail to carry out a series of directions completely, it is sometimes attributed by adults to noncompliance. Children with LI may only be able to understand one or two requests or directions at one time. This may be the last request made or the one the child is most interested in. When a child fails to comply, it may be interpreted by an adult as "This child only does what he wants to do." Moreover, in the classroom, children with LI have difficulty remembering steps in problem-solving tasks (e.g., in arithmetic computation) or instructions for homework. Children who miss or misunderstand one step in a procedure soon lose track of what is to be done. Furthermore, children with LI often fail to encode information so that on-line processing of information, such as is required on working memory tasks, is negatively affected. For all these reasons, it is not surprising that children with LI are often reported to have attention problems. Problems with auditory verbal memory can also strain the capacity of children when information that is emotionally loaded or syntactically complex or contains unfamiliar vocabulary spoken rapidly must be decoded and interpreted, as is the case in many social interactions and in therapy.

Communication

Most uses of language for learning and communication do not stop at the level of individual words or sentences. Once children have learned to combine words into grammatical sequences to form sentences, they must then learn to combine sentences into organized and coherent larger discourse units. Moreover, they must select the sentence patterns and gestures, body language, and communicative attitude that best serve their communicative task at the moment (pragmatics).

The terms discourse and narrative discourse are both used in the literature and have somewhat different meanings. *Discourse* skills are important for carrying on a conversation, expressing oneself, giving instructions, and describing thoughts and events. These activities involve linking sentences, integrating ideas coherently and cohesively, and using appropriate linguistic devices, such as "then," "now," and "but." Successful discourse also requires that speakers have some idea of the context and the state of knowledge or intention of the person to whom they are speaking. As Bishop (1997) has pointed out, when children have a conversation or listen to a narrative they do not react to isolated elements of what is heard. Rather, they build up a representation of situations, events, and objects and the relationships between these.

Narrative discourse refers to storytelling or retelling and is usually measured by asking a child to tell a story or to explain a procedure (e.g., how to make a peanut butter sandwich). The skills required for narrative discourse overlap with those required for discourse, but sequencing, cohesion, working memory, and perspective taking are especially important. Very young children describing a movie typically switch settings and characters without warning or informing the listener, ignoring psychological motives and reactions, and forgetting to resolve problems that were introduced. Their stories also tend to be shorter and to focus on action sequences. The stories of children with LI also have these features. For older children, and particularly for adolescents, narrative discourse involving figurative language (e.g., idioms, metaphor, humor, ambiguous language) becomes increasingly important. The finding that children with LI are deficient in figurative language means that handicaps associated with LI may get worse as children mature and are confronted with more complex tasks. Problems with narrative discourse have also been observed in children who have been abused (Coster & Cicchetti, 1993), in children diagnosed with Attention Deficit Hyperactivity Disorder (ADHD) (Tannock & Schachar, 1996), and in children with thought disorders (Caplan, 1996).

The *pragmatic* aspect of language, which includes rules for communication and use of particular forms of language in specific situations, involves an integration of specific skills, including (a) structural language, (b) knowledge of social rules, (c) social-cognitive skills, particularly theory of mind, and (d) executive functions (Baron-Cohen, 1995; Gallagher, 1999; Prutting, 1982). Pragmatic competence requires an on-line moment-to-moment recognition of the listener's needs, the demands of conversation, and estimates of the listener's knowledge and state of mind. Nonverbal as well as verbal pragmatic skills are essential for competent communication and include maintaining conversational distance, conversational turn taking, eye contact, appropriate use of social conventions such as greetings, knowing when to use slang, and knowing how to speak to people of different ages and status. Another aspect of pragmatics is conversational repair. Inevitably, some communications break down when a listener does not understand. Repairing these ruptures in conversation is complex because the child must be able to first notice the breakdown, then identify the root of the misunderstanding, and finally find an alternate way to express that which was initially miscommunicated. As we shall see, many problems in children referred for social-emotional disorders can be viewed in terms of violations of pragmatic rules (Hummel & Prizant, 1993). Moreover, there is relatively new evidence of a subset of children who have pragmatic communication impairments that extend beyond struggles with language structure (Bishop, Chan, Adams, Hartley, & Weir, 2000).

Classification of Language Impairment

Children with LI typically have problems with both receptive and expressive language in multiple domains. A number of means of classifying forms of LI have been pursued. The North American psychiatric classification system (American Psychiatric Association [APA], 1994) describes five types of language impairment: (a) Expressive Language Disorder, (b) Combined Expressive-Receptive Language Disorder, (c) Phonological

Disorder, (d) Stuttering, and (e) Language Disorder Not Otherwise Specified. These have minimal clinical usefulness, however, and do not represent the range of language difficulties that children present. Other schemes are linguistically and clinically based (Bishop & Rosenbloom, 1987; Rapin, 1996). For instance, Rapin (1996) suggested the following subtypes: (a) mixed receptive/expressive disorders, which are divided into verbal auditory agnosia and phonologic/syntactic deficit; (b) expressive disorders in the face of normal comprehension, which are divided into verbal dyspraxia (sparse verbal output and poor phonology) and speech programming deficit disorder; and (c) higher-order processing disorders, which are divided into lexical deficit disorder and semantic pragmatic disorder. Although the category of semantic-pragmatic disorder was previously applied to children with autistic features, as mentioned earlier, Bishop (2000) recently suggested that it might apply to a subset of the larger group of children with LI. Although Rapin's subtypes could provide a linguistically more powerful means for assessment and diagnosis, considerable work still needs to be done to validate them and to arrive at diagnostic criteria.

Neither of the above classifications systems takes into account developmental or contextual factors and the fact that the nature of LI may change with age (Bishop & Edmundson, 1987a, 1987b; Snowling et al., 2000; Stothard et al., 1998). Thus it is not clear whether a problem in middle childhood is a continuation of earlier LI in a different form or a new problem that emerges when demands on language increase (Bishop, 1997). Delineation of clear subtypes of LI is an important undertaking for understanding causal mechanisms and ultimately treatment. Although there has been some indication that the pattern of language impairment varies as a result of different causative factors, there is considerable overlap. For instance, phonological awareness has been identified as having a genetic basis, but only rarely do children have an isolated phonological processing problem. Most children who have problems with phonological awareness also have problems with other aspects of language (Bishop, 1991). In another arena, some investigators have found that low socioeconomic status is primarily related to vocabulary growth (Hart & Risley, 1995), but there is also evidence that children raised in low socioeconomic environments differ from middle-class samples in development of grammatic forms and narrative skills (Puckering & Rutter, 1987; Whitehurst, 1997). Although future research may ultimately permit making distinctions between specific subgroups, at this point there is no empirically or clinically meaningful way of subtyping LI. Therefore most clinicians and researchers simply describe the language strengths and deficits in individual children.

Prevalence of Language Impairment

Prevalence figures for LI have been applied primarily to structural language deficits. Throughout development, LI is more often diagnosed in boys (Whitehurst & Fischel, 1994). It is estimated that 8% to 12% of preschool children have some form of LI (National Institute on Deafness and Other Communicative Disorders, 1995). There are fewer data concerning the prevalence of LI in school-aged children and adolescents, but estimates of LI in the age range of 6 to 21 years are typically around 5%. Figures as high as 20% also have been reported, however (U.S. Department of Education, 1998). The exact prevalence is difficult to pinpoint because of differences between studies in the criteria for diagnosis of LI. This will be discussed in Chapter 5.

It is of note that even when less stringent diagnostic criteria have been applied, there are many associations between LI and both concurrent and later learning and social-emotional problems (Beitchman, Brownlie, Inglis, et al., 1996; Beitchman, Wilson, et al., 1996a, 1996b; Young et al., 2000).

PSYCHOPATHOLOGY IN INFANTS, CHILDREN, AND ADOLESCENTS: TERMINOLOGY AND DEFINITIONS

Most children come to the attention of mental health services because of social or emotional problems that interfere with adaptive functioning at home, at school, and in the community. Descriptors such as the following are often applied to infants and toddlers referred for mental health services: "can't be soothed," "difficult to read," "irritable," and "can't play." In the preschool through adolescent years, the following descriptors are typical: "noncompliant," "hyperactive," "has attitude," "unmotivated," "uncooperative," "bully," "aggressive," "rude," "mouthy," "moody," "shy," "unfriendly," and "irritable." Whether or not these problems warrant a formal psychiatric diagnosis depends on their severity, chronicity, and pervasiveness. There has been considerable debate in the literature regarding whether psychopathology is best measured by categorical systems that provide diagnostic labels or by standardized symptom rating scales that describe symptom patterns and severity on a continuum (Jensen, Brooks-Gunn, & Graber, 1999). Children who do not meet criteria for psychiatric disorder can nevertheless be impaired in their social-emotional functioning (Angold, Costello, Farmer, Burns, & Erkanli, 1999); because of this, there may be an advantage in using continuous scales. This is not the place to debate the pros and cons of these viewpoints; both are useful.

In most of the book, a developmental perspective is adopted (see Chapter 3) and the terms *social-emotional disorder* or *psychopathology* are used. Terminology from categorical psychiatric classification systems is most frequently used in clinical and educational settings, however, and a psychiatric diagnosis is often required to access services. In this section, the most common forms of psychiatric disorders observed in children referred for mental health service are briefly described. The aim of this discussion is not simply to define psychiatric diagnostic categories but to illustrate the overlap of language and communication impairments with social-emotional disorder.

The best examples of categorical classification systems are *Diagnostic and Statistical Manual–Fourth Edition (DSM-IV;* APA, 1994) and the International Code of Disorders *(ICD-10)* published by the World Health Organization (1993). These systems set criteria for specific diagnostic categories that are based, as much as possible, on empirical literature describing the phenomenology, correlates, etiology, and course of the condition. Although neither of these systems is explicitly developmental, developmental information has entered into their preparation.

LI is commonly associated with a number of psychiatric disorders, including Attention Deficit Hyperactivity Disorder (ADHD), Conduct Disorder, Oppositional Defiant Disorder, Anxiety Disorder, Depression, Selective Mutism, and Childhood Schizophrenia. As can be seen in Table 1.2, some of the criteria for a psychiatric disorder could reflect or be a consequence of difficulties with communication language processing and expression. Many of the symptoms that characterize the following syndromes could just as well be considered indicative of problems with language and communication by a communication specialist.

Attention Deficit Hyperactivity Disorder

Attention Deficit Hyperactivity Disorder (ADHD) is the most common diagnosis given to children with LI. This diagnosis is characterized by problems with inattention, hyperactivity, and impulsivity that impair social or academic functioning and have an onset before the age of 7 years. The potential overlap of psychiatric symptoms with problems with pragmatic communication or auditory verbal processing are illustrated in the following symptoms. For instance, among the criteria for attention problems are "often does not seem to listen when spoken to directly"; "often does not follow through on instructions and fails to finish schoolwork, chores, or other duties in the workplace"; and "often avoids, dislikes, or is reluctant to

TABLE 1.2　Overlap of Language and Communication Impairment and Psychiatric Disorder

Psychiatric Diagnosis	*Symptoms That May Indicate or Be a Reaction to Language and Communication Impairments*
Attention Deficit Hyperactivity Disorder	Often does not seem to listen when spoken to directly Often does not follow through on instructions and fails to finish schoolwork Often avoids or is reluctant to engage in tasks that require mental effort Often talks excessively Often blurts out answers before questions have been completed Often has difficulty awaiting turns Often interrupts or intrudes on others Clinically significant impairment in social or academic functioning
Conduct Disorder	Resorts to physical means of communication Clinically significant impairment in social, academic, or occupational functioning
Oppositional Defiant Disorder	Actively defies or refuses to comply with adults' requests or rules Often deliberately annoys others Often touchy and easily annoyed by others Often blames others for mistakes or misbehavior Clinically significant impairment in social, academic, or occupational functioning
Mood Disorders	Feelings of hopelessness Self-critical; feelings of inadequacy Social withdrawal Decreased productivity Poor social skills Loss of interest or pleasure in activities Clinically significant impairment in social, educational, or other areas of functioning
Anxiety Disorders	Embarrassed in public Excessive worrying Worry about quality of performance or competence at school Anticipatory anxiety about social situations in which child must perform or be evaluated by others Fear of public speaking Hypersensitivity to criticism or negative evaluation Underachievement in school due to test anxiety or avoidance of classroom participation Clinically significant impairment in social or educational areas Problems separating from attachment figures

(Continued)

TABLE 1.2 (Continued)

Psychiatric Diagnosis	Symptoms That May Indicate or Be a Reaction to Language and Communication Impairments
Selective Mutism	Consistent failure to speak in specific social situations in which there is an expectation for speaking (e.g., at school), despite speaking in other situations Disturbance interferes with educational achievement or with social communication
Childhood Schizophrenia	Disorganized speech (e.g., frequent derailment or incoherence) Failure to achieve expected level of interpersonal or academic achievement

engage in tasks that require mental effort (such as schoolwork or homework)." Under hyperactivity, "often talks excessively" is included, and under impulsivity are the behaviors "often blurts out answers before questions have been completed"; "often has difficulty awaiting turns"; and "often interrupts or intrudes on others, for example, butts into conversations or games."

Disruptive Behavior Disorders:
Conduct and Oppositional Defiant Disorders

A diagnosis of *Conduct Disorder* is given to children with symptoms such as aggression to people and animals, destruction of property, deceitfulness, theft, and serious violation of rules. To be diagnosed with this serious condition, children need to have shown some of these behaviors before the age of 10 years. Conduct Disorder, including delinquency, has been associated with LI (Moffitt, 1993). It is conceivable that a child with poor expressive language skills will encounter problems in communication early on and ultimately resort to physical means of communicating when more positive communicative means fail. Furthermore, it is well established that Conduct Disorder is associated with greater aggression and poorer prognosis when it occurs concurrently with ADHD (Hinshaw, Lahey, & Hart, 1993).

The diagnosis of *Oppositional Defiant Disorder* is given to children who are negative, hostile, defiant, and disobedient, more than is typical of children of comparable age and developmental level for a minimum of 6 months and leading to significant impairment in social and academic functioning. Children can be given this diagnosis as early as the preschool years, and it is often a precursor of Conduct Disorder (Loeber et al., 1993). The negativistic behavior may be expressed in a variety of ways, including resistance to directions or unwillingness to compromise, give in, or negotiate with adults or peers. Defiance may be shown by deliberate or persistent testing of limits, typically by ignoring orders, arguing, and not accepting blame for misdeeds. Hostility may include directly annoying adults or peers or verbal aggression. Language problems such as poor topic maintenance, poor negotiation skills, and inadequate interpretation of verbal and nonverbal signals of others often accompany a diagnosis of Oppositional Defiant Disorder (Audet & Ripich, 1994). Moreover, it has been shown that adults overestimate toddlers' language ability and may attribute problems with language comprehension to willful disobedience. Kaler and Kopp (1990) found that toddlers' compliance with adults' commands was directly related to the toddlers' receptive language competence. The same findings may also apply to older children with poor receptive language skills.

Mood and Anxiety Disorders

Children with mood and anxiety disorders are diagnosed in a way that is similar to that of adults. The two mood disorders of adults that are common in children are Major Depressive Disorder and Dysthymic Disorder. A third, Manic-Depressive Disorder, is diagnosed less frequently.

Major Depressive Disorder is characterized by marked episodes of children having at least five symptoms among the following: depressed mood most of the time; loss of interest or pleasure in activities; excessive weight loss or gain; sleep disorder (excessive increase or decrease); psychomotor agitation or retardation; fatigue or loss of energy; feelings of worthlessness or inappropriate guilt; diminished ability to think or concentrate; and recurrent thoughts of death that cause impairment in social, academic, and nonacademic activities. It is important to note that children who are depressed often manifest their distress in the form of an irritable mood and may also be agitated and restless. *Dysthymic Disorder* is a more chronic condition. Children with this disorder present some of the same symptoms as children with a major depressive disorder. *Manic-Depressive Disorder* usually has an onset no earlier than adolescence and is characterized by alternating cycles of depression and mania or irritability.

Depression can interfere with communication, memory, and auditory processing but can also be a result of children's feelings of inadequacy in the face of academic tasks that require these skills or stem from difficulties in language and pragmatic deficits that interfere with social competence. Children with depressive symptoms have been observed to have problems that reflect inadequate conversational discourse skills, including difficulties producing coherent and relevant utterances, describing story characters' internal states, distinguishing between old and new information, and sequencing events over time (Audet & Ripich, 1994; Baltaxe & Simmons, 1988).

There is also evidence that children rated as shy and withdrawn by their teachers have difficulties in communication that go beyond timidity and are related to poor structural language and pragmatic communication skills (Donahue, Hartis, & Cole, 1999; Evans, 1996).

Anxiety Disorder is characterized by excessive, generalized, and persistent anxieties and worries not apparently related to specific situations and that occur most days for 6 months. These may include unrealistic worries about the future, preoccupations with past events, overconcern about competence and extreme self-consciousness, and inability to relax. At least one additional symptom must be present for this diagnosis to be given to children, such as excessive restlessness, difficulty concentrating, or disturbed sleep. Somatic complaints also often accompany Anxiety Disorder. Anxiety Disorder can take a variety of forms, distinguished on the basis of the focus of anxiety, including Avoidant Disorder, Separation Anxiety, Social Phobia, and Post-Traumatic Stress Disorder. Although anxiety itself, like depression, may influence academic and social functioning, it also may be a reaction to problems in communicating in school and social settings.

Avoidant Disorder is characterized by persistent and excessive avoidance from contact with others that interferes with social functioning and relationships with peers and with adults outside of the family. This avoidance occurs in the context of a clear desire for affection and acceptance, which is displayed primarily within the family. Children who are avoidant may become excessively fearful and inhibited when confronted with even minor social or academic demands.

A diagnosis of *Separation Anxiety Disorder* involves anxiety manifested by an infant or child when placed in situations likely to lead to separation from major attachment figures, from home, or from other familiar surroundings. The anxiety experienced is extreme and often expressed as panic. Children with Separation Anxiety Disorder worry incessantly about the return of attachment figures and often have nightmares and associated somatic complaints. Problems with separation may be confounded by poor communication; that is, the children cannot express their feelings accurately, understand others, or successfully negotiate separation with their parents and peers.

Social Phobia is characterized by a marked and persistent fear of social or performance situations that might result in the child feeling embarrassed.

Children do not realize that their fear is excessive or unreasonable, although adolescents and adults typically do. The anxiety is such that it interferes with the child's daily activities. Common to this diagnosis is fear of public speaking and marked anticipatory anxiety concerning an upcoming social or public situation. Although such a phobia is considered irrational, children with LI may be reluctant to speak in class or be placed in situations where their poor language and communication skills will be noticed. Children diagnosed as having LI at the age of 5 years have been shown to exhibit Social Phobia as young adults (Beitchman et al., 2001).

It would appear that any of the above diagnoses could emerge when expectations of achievement stress children who are struggling with language-related learning tasks. Similarly, children may show school refusal or somatic complaints to avoid challenges in situations in which they feel less than competent. Anxiety is often observed in children presenting to speech-language clinics (Cantwell & Baker, 1991) and in children with LI seen in mental health clinics (Cohen et al., 1993), and in community samples (Beitchman, Nair, Clegg, Ferguson, & Patel, 1986). Moreover, the language and discourse problems described earlier might be the reason why some children are perceived as shy and reticent (Evans, 1996; Fujiki, Brinton, & Todd, 1996), and some of these children might meet criteria for a diagnosis of Anxiety Disorder.

Another form of Anxiety Disorder, *Post-Traumatic Stress Disorder,* comprises symptoms associated with observing or experiencing a traumatic event. Children show symptoms such as sleep disturbance, hypervigilance, aggressive behavior, and pain-seeking behavior. They may also have difficulties when routines are interrupted and engage in repetitive play in which themes or aspects of trauma are repeated. There is now considerable research showing an association of patterns of LI with both abuse and neglect. Problems with language development may arise because of both inadequate stimulation and the inability of parents to foster communicative experiences (Coster & Cicchetti, 1993). It also may be that children who have difficulty communicating are more likely to be targets of abuse and neglect.

Selective Mutism

Selective Mutism also needs to be mentioned, although it is a relatively rare disorder. This diagnosis is given to children who refuse to speak outside the home or only speak to a small select group of individuals. Until relatively recently, the possibility that at least some of these children are language impaired or exhibit other developmental disorders has not been considered. Rather, refusal to speak in some situations has been attributed to causes such as family dysfunction and Social Phobia. There are data, however, from recent studies of clinic samples suggesting an elevation of LI among children who are selectively mute (Kristensen, 2000; Steinhausen & Juzi, 1996).

Childhood Schizophrenia

Childhood Schizophrenia is a rare disorder characterized by two or more of the following symptoms: disorganized thinking, delusions, hallucinations, grossly disorganized behavior, and flattened affect. The presence of at least two of these symptoms observed for a minimum of one month is required for diagnosis. Of particular importance here is that disorganized thinking can only be observed through children's attempts at communication. The thought disorder may be reflected in children shifting from one topic to another, answering questions obliquely or giving completely unrelated answers, or being so incoherent that what is being communicated is incomprehensible. According to diagnostic criteria, childhood-onset schizophrenia must be distinguished from both language and communication disorders and other syndromes where disorganized behavior is a symptom (e.g., ADHD). Although the diagnosis of Childhood Schizophrenia is rare, it is possible that children with severe LI may be misdiagnosed, particularly during periods of high stress and anxiety.

Disorders of Infancy

In light of the dramatic increase in understanding of infant development and disorder over the past 20 years, there has been a move toward expanding and refining a diagnostic system for infants up to 3 years of age (Zeanah, Boris, & Scheeringa, 1997). The Zero to Three classification system (Zero to Three/National Center for Clinical Infant Programs, 1994) delineates a number of clinical disorders, some of which overlap with the *DSM-IV* system (e.g., Post-Traumatic Stress Disorder). Two disorders specific to infancy have been of particular interest: Regulatory Disorders and Reactive Attachment Disorder.

Regulatory Disorders include difficulties in emotion regulation, sensorimotor processing difficulties, and behavioral problems. These are manifested primarily as symptoms of sleep disturbance and problems with self-soothing, feeding, arousal, and emotional lability and are presumed to be related to maladaptive responses to sensory deficits (see DeGangi, Di Pietro, Greenspan, & Porges, 1991).

Although the diagnosis of *Reactive Attachment Disorder* has been part of psychiatric nosology for some time, there actually has been relatively little research on clinical samples of children who are insecurely attached. Rather, the bulk of information has come from examination of the links between early insecure attachment and later clinical disorders and the study of atypical populations such as children who have been institutionalized (e.g., Rutter, 1995; Zeanah, 1996). There are three major types of attachment disorders in the Zero to Three classification system: (a) Disorders of Nonattachment, (b) Disordered Attachment (distortions in the infant's secure base behavior), and (c) Disrupted Attachment Disorder (unresolved grief following loss of an attachment figure).

Although on the surface regulatory and attachment disorders may seem to be distinguishable, there is overlap. For instance, problems with regulation are commonly associated with insecure attachment. Moreover, of most relevance here, there is some evidence of an association between language functioning and both attachment and regulatory disorders. At as early as 2 years of age, language plays a role in self-regulation. Furthermore, there is evidence that infants' capacity to communicate may be both a contributor to and an outcome of attachment security. This is discussed at greater length in Chapters 2 and 3.

PROGNOSIS FOR CO-OCCURRING LANGUAGE IMPAIRMENT AND SOCIAL-EMOTIONAL DISORDER

Review of the literature on the long-term outcome for children with LI and co-occurring social-emotional disorder leads to rather sobering conclusions (Cohen, in press). Considerable evidence now points to the persistence of even mild LI. Children who have difficulties in multiple areas of language and whose LI continues beyond the age of 5 years are at the greatest disadvantage in terms of learning and social-emotional functioning (Mawhood, Howlin, & Rutter, 2000; Whitehurst & Fischel, 1994). Just as worrisome is that psychiatric disorder has been shown to increase over time even in children whose language functioning improves (Beitchman et al., 2001; Cantwell & Baker, 1991; Williams & McGee, 1996). The prognosis for children with receptive language problems is especially poor in terms of both language and social-emotional outcomes (Beitchman et al., 2001; Howlin, Mawhood, & Rutter, 2000; Rutter & Mawhood, 1991). Because receptive language problems are more subtle and difficult to detect than expressive problems, some children and adolescents are not identified as having LI unless a routine examination is done (Cohen, 1996).

An inevitable problem with examining data from longitudinal studies is that the context and knowledge base change over time and there are limited data on pragmatics, discourse, and narrative discourse in children with co-occurring LI and social-emotional disorder. This is particularly important because of the close association of poor pragmatic and discourse skills with many psychiatric disorders.

KEY POINTS

- Approximately 50% of children seen in mental health facilities and in special classrooms for children with social-emotional problems have LI. Conversely, a similar percentage of children seen in speech-language clinics or special classrooms for children with LI or language-related learning disabilities have a social-emotional disturbance.

- Examining both language structure and communication is important. Deficits in these areas interfere with learning and also prevent children and adolescents from understanding and expressing their thoughts and feelings and interacting socially.

- Children with pervasive expressive and receptive LI, and whose language problems continue beyond the age of 5 years, are most at risk for social-emotional disturbance.

- The relationship of language and communication impairments with social-emotional disorders can be confusing, and it is not always possible to make a clear differential diagnosis. Sometimes one disorder seems to lead to secondary symptomatology. In other cases, LI may be an inherent part of a social-emotional disorder.

- The evidence points toward the long-term persistence of LI in adolescents and adults, even among those whose language problems appear to be resolved. Furthermore, some children who early in development do not meet criteria for LI do so in later childhood and adolescence when language demands on academic tasks and social life increase.

2

LANGUAGE IMPAIRMENT AND ASSOCIATED CONDITIONS

Language is by definition a public behavior, wherein the child displays in exquisite detail the inner workings of the mind. . . . If we assume . . . that language acquisition participates in and displays the many other contents of mind, then . . . we can use information on language to understand far less accessible aspects of development, as children make the transition from infancy to childhood. (Bates, O'Connell, & Shore, 1987, p. 191)

Language and communication impairments do not occur in isolation. Beyond the obvious function of language as a means of communication, from early childhood LI is associated with cognitive deficits (e.g., thinking, memory, problem solving, concept development), poor academic achievement, immature social-cognitive skills, problems in social relationships, and difficulties in emotion and behavior regulation. The question naturally arises as to whether language should be the focus of study in child clinical populations, as it must be acknowledged that the processes indexed by any single measure are complex and there is probably considerable overlap in what is being measured. Whether there is something specific about language deficits is still open to question. On one hand, language may be just one of a range of deficits caused by a common underlying factor. On the other hand, language may have a central role to play in the development of social-emotional disorders in that internalized language and verbally mediated rules play an important role in both self-control and achievement across domains (Barkley, 1997; Denckla, 1996). Nevertheless, the risk in using language as a starting point and attributing too much to it as the favorite variable must be acknowledged at the outset since language and other developmental competencies are inextricably interrelated and interdependent throughout the course of development. The central role of language becomes clearer if we view it as a means of symbolizing experience and as a tool that allows for communication of one's own—and understanding of others'—thinking, experiences, emotions, ideas, and social and cultural rules.

The interrelationship of LI with other aspects of development is examined in two ways in this book. In this chapter, aspects of development associated with LI are briefly described. Then, in Chapters 3 and 4, a developmental model is applied to consider the dynamic transactional interplay of these with language and communication from infancy through adolescence. This approach is consistent with contemporary research and clinical work in child psychopathology that has moved toward evaluating principles of child development from an integrative perspective emphasizing the interdependence and dynamic, interactive relationship between various aspects of development and between biology and experience.

COGNITION

Thinking and Problem Solving

The term *cognition* is often used synonymously with thinking. It involves creating, acquiring, and applying knowledge to make sense of one's world and to function adaptively in it. Cognition also encompasses skills required for effective problem solving and abstract reasoning, such as being able to organize the world perceptually and to rapidly and efficiently process information, pay attention, and remember what has been observed and learned. Children with LI perform poorly on tasks that measure these functions (Johnston, 1988).

There is still debate over the degree of interdependence between language and cognition and whether one precedes or follows the other in development. Language and cognitive development appear to work in concert so that children are motivated to learn words or forms to communicate in a way that facilitates cognitive development. For instance, learning and generalizing the understanding that objects and people continue to exist when out of sight (object permanence) is accompanied by liberal use of the word "gone" (Gopnik & Meltzoff, 1986). In this way, language is seen as a "catalyst" of cognitive change (Nelson, 1996). As well, there is a reciprocal relationship between reading and learning. Over the course of development, children with good language and reading skills read more and consequently learn more (Stanovich, 1986). Although research on deaf children suggests that thought can be present without language, the finding that deaf children perform more poorly on verbal tests and tend to be less proficient readers suggests that language facilitates thinking (Reich, Hambleton, & Houldin, 1977).

Visual-Motor Skills

Children with LI have problems in areas of cognition that are not language based, including motor coordination (Bishop & Edmundson, 1987b; Powell & Bishop, 1992; Stark & Tallal, 1981) and visual-motor skills (Cohen, Barwick, et al., 1998; Cantwell & Baker, 1991; Johnston, 1988; Powell & Bishop, 1992; Tallal, Sainburg, & Jernigan, 1991). It has been suggested that the kinds of deficits observed in processing auditory information may apply to the nonauditory mode as well (Tallal, Stark, Kallman, & Mellits, 1981).

Memory

There is not a single memory system but separate systems that can function relatively independently (Gathercole, 1998). In the broadest sense, memory is divided into short-term memory, including working memory, and long-term memory, including procedural, autobiographical, and episodic memory.

Short-term memory refers to memory for recent events measured in spans of seconds and minutes. Current research on short-term memory is focused on *working memory* (Baddeley, 1986; Gathercole, 1998; Swanson, 1994). Working memory refers to the ability to hold a small amount of information in the forefront of the mind (cognition) for a short time to guide responses while simultaneously processing the same or other information (Swanson, 1994). Working memory has been particularly prominent in models of executive functions (Barkley, 1997; Pennington, Bennetto, McAleer, & Roberts, 1996) and is important for social interaction and for various aspects of academic achievement, including word decoding, reading comprehension, and mathematics. For instance, in social situations, the context of an interaction and the interactional partner's prior verbal and nonverbal messages must be held in mind to make an appropriate response. In reading, to answer questions about a story one must hold in mind what happened at the beginning of the story to make sense of the ending. A specific type of working memory, *phonological working memory,* has been implicated in LI and reading disability (Bishop, 1996; Gathercole & Baddeley, 1990). There is mounting evidence that the skills involved in one phonological working memory task, nonword repetition, play a role in learning new words. On nonword repetition tasks, children are asked to repeat nonwords of two, three, four, and five syllables (e.g., "blonterstaping"). It has been suggested that nonword repetition may be a genetic marker for LI that could provide a quick screening tool (Bishop, North, & Donlan, 1996).

Long-term memory refers to memory for events that occurred hours, days, months, and even years previously and is the storehouse for information transfer from short-term memory that can be called up on demand. Long-term memory is divided further into procedural, episodic, and autobiographical memory. *Procedural memory* involves representations of sensorimotor expectations based on past experience, such as tying one's shoes or riding a bicycle. *Episodic memory* involves recall of specific events that are remembered when the previous event context is reinstated and that can be expressed verbally (Nelson, 1993). For instance, on one's arriving in Paris, the memory of a wonderful meal eaten on a previous visit comes to mind but not the events of the day when the meal was eaten. *Autobiographical memory* emerges when children learn to talk about their memories, around the age of 3 years, and can formulate memories in the form of narratives (Fivush, Haden, & Reese, 1996; Nelson, 1993). Autobiographical memory goes beyond memory for specific events and provides a means by which children link sequences of events in narrative form and in this way learn about themselves in context. The quality of discourse shared between parents and their children, facilitated by children's increasing language competence, allows ideas to be exchanged and emotions understood (Nelson, 1996). Because these memories are built into conversations with important others, children are sensitive to the influence of deficits in narrative discourse (Vallance et al., 1999) and to others' mislabeling and distortions of events (Crittenden, 1996). Children with LI are at a disadvantage in recounting events and their personal stories to others, which may contribute to problems in social relationships and in therapy and be attributed to emotional factors.

Memory, which improves throughout childhood, is facilitated by language and cognitive development, including adequate executive function skills. Good memory is important both for achievement and for social and emotional growth. Over time, children show increasing capacity to create and use strategies to assist them in remembering. They also become aware that they use strategies *(metamemory)* (Brown, Bransford, Ferrara, & Campione, 1983). Many of these strategies are language based (e.g., rehearsal).

Executive Functions

To develop self-control and become socialized, children need to be able to plan, organize, and monitor their thoughts, communications, and actions (Luria, 1961). These skills have often been considered under the broad rubric of *executive functions*. There are a number of definitions of executive functions (Eslinger, 1996). The specific skills that are involved include setting a goal, inhibiting or deferring a response, making plans, taking in only information that is pertinent to the goal, planning and organizing, and being able to keep in mind plans and tasks until they are implemented. Problems with executive functions have been observed among children with LI (Cohen, Barwick, et al., 1998; Cohen, Vallance, et al., 2000; Purvis & Tannock, 1997) and with learning disabilities (Torgesen, 1994) and also among children with a psychiatric diagnosis who have co-occurring language problems, such as those diagnosed as ADHD (Tannock & Schachar, 1996), and children who are aggressive and noncompliant (Camp, Blom, Herbert, & vanDoorninck, 1977; Moffitt, 1993).

SOCIAL AND EMOTIONAL DEVELOPMENT

Affect and Behavior Regulation

Language is not only a tool for thought and social interaction but a means to control one's own behavior and emotions and those of others. Although definitions of affect and behavior regulation vary, these terms usually refer to behaviors that are used flexibly to guide, monitor, and direct one's behavior and social interactions (Fox, 1994). Children's capacity to regulate their emotions and behavior could also be considered elements of executive functions but are given special attention because of the relevance of affect and behavior regulation to social-emotional disorder. In fact, increasingly attention is turning to a broader descriptive view of psychopathology in which it is considered under the broad rubric of problems with emotion regulation. It has been suggested that specific psychiatric disorders could be translated into difficulties with overregulation (e.g., depression) or underregulation (Oppositional Defiant Disorder) (Cole, Michel, & O'Donnell-Teti, 1994). Well-regulated children are good problem solvers, more able to compromise and meet mutual needs when playing with peers, able to make new friends, and likely to develop peer interaction skills in play. Children must be able to understand, encode, organize, and retrieve rules that contribute to emotional and behavioral regulation and learn this in interactions with others. This important use of language is also a key feature of many therapeutic interventions such as social skills training and cognitive behavior modification. The skills required by such programs, however, are those with which children with LI are likely to be at a disadvantage.

Frameworks for Understanding Social Relationships

The ability to communicate for social purposes is a crucial part of development from birth onward. Children learn in and from a range of social relationships. Social influences and processes have been examined under two broad frameworks that on the surface appear to be unrelated. One framework is *attachment* and the other *social cognition*. Both contribute to understanding how children process information and represent reality in social interactions that may be both a contributor to and an outcome of language competence. This is particularly so when we adopt the broader definition of language to include pragmatics and discourse. The way in which attachment and social cognition may be related can be illustrated by considering an important developmental achievement that occurs around 9 months of age: the appearance of joint attention. Joint attention is the capacity to coordinate attention with a caregiver regarding objects and events (Mundy & Gomes, 1998). To this end, infants use communicative means such as gestures and vocalization to draw their communicative partner's attention to an object. To engage in joint attention, infants must be able to take in and process information from the environment and have some capacity to read cues, including the mental state of their caregiver (a social-cognitive skill) whose interest the infant is trying to engage. This is most evident in situations where the infant must repair a failed communication, that is, try another strategy when the previous one did not work. In some cases, the infant must do this more than once. It is also important that the infant has a secure attachment with a positive and sensitive caregiver who is appropriately responsive to the infant's bid to share attention and who facilitates the development of joint attention (Mundy & Willoughby, 1998).

Attachment

Attachment theory is one of the most important frameworks for understanding the origin and evaluation of social-emotional development across the life span (Bowlby, 1969). Essential to attachment theory is the formation of an emotional tie between infants and primary caregivers during the first year of life that is dependent on the way caregivers respond to the infant, especially when the infant is distressed. Attachment theory is usually associated with explaining the implications of different styles of caregiver response to infant emotions under stress. It also has contributed to thinking about language, communication, and cognition; features of caregiver-infant interaction shown to facilitate secure attachment are similar to those that facilitate competent communicative and language development. These include the capacity to follow the infant's lead, accurately read the infant's signals, and respond sensitively and appropriately to the infant.

Four different attachment patterns have been derived from an experimental procedure with infants and their mothers (Strange Situation Procedure) (Ainsworth, Blehar, Waters, & Wall, 1978) to capture the infant-mother relationship under conditions where the infant is mildly stressed. This well-standardized procedure comprises seven increasingly stressful episodes including infant separations and reunions with the mother. Using primarily the infant's responses during the reunion, they are classified according to criteria for secure, insecure avoidant, insecure ambivalent (Ainsworth et al., 1978), and disorganized (Main & Solomon, 1986) attachment relationships.

Infants who are *securely* attached are curious, explore their environment, and develop positive social relationships and self-esteem. When separated briefly and left with a stranger, they may become distressed but are quickly soothed when their mother returns. In mental health clinic samples, infants usually are not securely attached (Cohen et al., 1999; van IJzendoorn, Goldberg, Kroonenberg, & Frenkel, 1992). There are two types of insecure attachment relationships. One type is characterized by an infant displaying only limited or no expression of attachment needs (*avoidant* attachment). These infants often appear to be independent and typically do not seek comfort and protection from their caregiver even under distressing conditions. Infants with this type of attachment have a history of unresponsive caregiving. They do not expect to have their needs met and do not even try. The other type of insecure attachment, associated with an inconsistent caregiving style, is called an *anxious-ambivalent* or *resistant* attachment. These infants exhibit an exaggerated expression of attachment needs, showing extreme distress when separated from their caregiver and being difficult to comfort by their caregiver when reunited. Such infants have a history of getting attachment needs met only when they heighten affect to get the attention of their caregiver. A fourth attachment category, *disorganized,* is associated with a frightening caregiving style and applies to children who show no consistent pattern of attachment but often exhibit odd behaviors such as freezing and stilling when reunited with their mother following separation. A disorganized attachment is frequently observed in children referred to mental health clinics who have been neglected and abused (Cicchetti & Toth, 1995).

Attachment may be associated with language, communication, and cognition in both direct and indirect ways. Bowlby (1973) maintained that the way that caregivers talk to their infants and children about early experiences and about emotions is critical to later adjustment and that children use these experiences to construct a working (mental) model or representation of the caregiver and of the self in relation to the caregiver (Main, Kaplan, & Cassidy, 1985). Although this construct is still speculative, it is presumed that working models serve to organize emotion and behavior and set predictions or expectations of others' behavior specifically in relation to attachment goals. Understanding working models may be facilitated by research on aspects of children's cognition (i.e., reasoning, event representation, episodic and autobiographical memory) and social cognition. Main et al. (1985) suggest that working models operate by directing attention, memory, and the appraisal of experience (Bowlby, 1969, 1973); thus working models provide an operative framework for evaluating new experiences that include both affective and cognitive components (Main et al., 1985). These working models become increasingly stable and automatic over time and less accessible to conscious awareness. By the middle of the second year, infants can routinely abstract from repeated daily events mental representations of their sequences and form expectations about their outcome (see, e.g., Fivush et al., 1996). When later experiences are referred back to these representations and expectations, they enhance memory (Nelson, 1986). Children's experience and expectations of consistency in interactions with their caregiver are also related to coherence and elaboration of personal narratives (Crittenden, 1996).

Attachment security may also have indirect effects on language development. First, securely attached infants are more readable and react more positively to input. Second, securely attached infants are more socially competent and consequently both elicit and respond to social communication. Finally, for securely attached infants, attachment figures provide the stable emotional base from which they can exercise curiosity, explore their environment, and have confidence to take on challenges without giving up prematurely. Having this base from which to explore is presumed to exert a salutary effect on the cognitive, language, and social development of securely attached infants and a negative effect on the development of insecurely attached and disorganized infants. It would seem that qualities of maternal interactive style that are important to infant and toddler language development are similar to those important to social-emotional development.

Although there is evidence of an association of attachment security with language development, this has been observed only in high-risk samples (Kelly, Morisset, Barnard, Hammond, & Booth, 1996; Meins, 1997; van IJzendoorn, Dijkstra, & Bus, 1995). In clinical samples with moderate risk, language and communication are not associated with attachment security as measured by the Strange Situation Procedure, but they are with qualities of the mother-child relationship, such as maternal sensitivity and dyadic reciprocity (e.g., Barwick et al., 2000; Bates, Benigni, Bretherton, Camaioni, & Volterra, 1979). It would appear that when environmental risk is moderate, infants receive enough quality social input to maintain a normal course of language and communicative development. It is important to say at this juncture that, although obviously attachment security is important, neither Bowlby nor other attachment researchers suggest that early insecure attachment causes later psychopathology or language or learning problems. Such problems are considered a cumulative product of both early experience and ongoing supportive (or unsupportive) circumstances.

Social Cognition and Social Skills

Attachment theory focuses on child-caregiver relationships, particularly caregiver responsiveness in times of distress. There are clearly other kinds of relationships that function in a variety of situations (Rutter, 1995). This is where social cognition comes in. Social cognition refers to the cognitive processes individuals apply to understand social situations; they have a predictable progression throughout childhood (Staub & Eisenberg, 1981). Social-cognitive development contributes to communication because effective communication relies not only on linguistic competence but on the capacity to integrate language with awareness of the emotions, intentions, and beliefs of others.

As for other aspects of cognition, the direction of the relationship between development of language and social cognition is controversial. Bishop (1997) has outlined three possible links between social skills, social cognition, and language that could contribute to treatment planning, all of which have had some research support. The first is that both language learning and social communication problems arise because of limited information-processing capacity. The second is that children with LI have limited opportunities for social learning given that they tend to be rejected by both adults and peers. Consequently, they have less opportunity for learning and practicing social skills. Finally, children with LI could have primary deficits in social cognition that influence communication skills and increase social rejection. Regardless of the direction of causality between LI and social cognition, many intervention programs for children and adolescents aim to improve social-cognitive skills but have been remiss in assessing language as a contributor to the outcome of treatment.

Four aspects of social cognition have been most commonly examined: (a) emotion recognition and understanding, (b) theory of mind, (c) social problem solving, and (d) self-cognition.

Emotion recognition and understanding. The ability to recognize and understand others' emotion expression and appropriately respond to social and emotional cues is an important component of social cognition. By 2 years of age, children can identify basic emotions in themselves and others. The capacity to identify more subtle emotions and conflicting feelings grows through the school years (Dunn, Bretherton, & Munn, 1987). In the past, emotions were viewed solely as an internal experience or feeling state rather than as a relational experience. It is now assumed that the way children conceptualize and reason about others' emotions influences social interactions and as a result the development of psychopathology (Crick & Dodge, 1994; Yeates, Schultz, & Selman, 1990). Children with LI have been shown to have no difficulty identifying emotion from pictures but do have difficulty identifying emotion in social situations (Cohen, Menna, Vallance, Im, & Horodezky, 1998).

Theory of mind. Theory of mind refers to children's ability to understand and make inferences about their own and another person's mental state, including desires, thoughts, beliefs, and emotions (Baron-Cohen, 1995; Dunn, 1996). It also involves understanding that someone else may believe something that is not true and act on that false belief. Although elements or precursors of theory of mind appear in infants, it is generally thought to be established around the age of 4 years, once children grasp that what one has in mind is a representation of reality and not the reality itself. Theory of mind is usually measured in preschoolers with a task intended to determine whether they are able to recognize that other people possess beliefs that are different from their own. In these false-belief tasks, situational circumstances are arranged so that the child's beliefs are true and the other's beliefs are false. The original Wimmer and Perner (1983) false-belief task was based on a story that was acted out for a child using a boy doll. The boy doll puts some chocolate in an area and then leaves that area. While he is gone, the child witnesses the chocolate being moved. The boy doll returns and wants to eat his chocolate. At this point, the child observing the story is asked where the boy doll will look for the chocolate. Most 3-year-olds will say that the boy doll will look in the new place where the chocolate was moved; they are unable to take into consideration the boy doll's perspective and the fact that he was not witness to the chocolate being moved from its original location. Four-year-olds will say that the boy doll would look in the original location, thereby taking into consideration the fact that the boy doll did not witness the chocolate being moved. The majority of research has been devoted to examining the emergence of theory of mind in the course of normal development. There is considerable research showing that theory of mind is deficient in children diagnosed as autistic (e.g., Tager-Flusberg, 1999), but only a few studies have provided evidence that language is associated with theory of mind in normally developing children (Astington & Jenkins, 1999; Cutting & Dunn, 1999), children with LI (Farmer, 2000), and children with social-emotional problems (Happé & Frith, 1996; Hughes, Dunn, & White, 1998).

Social problem solving. Competent social problem solving has been examined from two broad perspectives. One perspective focuses on deficits in social problem solving ability (Dodge, Pettit, McClaskey, & Brown, 1986) and the other on developmental lags in social problem solving (Yeates, Schultz, & Selman, 1991).

Dodge and colleagues (1986) are most closely associated with the first approach. These investigators studied social cognition by asking children to respond to a vignette by imagining that they are the protagonists in a situation involving two children who ultimately engage in a verbally and physically aggressive interchange. A series of questions is asked according to steps involved in the social problem solving process: (a) encoding external and internal cues, (b) interpreting and mentally representing those cues, (c) clarifying or selecting a goal, (d) accessing or constructing a response, (e) deciding on a response, and (f) enacting a behavior (Crick & Dodge, 1994). This model assumes that feedback loops influence and modify social-cognitive processes across the six steps. Normally developing children are able to repair a rupture in social problem solving to maintain a harmonious relationship. When social cues are ambiguous, children tend to perceive what they expect to see, presumably based on prior experience. Aggressive children, for instance, are more likely to perceive hostile intent (Lochman & Dodge, 1994). If children with LI have been rejected and also have deficits in social information processing, this may lead to more negative interchanges with peers. Dodge and colleagues have focused on preadolescence and early adolescence because it is during this time that cognitive processing becomes more hypothetical.

Selman and colleagues have been the only researchers to place social problem solving in a developmental framework, examining stages of social problem solving from early childhood to adulthood (Selman, 1980; Yeates et al., 1991). This model considers how children process social information to coordinate their understanding of others' thoughts, feelings, and motives in conjunction with their own in attempting to balance inner needs and interpersonal conflicts. Each successive developmental stage reflects increasing differentiation and coordination of the social perspectives of self and other. This developmental framework is applied to four sequential steps in the process of social problem solving: (a) defining the problem (which includes understanding that the perceptions, beliefs, and feelings of the partners in conflict are different), (b) generating alternate strategies, (c) selecting and implementing specific strategies, and (d) evaluating outcomes. Although an iterative transactional process is not explicitly described, it is inevitable that one exists. At the most immature level (3 to 7 years of age), children are aware of feelings, but they lack understanding of the possibility that another person may interpret the same situation differently. They are egocentric and focus on physical rather than psychological characteristics. Impulsive solutions such as physical aggression or social withdrawal, which fail to coordinate social perspectives, are often articulated. The most mature perspective, characteristic of adolescents, acknowledges reciprocity and recognition of the need for mutual coordination in arriving at a solution to maintain the relationship. Interpersonal negotiating strategies reflect awareness of the need to coordinate perspectives where compromise and discussion are in order. Evidence concerning the association between maturity of social problem solving, LI, and social-emotional disturbance is limited but has been observed in one study of a mental health clinic sample (Cohen, Menna, et al., 1998).

Self-cognition. Over the past 20 years, the study of what has been called the "self-system" has moved from examination of personality traits to consideration of cognitions or beliefs about oneself, relationships, and interactions (Harter, 1999). Important components of self-cognition include self-esteem and feelings of efficacy. A major development in young children is the capacity to use language intentionally, that is, to communicate an observation, thought, or feeling. This also requires monitoring of whether one is, in fact, understood. Bruner (1984) has suggested that self is defined by the way intentions are organized and sequenced and by awareness of one's communicative efficacy. Self-esteem is important because it determines whether children will act on knowledge they have or take a calculated risk when they do not know the answer.

Play

Children practice and consolidate their cognitive and social skills in play. Moreover, through play children master their environment and work through challenges to development. The appearance of pretend play is linked with language development and the capacity to represent events and relationships. In normal development, language and play are closely linked. Immature forms of play are associated with children using only single words, whereas complex pretend or symbolic play is associated with multiword verbal expression (Bates et al., 1979; McCune-Nicolich, 1981). Given the many functions of play, it is notable that children with LI exhibit immature forms of play.

MODELS FOR UNDERSTANDING THE DEFICITS OF CHILDREN WITH LANGUAGE IMPAIRMENT

As yet, there is no comprehensive model that simultaneously addresses the interrelation of language, cognition, social cognition, and behavior. From a theoretical perspective, in recent years there has been increasing interest in examining the neuropsychological and cognitive-processing correlates of psychiatric disorder (Szatmari et al., 1990) and particularly Conduct Disorder and ADHD (Hinshaw, 1992; Moffitt, 1993). Whether there is something specific about language deficits is still open to question. On one hand, language may be just one of a range of deficits caused by an underlying neurodevelopmental factor. On the other hand, language may have a central role to play in the development of psychiatric disorders in that internalized language and verbally mediated rules play an important role in both self-control and achievement across domains (Barkley, 1997; Denckla, 1996). Looking more closely at the underlying nature of LI, Bishop (1992) concluded that the concept of *limited processing capacity* provides a framework for interpreting the wide range of deficits in children with language impairments. She contends that the fundamental deficit in language-impaired children is a slowed rate of information processing that leads to impairment on any task that requires integration of rapidly presented information. Language may play a more critical role because auditory information is more vulnerable to processing problems than visual information since auditory stimuli are typically brief and sequential whereas visual information persists. Bishop does not discuss social-emotional disorder, but the notion of a limited processing capacity could have implications for processing social and emotional information as well, particularly auditory information. Another framework for understanding why children with LI have difficulty processing social information can be found in the work of Vygotsky (1962). Central to Vygotsky's work is that language is a tool for thought. During development, children first engage in dialogues that then become internalized for future use. Disruptions in language development thus can interfere with children's formation of internal representations of their social environment and consequently their behavior.

Although researchers have yet to pinpoint the precise explanation for the relationship of language with other aspects of development, the preponderance of current evidence suggests that there is a bidirectional interaction between language and these other aspects of development and between these developmental domains and experience. This is the subject of the next two chapters.

KEY POINTS

- Language and communication impairments are associated with deficits in cognition, social-emotional functioning, social cognition, play, and affect and behavior regulation.

- With respect to cognition, children with LI exhibit problems with cognitive processes associated with problem solving, executive functions, and memory. Problems in working memory and autobiographical memory are especially pertinent to these children's functioning in school and in social situations.

- The ability to communicate for social purposes is crucial to development. One framework for understanding social and emotional development is attachment; another is social cognition.

- Children hone their cognitive and social skills in play with other children. Children also use play as a means to work through challenges to development. Immaturity of the play of children with LI contributes to problems in their overall developmental functioning.

- There is considerable interest in the role of language in affect and behavior regulation for self-reflection, planning, and organization. It has even been suggested that social-emotional disorders could be conceptualized as difficulties with overregulation or underregulation.

3

DEVELOPMENTAL CONSIDERATIONS
Infants

> When maladaptation is viewed as development rather than as disease, a transformed understanding results. . . . It is not something a person "has" or an ineluctable expression of an endogenous pathogen. It is the complex result of a myriad of risk and protective factors operating over time. (Sroufe, 1997, p. 251)

Increasingly, the perspective of developmental psychopathology is being adopted to understand and treat child psychopathology. This perspective emphasizes examining mechanisms and maladaptive processes in terms of transactions between characteristics of children and their psychosocial environments across the life span (Cicchetti, 1993; Sroufe, 1997). Using a developmental transactional approach for assessment and treatment is preferable to a categorical diagnostic approach for a number of reasons. First, current diagnostic schemes separate LI and social-emotional disorder. It is now apparent, however, that in some cases they are not separable and in fact one may be an inherent part of the other. Second, psychiatric and language diagnostic schemes do not consistently point to the developmental processes that inform assessment and treatment. Third, there can be multiple pathways to the same end point, and this is not reflected in a categorical system that only classifies disorder. Thus the co-occurrence of LI with social-emotional disturbance is unlikely to be attributable to language alone but to a combination of LI with adverse relationships and environmental events that must be taken into consideration.

Certain principles of developmental processes are typically applied to understand the perspective of developmental psychopathology (Rutter et al., 1997; Sroufe, 1997) as well as to provide clues about how one might intervene. These principles, listed below, are consistent with current interactionist views of language acquisition and development that integrate understanding of experience, and especially social interactional experience, with changes in brain organization and function associated with learning (Chapman, 2000). Thus although there is evidence of the genetic and neuroanatomical underpinnings of language development and impairment (e.g., Tager-Flusberg, 1999; Bishop et al., 1995; Grigorenko et al., 1997), the quality of the interactional environment throughout development is critical.

1. The interaction of children with their environment goes two ways. Biological factors, such as genetic endowment, influence individual differences in how children react to others and how others react to them. Multiple pathways could also lead to the same outcome, as is the case with a symptom such as inattentiveness.

2. The two-way interaction between children and their environment needs to be viewed within the larger social or cultural context. For instance, children raised in impoverished and stressful family circumstances are at greater disadvantage than those who are not.

3. Children's characteristics change over time as a function of the interplay between biological and environmental influences such that there are both continuities and discontinuities in development. Longitudinal research has helped see where a child may get on and off track at various developmental turning points. Consequently, the timing of intervention may be important.

4. Behavior may change in form while still reflecting the same underlying process. This was illustrated in the Stothard et al. (1998) and Snowling et al. (2000) studies described in Chapter 1, which showed that even when preschool children's LI seemed to resolve, difficulties related to literacy skills were observed in adolescence when the demands on language increased.

5. Both risks and protective factors need to be considered in understanding the developmental trajectory for children with LI. Not all children with LI have social-emotional problems, and it is important to understand how this has come about.

Adopting the model of developmental psychopathology means that, optimally, links between LI and social-emotional disorder are understood in terms of the sequence of problem onset and the relationship between language, cognition (including social cognition), and social-emotional functioning during different developmental periods. This full range of information is rarely available. Some longitudinal studies have traced a developmental trajectory, but only a few studies have simultaneously examined relationships among multiple skills in atypical populations. Therefore it must be understood that the research on LI and social-emotional disorder reviewed in this chapter and in Chapter 4 provides an incomplete picture of interrelated developmental processes. I hope that what is described will stimulate the reader's thinking about both their clinical work and future research. Four developmental periods are discussed separately. Major milestones in language, communication, and associated skills, along with factors in the child and in the environment that may interrupt or facilitate the normal developmental course, are described. In this chapter, infants from the ages of birth to 3 years are considered. Then, in Chapter 4, the preschool, middle childhood, and adolescent periods are described in a similar way. Both clinical cases and descriptions of research on atypical populations, where available, are used to illustrate the interrelation of LI, social-emotional disorder, and other aspects of development and the multiple pathways to adaptive and maladaptive outcomes.

DEVELOPMENTAL TASKS OF INFANTS: BIRTH TO 3 YEARS

Language and Social-Emotional Development

In infancy, the overlap of communicative and social-emotional development is perhaps most evident. In the first 2 years of life, the evolution of social interaction and communication can be divided into three main periods (Adamson & Chance, 1998). The first period begins at birth. Infants are primed to orient socially to the human face and motivated to communicate, first through their cries, gazes, vocalizations, and early gestures or "protolanguage" (Trevarthen, 1979). By 8 to 12 weeks, infants can discriminate attachment figures reliably and begin to communicate about when they do and do not want to interact and what they do and do not like by showing pleasure through smiling and alertness, on the one hand, and displeasure through fussiness or crying, on the other hand. From these cues, parents come to understand their infants, and infants develop expectations of how their parents will respond to their signals. These early communicative behaviors are not intentional (although parents often think that they are) but set the stage for intentional communication later on. Most infants are good at sending clear signals, but those who are ill or have even a mild developmental handicap may pose extra challenges to parents. Thus for some parents and infants, this interactive process can be easy and a source of feelings of pleasure and competence. For others, it is frustrating and requires patience and the capacity to tolerate intense feelings while testing a variety of responses to the infant.

In a second period of communicative development, from 6 to 18 months, infants make significant gains in their capacity to communicate by actively engaging and taking turns with parents (Bornstein & Tamis-LeMonda, 1990; Cohn & Tronick, 1987). Infants initiate, maintain, and stop face-to-face interactions through such behaviors as smiling and gurgling or turning away and showing distress. These are among the precursors for both intentional communication and attachment formation. Although parents talk to their infants from birth, typically by trying to imitate or comment on what their infants are doing, it is not until some time around the midpoint of the first year that vocal exchange becomes reciprocal and infants take on responsibility for initiating and maintaining interactions such that their communicative gestures can be considered intentional. Developments in babbling illustrate the importance of prelinguistic communication for both language and social-emotional development. Infants begin to produce combinations of vowels and consonants (i.e., babble) around the age of 3 or 4 months. They also play with their babbling; infants listen to themselves and show pleasure at the various sounds that they make. Not only do infants enjoy hearing themselves, but parents are more likely to speak to babbling infants, which increases babbling further (Locke, 1993). For instance, a dialogue may be established when an infant babbles and the mother responds with a pleased "You're trying to tell me something. You want me to shake this again, don't you?" If the infant smiles in response to the mother's voice, then the mother smiles back. After a series of these interactions, the infant may turn away and the mother may say, "You need a rest. That was a lot of talking." There also is an association between preverbal communication such as babbling and language development. Babbling indicates that infants have learned to segment a stream of sound into communicatively meaningful chunks (Rapin, 1996). Infants who are ultimately delayed in language, as indicated by a low rate of vocabulary growth and limited phonological skills, have fewer consonant-vowel utterances that characterize babble during infancy (Stoel-Gammon, 1998).

This second period of infant social communicative interaction is also marked by the appearance of *joint attention,* a turning point in development that changes the nature of social interaction profoundly (Bakeman & Adamson, 1984; Bruner, 1975). Joint attention is associated with later language development as reflected in vocabulary and pragmatic competence (Bates, Bretherton, & Snyder, 1988). Joint attention requires coordinating motor skills and visual attention with those of another person regarding objects and events (Mundy & Gomes, 1998). Beginning in the fourth or fifth month, infants become increasingly attentive to objects, and from then on social interactions expand to include attention to self, the social partner (usually a parent or other caregiver), and objects. At 6 months, infants are able to localize the general area of their parents' (or other caregivers') visual attention and begin to be able to point to an object of interest. By 9 months, infants gain the attention and help of caregivers by looking and combining looks at the parent with fussing and wiggling and handing things to them (Bates et al., 1979). At 12 to 18 months, infants' communication becomes more accurate and parents find their infants' signals easier to read. From then on, a large proportion of infant-parent interacting includes objects in joint attention episodes. The communication skills observed in joint attention episodes reveal early signs of a number of important capacities. These include appreciation of the perceptions of others, understanding that these can be influenced by the infants' own behavior (a possible precursor of theory of mind), and perceiving and sharing thoughts and feelings and thus a sense of connectedness during social interaction *(intersubjectivity)* (Stern, 1985). The beginning of pragmatic competence is shown in infants' attempts to *repair* communications when they fail to get the intended response from a caregiver. For instance, competent infants who do not get their caregivers' attention with a glance may make a sound or touch the caregiver to do so. Difficulties with repair may occur in the presence of otherwise normal language development, as we shall see in the case example presented later in this chapter.

All these important early gestural communicative behaviors depend simultaneously on competent infant behavior and having sensitive, responsive caregivers. They also are influenced by individual differences in the tendency to initiate social behavior (Slomkowski et al., 1992), attention, and self-regulation (Kaler & Kopp, 1990). In fact, after approximately 9 to 10 months of age, problems with joint attention may foreshadow social-emotional difficulties (Mundy & Willoughby, 1998). First, infants who do not respond to or initiate joint attention activities may foster disturbance in the infant-caregiver relationship (Wetherby & Prizant, 1993b). Second, joint attention is related to social-cognitive capacities, including the capacity for repair (Bretherton, McNew, & Beeghly-Smith, 1981; Tomasello, 1995). Finally, joint attention may be associated with infants' capacity to initiate shared positive affective states with others in relation to a third object (Adamson & Bakeman, 1985) and thus to engage in affective intersubjectivity (Mundy, Kasari, & Sigman, 1992).

Here we come to the third period of communicative development. From 18 months to 2 years, the rapid growth of language marks a major turning point in infants' capacity to communicate, learn, engage in social interactions, and regulate emotions and behavior. Normally, infants say their first words around their first birthday, usually labels for familiar people and objects in context. From then on, language development escalates, and at 30 months of age infants show their most rapid increase in vocabulary, in what has been called the "vocabulary burst" (Bates et al., 1988). By the age of 2 years, infants have a vocabulary of 50 words; by the age of 3, they have a vocabulary of around 1,000 words (Nelson, 1973). Even infants who have not begun to talk by their first birthday understand words and simple commands and are sensitive to the emotional intonation of language. Around 2 years, most infants are in the process of a "grammar burst" (Bates et al., 1988), when they use increasingly more word combinations.

Interwoven with developments in cognition, language becomes a tool for infants' continuing awareness of themselves and differentiation of self from others when they begin to use the words "I," "me," and "mine" at 2 to 3 years to refer to themselves. Toward the end of this period, infants begin to be able to organize narratives to talk about their experiences and inner life and share them with others both verbally and through play. These narratives represent a convergence of skills that include using language to retell memories, anticipate experiences, process emotional events, problem-solve, practice questions, and reflect on relationships with others (Nelson, 1989). Narratives of 3-year-olds have the basics of a story structure such as characters, a beginning, a sequence of events, and an ending (Engel, 1996). Narrative skills also are used to talk through things that are puzzling or troubling (Nelson, 1989). A significant factor contributing to the capacity to engage in these narratives is "memory talk" with parents, which structures infants' memories in narrative form (Dunn & Brown, 1991). Undoubtedly, these social interactions with parents and other caregivers, as well as competence in structural language and communication, are important.

There is also an association between the early quality of mother-child conversations and children's later narratives (Dunn et al., 1987; Stern, 1985). Narratives convey both what has happened and how children feel about the narrated event (Fivush, 1991). Dunn, Brown, and Beardsall (1991) observed a relationship between 3-year-olds' conversational discourse about feeling states with their mother and siblings (but not structural language) and their ability to recognize emotions on an affective perspective taking task at 6 years. These personal narratives are also important for development of autobiographical memory (Fivush, 1991), integration of children in their sociocultural context (Miller, Mintz, Hoogstra, Fung, & Potts, 1992), and working out feelings about troubling experiences (Dunn et al., 1991).

Infants' quality of interacting in a range of situations is related to sensitive and responsive caregiving, which is important for later language, social, and cognitive development (Ainsworth et al., 1978; Bornstein & Tamis-LeMonda, 1997; Nicely, Tamis-LeMonda, & Bornstein, 2000). For instance, Murray and Hornbaker (1997) followed infants and their mothers at 3-month intervals from birth to 30 months. They found that an early elaborative style of interacting, which involved mothers following their infant's lead, responding sensitively to their infant's cues, and extending or expanding on their infant's activity, positively predicted cognitive development at 24 months. With respect to language, mothers' intrusive direction of their infants at 12 months was negatively related to receptive but not expressive language at 24 months. These findings are important in light of the relatively poorer prognosis for infants and children with receptive language problems. In this context, it is important to emphasize that infants with receptive language impairments evoke or respond to interactions in ways that may have a maladaptive outcome, particularly if parents are unaware of their infant's problems in comprehension.

Sensitive and contingent responding means different things at different developmental periods (Yoder, Warren, McCathren, & Leew, 1998). In young infants, from the newborn to 6-month period, parents' nonlinguistic contingency to infants' cues (e.g., smiling at their infant) is important. Once infants begin to use language to communicate, growth of noun vocabulary is facilitated by parents talking about objects that are in their infant's focus of attention. Between 16 and 22 months, as the frequency of verbal communication increases, continuing the infant's topic with recasts (e.g., *Child:* "Baby eating." *Adult:* "The baby is eating.") and expansions (e.g., *Child:* "Truck." *Adult:* "A big red truck.") facilitates multiword combinations.

Sensitive and contingent responding also means different things to infants in different affective states. Outcomes differ for infants responded to when in distress and when not in distress. Bornstein and Tamis-LeMonda (1997) observed that at 5 months, maternal responsiveness to infants who were in a nondistressed neutral state, in which they are quiet and alert, predicted attention and symbolic play at 13 months. Responsiveness at 9 months predicted language development, and particularly language comprehension, at 13 months. Although in nonclinical samples there is a different response to distress and nondistress states, this is not so in clinical samples, where a high proportion of infants are insecurely attached. In fact, parents of insecurely attached infants have been found to be less sensitive to their infants during both distress and nondistress situations. Infants who are brought to mental health clinics are often chronically distressed, and their parents report that they have frequent tantrums and are difficult to soothe. There are a number of reasons why some infants spend less time in neutral affect. Difficulty with maintaining neutral affect may be related to risk for language delay when infants have problems communicating to caregivers. But there are other potential reasons. Research on attachment suggests that some infants need to heighten or dampen affect to ensure that they can maintain the care of their attachment figures (Main et al., 1985). Temperament may also play a role; infants who have a predisposition to be fussy and inattentive or to be introverted rather than extroverted are at a disadvantage (Dixon & Shore, 1997; Slomkowski et al., 1992). In any of these scenarios, infants are less likely to be in a state where they are responsive to their environment and may be less likely to have caregivers who are sensitive and responsive to their affective states and attempts to communicate.

Language, Play, and Cognitive Development

Growth in memory skills means that infants and toddlers are increasingly aware of connections between the past and present and able to predict future events based on past experiences (Kagan, 1984; Rovee-Collier, 1990). In the middle of the first year, this capacity contributes to forming mental representations of familiar and unfamiliar individuals and accounts for the timing of separation anxiety, which signals formation of attachments. At the same time, infants' emerging cognitive and intentional communicative capacities are apparent in their play, as play becomes both more symbolically complex and interactive over their first 3 years.

By their first birthday, infants' representational pretend play emerges, some of which involves simple interactions and play sequences (e.g., patty-cake). This play involves infants engaging in familiar activities with toys, such as pretending to feed themselves with a spoon or labeling baby dolls "baba." By 18 months, infants are able to perform these acts on another object—for instance, feeding a doll rather than themselves. Even later, they can take on an autonomous role—for instance, enacting a doll feeding the infant. From 1 to 3 years, play becomes more complex in that sequences of events come to be represented mentally. Moreover, as infants' attention increases so too does their capacity for extended exploration and sustained pleasurable and reciprocal play interchanges with caregivers. Infants' ability to symbolize through play, show signs of logic, take another's perspective, classify objects by form or function, and begin to understand causal relationships grows exponentially. Infants and toddlers engaged in symbolic play are developing basic mental representations of roles, objects, and the sequence of actions called for in a situation, often referred to as "scripts" (Nelson, 1981), which are then verbalized. Symbolic play, in turn, enhances language, cognitive, social, and emotional development by providing infants with an opportunity to practice these skills. In the process of pretend play with others, infants have the opportunity to share feelings and to sharpen their understanding of them. Given the multiple domains of development involved in play and the role of play for learning and for social and emotional development, it is notable that LI is associated with delays in the capacity for symbolic play (Westby, 1999).

Once infants can crawl, they more actively explore their environment. Active exploration may influence both language and cognitive development because infants are in a position to learn about objects and their relationships (Bloom, 1993) and feel confident to take risks and challenges in learning. Parents and other adults foster infants' exploration and curiosity through activities referred to as scaffolding (Bruner, 1983) and working in the zone of proximal development (Vygotsky, 1978). *Scaffolding* involves teaching interactions that support and enhance infants' capacities a step further. The *zone of proximal development* refers to infants performing beyond the limits of skill when supported by an adult. With practice, infants' performance advances to the next zone and they no longer require adult support. Keeping in mind that infants contribute to their own development, there is a dynamic interplay between parents' ability to evaluate and facilitate their infants' development, withdraw support to test infants' competence, and provide the circumstances in which infants' competence can advance. Over time, verbal instruction replaces the active participation of parents and parents encourage their infant's development by explaining and facilitating communication, providing reassurance at times of anxiety and separation, talking through emotions, and working out conflicts (Lieberman, 1993). For infants with poor language and communication skills, these communicative interchanges can prove frustrating, resulting in slower cognitive and communicative development.

Language and Affect and Behavior Regulation

One of the most important tasks in the first 3 years of life is achieving physiological, emotional, and behavioral regulation, for example, sleepwaking, feeding, and distress-soothing cycles, which are interrelated with neurophysiological development. Infants who experience responsive caregiving, from caregivers who provide a model of regulation, become confident knowing that their needs will be met. Over time, parents take diminishing responsibility for their infants' regulation. Important to this process is *social referencing,* an aspect of pragmatic capacity that appears at about 10 months of age. Infants monitor the facial expression and vocal tone of a familiar adult in unfamiliar situations and approach or retreat based on the adult's emotional response (Klinnert, Campos, Sorce, Emde, & Svejda, 1983). Thus from early on, normally developing infants are able to interpret facial expressions and their affective and communicative significance. By 9 to 12 months, infants are better able to regulate their own emotional and physiological states. Their affect and behavior regulation is also intimately related to communicative development. Strong emotions disrupt infants' behavior and capacity to communicate their needs. Conversely, competent communication is related to affect and behavior regulation. Behavior regulation also plays a role in joint attention and repair and this is important for ongoing infant communication and social-emotional functioning.

Although emotions do not come under verbal control until the preschool years, nevertheless, the ability to talk about emotions supplements emotion expression in infants and this is an important contributor to self-regulation (Bruner, 1983; Vygotsky, 1978). Infants learn the language of emotions around the age of 2 years (Dale, 1996; Dunn & Munn, 1987) and can refer to a range of feeling states in themselves and others. They also discuss the cause of feeling states in a range of contexts, including pretend play (Dunn et al., 1987). By 2½ years, words about sensory perception, physiological states, and volition are common, followed next by words for the basic emotions of joy, anger, sadness, fear, and disgust and words referring to moral approval (e.g., "good boy"). Reference to the causes of emotional states also increases between 2 and 3 years of age (Brown & Dunn, 1991, 1992). Words concerning moral obligation, such as "have to," and those concerning cognitive processes, such as knowledge and memory ("I know"), do not appear until around 3 years (Shatz, Wellman, & Silber, 1983).

Data obtained from infants not at risk for LI or social-emotional disorder raise some interesting possibilities in relation to those who are at risk. Bloom and colleagues have outlined the temporal order of communication modalities around expression of emotions (Bloom & Beckwith, 1989; Bloom & Capatides, 1987) and use what they call a "trade-off" model to explain the relationship between expressing words and expressing affect. In the one-word stage, infants tend to say a word and then show emotion. Acquiring words for labeling emotions occurs later, and, over time, emotion expression and emotion word use become integrated. Utterances that show affect tend to be shorter and less cognitively complex than utterances produced when affect is neutral. Bloom and colleagues suggest that when toddlers are in the process of acquiring the language of emotions they cannot simultaneously express emotions and talk about them, an integrative skill that comes later in development. For instance, when 9-month-old infants were followed to 2 years, those who had spent more time in neutral affect, as opposed to either positive (e.g., laughing) or negative (e.g., crying) affect, were younger at the time of speaking their first words and their vocabulary spurt (Bloom & Capatides, 1987). These investigators argued that the cognitive requirements for learning words and expressing emotion are different. Whereas affect expression is automatic and immediate, learning words requires a reflective stance. The mental representations that underlie linguistic expressions and interpretation are recalled from memory; language emerges in infants' endeavors to remember and recognize words that express what they are thinking and feeling. This takes considerable effort on their part and cannot be accomplished in a highly emotional (unregulated) state. Such findings are consistent with those of Bornstein and Tamis-LeMonda (1997) cited earlier and suggest further that infants who are chronically distressed may be slower to develop language.

Another major shift in the capacity to regulate emotion and behavior occurs during the second year when infants begin to talk out loud either to themselves or to no one in particular as an accompaniment to ongoing activity. There is an orderly progression from conversational task-irrelevant and sometimes self-stimulating talk in infants to descriptive task-relevant language to prescriptive and self-directed talk in the preschool years (Berk, 1994). Self-directed talk may be used to influence performance on cognitive tasks (e.g., "Put block now"), control and modulate arousal to accomplish a goal (e.g., "Go slowly, slowly"), express emotional states (e.g., "Broke glass. Mommy angry?"), and comfort themselves (e.g., "No more sad"). Later, self-directed talk also can provide a tool for reflection, description, and self-questioning that contributes to both cognitive and social-cognitive problem solving (Barkley, 1997). It is not a stretch of the imagination to consider that disruptions in language development can interfere with children's development of self-directed talk and consequently formation of internal representations of their social and learning environments and of their behavior (Kopp, 1989).

Although labeling, describing, and talking about their feelings helps infants understand those feelings, it is also important for them to gain experience in regulating the behavior of others (Vygotsky, 1962). Thus the interaction pattern encompassed in joint attention episodes—for instance, where infants gain not only the attention but the interest and affect of their caregivers—is important for the development of self-regulatory capacity as well as for language and social-cognitive development (Greenberg, Kusche, & Speltz, 1990).

Although infants begin to use language for self-regulation, they still need parental support and responsiveness. Attachment figures continue to be a source of comfort and help when the child is distressed or frustrated (Sroufe & Waters, 1977). In a secure attachment relationship, attachment figures facilitate emotion and behavior regulation, along with communication and cognition, by explaining things to their infants. Attachment security at one year is associated with the ability to use attachment relationships as a base from which to explore and master the environment. Language about emotions also is facilitated in child-focused family discussions about emotions and negotiations around conflicting goals (Dunn & Brown, 1991). For instance, references to feeling states made by mothers and older siblings are related to 2-year-olds' language around feeling states in infancy (Dunn et al., 1987). Moreover, later in development children who are securely attached have a more positive mood, tolerate frustration, and have better problem-solving skills than those who are insecurely attached (Easterbrooks & Goldberg, 1984). When caregivers avoid discussion of feelings or mislabel or distort them, then it is not surprising that children suffer in their own capacity to do so (Crittenden, 1996).

Infants have some capacity to use language as a tool for problem solving, self-expression, and affect and behavior regulation. This can be a frustrating process, however, because they do not yet have all of the words to express what they are feeling. For infants with language and communication problems, the awareness that others do not understand them and their limited capacity for repairing communications or rephrasing sentences can lead to anger and conflicts with siblings, parents, and peers. There are also numerous frustrations for adults and opportunities for misinterpreting infants' behavior. As will be recalled, infants' compliance with adults is directly related to their verbal comprehension skills (Kaler & Kopp, 1990).

Toward the end of the first year, infants become noticeably aware that others have a point of view and intentions that differ from their own. Subsequently, between 18 and 30 months, the first signs of what Bowlby (1969) called the *goal-corrected partnership* emerge. Both parents and children increasingly take into account the others' attitudes, wishes, and needs in negotiating outcomes. Whenever there is a goal-corrected system, there is the potential for conflict when parents and children have opposing goals and plans. Inadequate language skills rob infants of the capacity for versatility in negotiating relationships and establishing a sense of self as independent from others. Moreover, because infants at risk for LI are likely to be immature in social-cognitive understanding and perspective-taking abilities, there is room for even greater misunderstanding. From a developmental perspective, it is not surprising that parents seek help with managing and understanding behavior problems when there is a clash between infants' developmental needs and parental expectations. Infants who are able to say "I am mad" or "I am sad" are more likely to gain the support and understanding of adults than those who throw tantrums or break toys.

LANGUAGE IMPAIRMENT
AND SOCIAL-EMOTIONAL DISORDER:
RESEARCH FINDINGS ON ATYPICAL POPULATIONS

There is evidence that genetically determined normal maturational processes protect children in their first 18 to 24 months when they are most vulnerable. Thus infants' development takes a normative course except under exceptional conditions, such as extreme deprivation (Skuse, 1984). Moreover, even infants exposed to extreme conditions show a remarkable degree of developmental catch-up, as was recently illustrated among infants and children adopted from institutions in Romania (Fisher, Ames, Chisholm, & Savoie, 1997; O'Connor, Bredenkamp, Rutter, & English and Romanian Adoption Group, 1999). Although there is built-in protection, at the same time there is variation in development associated with environmental and relational factors, such as those reviewed earlier in this chapter, that have implications for adjustment.

Infants With Expressive Language Impairment (Late Talkers)

The first signs of LI are typically observed in 2- to 3-year-olds, with prevalence estimates falling between 9% and 17% (Whitehurst & Fischel, 1994). From this early age, infants who fail to develop adequate receptive language skills are of clinical concern (Bishop, 1997; Thal, Tobias, & Morrison, 1991). The majority of referrals during this period, however, are for problems in expressive language ("late talkers") (Whitehurst & Fischel, 1994). Although many late talkers' language abilities are within normal limits when they begin school, approximately 50% identified at 2 to 3 years continue to have problems after the age of 3 (Paul, 1993; Rescorla & Schwartz, 1990) and 25% in kindergarten (Paul, 1996; Paul, Spangle-Looney, &

Dahm, 1991). Moreover, narrative skills of 4-year-olds with a history of late talking are less well developed than those with normal language (Paul & Smith, 1993). Recently, Rescorla (2000) reported that although late talkers from middle-class backgrounds did not differ from controls on language measures when followed in the early school years, they did differ when followed again at 8 to 9 years and at 13 years.

There is some difference in opinion regarding whether intervention should be provided for late talkers (Bishop, 1994; Whitehurst & Fischel, 1994). When resources are limited, it is usually only those at risk for the poorest outcome who receive treatment. For instance, having a marked delay, such as no spoken words by 36 months, would indicate a need for intervention (Bishop & Edmundson, 1987a). Multiple risk factors such as delays in addition to expressive LI, low socioeconomic environment, and insensitive parent interactional style are also risks that are taken into consideration (Thal & Katich, 1996).

Late talkers also have poorer nonverbal communication skills. They are less likely to initiate joint attention acts than infants with normal language and are more likely to engage in social interactions for instrumental than for social communication (Lord & Pickles, 1996; Paul et al., 1991). This is consistent with the observation that the short-term outcomes were more positive for 2-year-olds with expressive LI who were able to engage in quiet interactive play with their mother (Fischel, Whitehurst, Caulfield, & DeBaryshe, 1989).

Social skills deficits and poor peer relationships have been observed as early as 18 months of age. Paul et al. (1991) found that 48% of 18- to 31-month-olds identified as late talkers continued to exhibit social skill deficits 12 to 18 months later. Moreover, even though some of these late talkers' language improved to the point where they were in the normal range, they still showed social skills deficits. Poor peer relationships can exert a negative effect on social-emotional development at two interrelated levels. First, young children who cannot express themselves make fewer social initiations with peers and are more often rejected than those with normal language (Carson, Klee, Perry, Muskina, & Donaghy, 1998; Paul et al., 1991). In time, this may isolate them and provide less opportunity to practice important social-cognitive skills. Second, problematic peer relationships reduce opportunities for engagement in play that stimulates cognition and language (Skarakis-Doyle & Prutting, 1988). Moreover, scripted play around social relationships, roles, objects, and actions, although present, is briefer; late talkers repeat familiar schemes rather than devise new ones and are less elaborative. The brevity, repetitiveness, and limited organization of play may reflect limited knowledge about roles, actions, and objects and constrains the child's ability to integrate and organize that knowledge. Social-emotional problems are also common in late talkers. Although many late talkers have behavioral problems, this early period may offer a window of opportunity. When 27-month-old infants were examined, Caulfield, Fischel, DeBaryshe, and Whitehurst (1989) found that those with expressive LI exhibited more negative behavior, such as throwing toys and having tantrums, when confronted with a language-based task (naming) on which performance was worse than controls. This suggested that their behavior was related to performance on a task that was frustrating to them. Mothers' ratings indicated that late talkers were perceived as more shy and exhibited more problem behaviors at bedtime compared with controls with normal language. Ratings of problem behavior were more marked, however, when trained observers rated the children's behavior. Parents may have a relatively more benign view of their late-talking infants and therefore have lower behavioral expectations when they know that they are struggling to communicate (Whitehurst, Fischel, Lonigan, Valdez-Menchaca, DeBaryshe, & Caulfield, 1988). This might be capitalized on in programs that enhance parent-infant interaction in a way that facilitates language development.

This discussion has focused on infants with expressive LI. It is important to reiterate that outcomes for infants with LI that include receptive language problems are consistently poor (Benasich, Curtiss, & Tallal, 1993; Carson et al., 1998; Mundy & Willoughby, 1998; Richman, Stevenson, & Graham, 1982). The clearest results regarding prevalence and persistence of social-emotional disturbance in infants with LI come from studies of community samples. In a randomly sampled group of 3-year-olds, Richman and Stevenson (1977) observed that 14% of children had LI, and of these, 58% had behavior problems. In another sample of 3-year-olds, Silva and colleagues (Silva, 1980; Silva, McGee, & Williams, 1983; Silva, Williams, & McGee, 1987) found that 40% of infants with language difficulties at the age of 3 years still experienced problems at 5 years, and of those who experienced language difficulties at 5 years, 31% continued to do so at 7 years. At each of these test points, children with language difficulties were at higher risk for social-emotional disturbance.

Infants Referred for Social-Emotional Problems

Parents increasingly are seeking help from mental health professionals for their infants' social-emotional problems. The reasons for such referrals include functional problems with sleeping and feeding that cannot be attributed to medical cause, concerns about affect and behavioral regulation (i.e., excessive tantrums and difficulty being soothed), and attachment and relational problems (Zeanah et al., 1997). Parents also often complain that their infant does not play. Although complaints about language, communication, and cognitive development are typically not the primary reasons for referral to mental health settings, it is often the case that such concerns arise when parents are interviewed or when communication problems are identified once an assessment is done (Barwick et al., 2000).

Case Example

Tina was the 14-month-old daughter of a single mother living at home with her own parents. A referral was initiated because of signs of anxiety in Tina, including grinding her teeth, clinginess, and waking frequently at night. Tina's mother made the referral herself because she thought that her daughter might be insecurely attached. The mother felt she had an insecure attachment relationship with her own mother and was worried that this would affect Tina. Tina's mother recalled being taught by her mother to exhibit "proper" behavior but did not remember her own feelings as ever being acknowledged.

Tina was a child of an unplanned pregnancy, and there was no contact with her father. The mother was distressed throughout the pregnancy because of her relationship with Tina's father and the possibility that she would have to quit school. Following a planned cesarean section, she developed an allergic reaction to the bandage, causing her incision to become infected. Subsequent treatment with medication led to interruption of breast-feeding, creating further distress. Although living with her parents meant that the mother could return to school, she felt very unsure of herself in her mother's presence.

On the Bayley Scales of Infant Development, Tina scored in the average range. On ratings of behavior during testing, however, she was considered to have questionable orientation to and engagement with the tasks and the examiner and nonoptimal emotion regulation. Tina's mother, who attended the assessment, appeared distant and unperturbed by her daughter's distress. When she did try to calm Tina, she gave her a bottle rather than touching or talking to her.

When asked about language development, Tina's mother reported normal development except for number of words produced (5th percentile). During the language assessment, Tina repeatedly got off her chair and threw things off the table. Although scores on the Preschool Language Scale–3 fell within the average range of ability, concerns about Tina's nonverbal communicative competence were raised during testing with the Communicative and Symbolic Behavior Scales, where Tina was delayed in using intentional communication.

On this test, infants are presented with "communicative temptations" such as an interesting windup toy and blowing bubbles. When the examiner presented a windup toy, Tina briefly manipulated it and then started whining and crying. She showed only fleeting eye contact and a small gesture that the examiner took as a sign that she wanted the toy wound up again. When the examiner did this, Tina looked at the toy with calm interest and then knocked it toward the examiner with a sweep of her hand. This, too, was interpreted as a request. In another episode, after giving a bottle of bubbles to her mother and whining and crying until it was opened, Tina abruptly walked away. When the examiner asked if Tina needed help, Tina returned and touched the examiner's hand. When the examiner blew the bubbles again, Tina watched with fascination. Even when she was not distressed, Tina's affect was flat and she smiled only once. It was easy to understand how Tina's bids for communication may have been missed or misinterpreted by her mother.

When observed in play, although the mother showed signs of pleasure toward Tina in her looks and voice, there was little pleasure or give-and-take in the interaction between them. Although Tina's mother often waited for Tina to initiate play, she would then become directive, for instance, labeling toys and speaking for Tina ("Nice baby—drink your milk").

Questionnaires completed by the mother indicated that she was significantly depressed (Beck Depression Inventory) and regarded herself as ineffective in and unsatisfied with her parenting role. Difficulties reading Tina's communicative signals compounded these feelings. It was concluded that unresolved issues made it difficult for Tina's mother to feel adequate as a mother, to deal with her daughter's distress, and to be emotionally available in a consistent way. This influenced and was compounded by Tina's ambiguous communications. The mother's alternating between lack of responding and being intrusive was frustrating to Tina, who was not secure that her needs would be met, which in turn made it difficult for her to regulate her own emotions and behavior. Psychotherapy was undertaken with Tina's mother. The therapist helped the mother understand Tina better by including Tina in the sessions. Including Tina also helped the mother make links between her current parenting behavior and her experience of being parented in the past.

This case illustrates how affective and behavioral dysregulation may become associated or even synonymous with psychopathology and poor communication. As discussed earlier, regulation is important for the capacity to communicate and socialize. Conversely, how infants communicate and socialize contributes to their capacity to regulate emotions and behavior.

Tina was part of a sample of 50 infants referred to a mental health clinic participating in a study in which both structural language and communicative competence were examined in relation to characteristics of infants' interaction with their mothers (Barwick et al., 2000). These clinic-referred infants, who were, on average, 20 months of age, had language skills at the lower end of the average range but exhibited poorer expressive and receptive language than controls, confirming that children referred for mental health services are at risk for LI at an age younger than has been previously studied. Furthermore, the clinic infants engaged in less social-affective signaling (e.g., gaze shifting from person to object as required for joint attention episodes; showing positive affect in conjunction with verbalization) and had poorer overall prelinguistic skills than controls. This finding supports research showing that chronically distressed infants' language is slower to develop (e.g., Bornstein & Tamis-LeMonda, 1997). Moreover, in clinic and nonclinic samples both structural language and communicative competence were associated with qualities of mother-infant interaction. Most notable in the sample studied by Barwick et al. (2000) was that it was aspects of preverbal communication rather than structural language that were associated with qualities of the mother-infant relationship.

Maltreated and Neglected Infants

Maltreated infants exhibit difficulties in language and communicative functioning and are at risk for behavioral and emotional problems (Coster & Cicchetti, 1993). With respect to structural language, they have been shown to have problems with vocabulary and syntax and to speak in shorter sentences. Functional communication and discourse also were significantly impaired in maltreated infants. For instance, they were less able to convey messages clearly, less likely to describe their own activities or features of objects, and less likely to seek information from their mothers. Furthermore, they were more likely to give minimal replies and use filler devices such as "hmhm" or "oh." Although these fillers acknowledged conversations, they did not add to them. Moreover, maltreated infants were less contingent in conversation and tended to end conversations abruptly, which interfered with sustained dialogue. As well, they used less decontextualized speech; that is, they made fewer references to persons and events not present (Coster, Gersten, Beeghly, & Cicchetti, 1989).

The language of emotions in maltreated infants also has been shown to be different. Maltreated infants used fewer labels for emotion states even when overall language level was controlled (Beeghly & Cicchetti, 1994; Coster et al. 1989). In particular, they used fewer words to express physiological states (e.g., hunger, fatigue), negative affect (e.g., sadness, anger, fear, disgust), and obligation (e.g., permission). No differences were observed, however, for words used to direct or guide behavior during task-oriented interactions. Beeghly and Cicchetti (1994) suggested that maltreated infants may keep conversations impersonal to protect themselves from a volatile environment. If this is the case, unfortunately at the same time it limits both language and social communication and is likely to have a detrimental effect on development of self. Infants who were both maltreated and insecurely attached exhibited more compromised internal state language and conversational relatedness than did either infants with more moderate risk (insecure/nonmaltreated or secure/maltreated) or at low risk (secure/nonmaltreated) group. Since it has been found that learning words requires a neutral reflective stance (Bloom & Capatides, 1987; Bornstein & Tamis-LeMonda, 1997), abused infants, who were chronically distressed, were at a clear disadvantage. Moreover, these infants were raised in environments that included multiple psychosocial stressors. Thus the findings likely reflect the effects of cumulative risk on the organization of social-emotional and communicative development (Beeghly & Cicchetti, 1994).

On the more positive side, attachment security has been shown to exert a protective effect on language development of low socioeconomic status, maltreated 24-month-old infants (Gersten, Coster, Schneider-Rosen, Carlson, & Cicchetti, 1986), a finding also observed in other extremely disadvantaged samples (Morisset, Barnard, Greenberg, Booth, & Spieker, 1990). Gersten et al. (1986) found that, although maltreated infants were more likely to be insecurely attached, those who were securely attached were more likely to use syntactically complex utterances; an elaborate vocabulary; and a high frequency of utterances that referred to objects, events, themselves, and others. In these latter respects, they were similar to nonmaltreated securely attached infants. Of note is that language development and abuse were related in 31-month-old infants (Coster et al., 1989) but not in 25-month-old infants (Cicchetti & Beeghly, 1987), supporting the conclusion that language development is protected in the first 2 years of life.

Older children and adolescents who have been maltreated earlier in their lives also exhibit an increased incidence of LI (Blager & Martin, 1976; Tarter, Hegedus, Winsten, & Alterman, 1984). Furthermore, retrospective accounts of adolescents who as younger children had been physically abused showed a higher likelihood of cognitive impairments (Tarter et al., 1984), reading deficits, and receipt of speech-language services, especially among those children exhibiting aggressive behavior (Burke, Crenshaw, Green, Schlosser, & Strocchia-Rivera, 1989). It has been proposed that long-term sequelae result from early maltreatment experiences on brain structure, function, and organization (Cicchetti & Cannon, 1999; Pollak,

Cicchetti, Klorman, & Brumaghim, 1997). This may arise from a number of potential factors such as lack of sensory experiences during critical periods or distortions of cues in the context of extreme relational experiences (Crittenden, 1996; Perry, Pollard, Blakley, Baker, & Vigilante, 1995). Perry et al. (1995) hypothesized that severely abused and neglected children become hypervigilant and spend much of their time in a state of fear. As a consequence, they focus on nonverbal cues and do not develop the verbal skills necessary for mature problem solving. Moreover, Perry et al. suggested that chronic fear, even low-level fear, creates changes in brain functioning so that inappropriate affective experiences in early life result in "malorganization" that disrupts the ability to develop empathetic responding.

Maternal Depression

A substantial body of research shows the impact of maternal depression on infant and child development. Longitudinal studies of mothers with postpartum depression have indicated that the quality of mothers' communication with their infant at 2 to 3 months of age has an impact on infants' language and cognitive development at 18 months (Kaplan, Bachorowski, & Zarlengo-Strouse, 1999; Murray, 1992; Murray, Kempton, Woolgar, & Hooper, 1993; Sharp, Hay, Pawlby, Schmucker, Allen, & Kumar, 1995). Further follow-up at 5 and 11 years showed that early insensitive maternal interactions predicted persistence of poorer cognitive functioning (Hay et al., 2000; Murray, Hipwell, Hooper, Stein, & Cooper, 1996). Along these same lines, Kaplan et al. (1999) found that depressed mothers did not promote associative learning in their infants.

In a community-based study that is following a large group of infants and their mothers, maternal report of depressive symptoms was obtained at 1, 6, 15, 24, and 36 months after the birth (NICHD Early Child Care Research Network, 1999). At 36 months, infants whose mothers reported feeling chronically and intermittently depressed performed more poorly on measures of cognitive and language functioning and were rated as less cooperative and as exhibiting more problem behaviors. When observed directly, depressed mothers interacted less sensitively with their infants. Furthermore, these mothers showed a decrease in sensitive interactions with their infants over time. Differences in measures of school readiness and language comprehension were accounted for by the measures of maternal sensitivity. The authors note that the greater demands of infants as they mature may challenge mothers with limited resources and lead to exacerbation of problems.

Low socioeconomic status also exacerbated insensitive maternal interactions. Despite the powerful effects of depression on infants' development and maternal sensitivity, some depressed mothers were able to be sensitive in play with their infants and this had a salutary effect on the infant's development and maternal ratings of cooperation. Programs that aim to enhance maternal sensitivity would appear to be an important component of treatment for these mothers. Although such programs have been tested (e.g., Cicchetti, Rogosch, & Toth, 2000; Lieberman, Weston, & Pawl, 1991), the effects of treatment on infants' language, communication, and cognition have rarely been examined (Cohen et al., 1999; Cooper & Murray, 1997). Elsewhere, infants have been shown to benefit when they have access to nondepressed caregivers, as it has been observed that infants' interactions improve with nondepressed fathers and familiar caregivers (Hossain, Field, Gonzalez, Malphurs, & Del Valle, 1994; Pelaez-Nogueras, Field, Cigales, Gonzalez, & Clasky, 1994). This suggests that positive environmental factors can ameliorate some of the harmful effects of interacting with a depressed mother.

Longitudinal studies with multiple assessments tracing the trajectory of language and social-emotional development in the early years, such as the ones described above, are important because they indicate that infants' behaviors are open to change under the right environmental circumstances. Interventions need to take into account multiple developmental and psychological factors, but clearly the most effective treatments are likely to be those focusing on infants' relationships with parents and other caregivers.

Temperament and Language Development

The preceding discussions of atypical samples have considered infants at moderate or high risk for social-emotional disturbance. Milder forms of individual variation, such as infants' temperament, also can be influential. Infants with different temperamental traits have different styles of interacting, which may influence language development. In one study, observers rated 2-year-olds' temperament along the dimensions of Affect-Extraversion, Task Orientation, and Activity and examined the relation between these measures and language characteristics at 2, 3, and 7 years of age (Slomkowski et al., 1992). There was a significant correlation between receptive language and both the Affect-Extraversion and Task Orientation dimensions at the age of 2 years. Moreover, there were significant associations between the language and temperament measures at the age of 2 years with language measures at ages 3 and 7 years. Although the temperament dimensions were associated with both receptive and expressive abilities in infancy, the association with receptive language was stronger in middle childhood. As well, in some cases specific temperament dimensions in infancy, in this case Affect-Extraversion, made a unique contribution to individual differences in language abilities at the age of 7. Slomkowski et al. (1992) suggested that extraverted children are not simply talking more but also have better receptive language skills than children who are less extraverted. Given that temperament also has been involved in studies of behavior problems and cognition, goodness of fit between extraverted children and their caregivers' style of interacting may either enhance or detract from both language development and social-emotional development.

KEY POINTS

- Competent language and communicative development is associated with pleasurable reciprocal interactions that are sensitive and responsive to the infant. When caregivers are intrusive and unresponsive, language and communicative development are likely to suffer.

- In the first year of life, a series of milestones mark important turning points in infants' capacity for communication and feelings of efficacy. In the first 6 months, infants develop patterns of attending and responding to caregivers. It is only after that, however, that infants' communication becomes intentional. Contingency learning, exploratory behavior, object play, joint attention, capacity for communicative repair, affect and behavior regulation, motor coordination that facilitates communication, and secure attachment are each empirically related to some aspect of later communication or language development.

- Around 18 months of age, infants develop greater capacity to communicate with language and to use language to learn about their world, participate in social relationships, think and problem-solve, and regulate affect and behavior. Symbolization, including use of language, plays a role in communication and play. Although they are still egocentric in their social relationships, their capacity for reciprocity in relationships with both adults and other children increases.

- Older infants also exhibit an increased capacity to use language to regulate their own affect and behavior, although they still rely on attachment figures for help.

- Continuing sensitivity and appropriate responsiveness of attachment figures is essential for reciprocal interaction and development of working models of attachment relationships that facilitate infants' capacity for self-regulation. Securely attached infants who can use their attachment figures as a base from which to explore, and who have the support and pride of attachment figures in their endeavors, gain a positive sense of self that fosters exploration and learning about the environment and other social relationships.

- Coalescing evidence from a number of atypical populations and populations at risk for social-emotional problems suggests that a variety of caregiving characteristics related to insensitive, intrusive caregiving and including abuse and neglect and maternal depression can negatively affect language and communication. Interventions for infants with co-occurring language or communication and social-emotional disorders are likely to be most effective when the relationship with caregivers is the focus.

4

DEVELOPMENTAL CONSIDERATIONS
Preschool Through Adolescence

Preschoolers behave as if they know who talks well and who doesn't and they prefer to interact with those who do. (Hadley & Rice, 1991, p. 1315)

DEVELOPMENTAL TASKS
OF THE PRESCHOOL YEARS:
3 TO 5 YEARS

Case Example

Joey, aged 5 years, 1 month, was referred because of difficulties in behavior and learning. Described as an introverted child, he enjoyed imaginative play and did not readily engage in conversation. Sometimes Joey appeared to be so much in a world of his own that he was unaware of others. Although occasionally he could play well with other children, more frequently he annoyed them by being silly and scribbling on their drawings. Because of this, Joey was routinely teased or ignored. In group activities, Joey had difficulty concentrating and put up his hand even when he had nothing to say. The teacher in the school that Joey had attended since age 3 observed that his development seemed slower in autumn and winter but accelerated in the spring. His parents attributed the seasonal pattern to Joey's temperament, saying that he was slow to warm up and that his performance improved when he became familiar with his environment.

Generally, Joey's parents saw him as a serious, independent, and creative child and were proud that he could entertain himself for hours. They were most concerned about his social relationships, that his feelings were easily hurt, and that he did not seem to feel good about himself. When upset, he usually withdrew to his room and only rarely articulated his feelings. They also reported that sometimes Joey lied about not feeling well to avoid going to school. Parent ratings on the Child Behavior Checklist indicated that Joey was functioning within normal limits in most respects, although on the Withdrawn subscale he was rated in a range for clinical concern.

Joey was the only child of two professionals who had high aspirations for their son. Both parents had been educated in a strict, regimented learning environment and wanted Joey to attend a school where he could enjoy learning and express himself freely. His parents were pleased when an art teacher told them that Joey had a unique way of drawing abstract pictures.

Joey was born early and initially had difficulty establishing a sleep cycle. He crawled at 8 months and walked at 1 year. His parents did not recall when he said his first word but felt that he could not really talk until he was 4 years old. Joey had a history of ear infections, but a hearing test revealed no sign of impairment. Joey did not enjoy books or being read to. Rather, he preferred fantasy play and television.

Joey presented as a friendly and eager-to-please child who was small for his age. It was difficult to engage Joey in extended conversation even about things that he enjoyed. During testing, he was initially cooperative, but when items became difficult he complained of being tired, put his head down on the table as if to sleep, and said he wanted to go home. When the examiner persisted, Joey repeatedly asked to go to the washroom.

Testing indicated overall intelligence in the lower end of the average range, with stronger performance on nonverbal (average) than on verbal (low average) tasks. Joey's ability to copy geometric designs, a skill that is an important precursor of learning to copy alphabetic letters, was at the lower end of the average range. When asked to draw a picture, Joey simply made a multicolored border on a page (no doubt the abstract style described by his art teacher) and refused to draw a human figure.

Joey's performance on receptive and expressive vocabulary tests was average for his age. In other areas, however, his scores fell in the mildly to moderately delayed range. Joey's understanding of grammatical rules was poorer than expected for his age, and he had difficulty understanding linguistic concepts such as "either-or" and "some." When asked to follow a sequence of an increasing number of directions, Joey could recall only two steps correctly. On expressive language tests, Joey had difficulty remembering details of a brief story read aloud to him. He did not show readiness for reading on a test of phonological awareness or on a nonverbal test of the understanding of concepts. Finally, when he was asked to tell a story from pictures, Joey's stories were brief and included repetitions, grammatic errors, and poor cohesion. One of Joey's stories went as follows: "The kangaroos wants to having a picnic. But the other kangaroo is riding his bike because they're going to have a picnic but not having a picnic today."

It was concluded that both expressive and receptive language processing problems had been overlooked and attributed solely to temperamental style.

These language problems were interfering with Joey's ability to learn and engage successfully with peers. When feedback was given to Joey's parents, they were disappointed that Joey's potential was lower than expected and that some of what they had regarded as creative activity was an indication of his difficulties processing incoming information and poor visual-motor skills. Nevertheless, they were encouraged to continue with art lessons as this was something that Joey enjoyed.

Joey's parents were offered counseling to help them better understand Joey's learning needs and help him feel better about himself. Written recommendations also were given to them on how to use interactive reading techniques with Joey that would encourage him to take an active role in storytelling and provide opportunities for them to expand his verbal skills. As well, recommendations were made to Joey's parents on how to model correct grammatic forms and help Joey to process sequences of multistage directions by initially keeping them short and specific, gradually building them in length and complexity over time. It was also important to help them mourn their unmet expectations for their son. Feedback to the school led to special services being implemented. A speech-language pathologist developed in-class strategies for helping Joey with language and communication skills and with communicating more effectively with peers. Additionally, twice weekly, a student teacher worked one-on-one with Joey to help him gain confidence. As Joey had never had any remedial assistance, it was recommended that his language, learning, and peer relationships be monitored and that he be retested in one year's time.

Joey's problems can be seen in the context of the developmental tasks of the preschool years that enable children to explore their environment in new ways and to gain an increasing sense of competence, independence, and self-control.

Language and Cognition

In the preschool years, language overtakes action as children's primary means of learning and communication. After reaching approximately 1,000 words by the age of 2 years, vocabulary continues to grow by about 50 words per month. Preschoolers' sentences are longer and more complex and include relative and dependent clauses, grammatic inflections to indicate verb tense and plurals, and passive sentences. Although the rudiments of conversation appear in older infants as they learn to continue a topic with repetition, preschoolers do this by adding new information. Preschool children gain many important cognitive skills, such as the ability to classify objects, understand identities (e.g., three trucks is the same as three cows), and appreciate cause and effect ("Today is a holiday, so I don't go to day care"). They can manipulate language symbols internally, process information more rapidly, and remember more (Blake, Austin, Cannon, Lisus, & Vaughan, 1994). Moreover, there is increased capacity for planning and controlling thoughts and actions (executive functions), including using rudimentary strategies to remember, for instance, verbal rehearsal (DeLoache, 1989). Like Joey, children with LI have smaller vocabularies and make grammatical errors, use shorter and less complex sentences, and have less coherent and detailed narratives. They also have a poorer grasp of concepts and more difficulty processing and retaining information.

Long before children enter school, they are exposed to printed material, and some can read labels and signs. Children in "high print-high talk" homes, who are exposed to parents and siblings who read, are more prepared for school (Kuvshinoff & Creaghead, 1994). Children with LI are less interested in reading (Gillam & Johnston, 1985) and, as was the case with Joey, less likely to interact with books and with adults around literacy (Terrell, 1994). In turn, adults are less likely to initiate or persist with such activities.

Language and Social-Emotional Development

Preschoolers rely less on emotional or physical action to indicate attachment needs. They can ask for help or succor and express feelings in words in a way that others will understand. Children who are securely attached and have good verbal skills are confident that they will be understood by parents and other caregivers. For their part, parents must allow children appropriate autonomy and encourage and respect verbal expressions of feelings. Associations have been found between the quality of mother-child conversations about emotions and later differences in social-cognitive skills, including discussion of affective states (Dunn et al., 1987), perspective-taking abilities, and the beliefs and feelings of others (Dunn, Brown, Slomkowski, Tesla, & Youngblade, 1991). Although signs of negotiating a goal-corrected partnership begin earlier, they are especially prominent in preschoolers. When conflicts arise, preschoolers without good language skills have less capacity for such a partnership, which calls for both social-cognitive skills and the ability to negotiate verbally. Without this ability, they often resort to immature means of negotiating, such as tantrums or aggression (Bloomquist, August, Cohen, Doyle, & Everhart, 1997). Although the association between attachment security and language development in infancy appears to be limited to high-risk dyads exposed to significant interpersonal and psychosocial stress (Morisset et al., 1990), a link between attachment security at 2 years of age and children's reading interests at the age of 5 years has been reported in lower-risk samples. This association has been attributed to the capacity of mothers of securely attached children to foster curiosity and exploration (Bus, Belsky, van IJzendoorn, & Crnic, 1997; Bus & van IJzendoorn, 1988, 1992).

Just as in their earlier years, children develop a sense of self through the way in which they receive social feedback with attachment figures, other adults, and peers. When the feedback is inaccurate or critical and questioning, it elicits feelings of anxiety and low self-esteem. Inaccurate feedback may arise from misattributions for children's behavior, such as when children withdraw or are accused of willful misbehavior when in fact they do not understand or remember what was said. One outcome of the development of theory of mind is that preschoolers begin to be capable of masking their true feelings. To avoid the discomfort of anxiety that interferes with positive self-regard, some children give the impression of not caring. This may be expressed through depression and withdrawal or by angry, aggressive acting out, which further impedes development of a sense of self. It was Joey's withdrawal and low self-esteem that first signaled to his parents the need for help.

Preschoolers' play is imaginative and interactive and functions to explore reality, practice social roles, express fantasies and wishes, and master or work through stressful events. Occasional turn taking is observed, and conversations and role plays become lengthier. The finding that children with LI exhibit less mature forms of play (Westby, 1999) has implications for social, cognitive, and language development, as peers are a valuable source of learning and social partnership, including ways of dealing with conflict and disagreement. Joey lacked important social-cognitive and social-interactional capacities, and this likely contributed to his exclusion from play by peers.

Beginning at the age of 4 to 5 years, children form a broader range of social relationships, and there is an impetus to maintain individual friendships over time, although friendship is still defined by who is or is not a playmate and by physical attributes (Selman & Schultz, 1990). Growing social-cognitive maturity and language skills are reflected in the ability to see and report circumstances from another's perspective, recognize and label emotions, reflect on and talk about feelings, express empathy, talk about the consequences of one's actions on others, and discriminate imaginary from real. Emergence of a theory of mind means that children recognize that others can have different interpretations of the same situation.

Therefore it is notable that language development, including discourse, is related to performance on false belief (theory of mind) tasks in normally developing preschoolers (Astington & Jenkins, 1999; Cutting & Dunn, 1999).

Language and Affect and Behavior Regulation

Preschoolers make tremendous strides toward self-control, and episodes of negative emotion expression, such as tantrums, diminish (Kopp, 1982, 1989). During this period, children use language for self-control as well as for learning and social-emotional communication. One way they do this is by engaging in private speech (self-talk), that is, talking out loud to themselves as an accompaniment to ongoing activity. Although self-talk begins in the later part of infancy, for preschoolers it is more effective for planning and self-regulation (e.g., "Now I put the bridge here. The truck is too tall [to go under the bridge]. The block. Where are the blocks?" [child puts blocks under the bridge to make it tall enough for the truck to pass through]). Over time, private speech becomes internalized, and children begin to "talk to themselves inside their head." In this context, it is interesting to note that children diagnosed as ADHD often continue to use external speech longer than children without this diagnosis (Berk & Potts, 1991).

LANGUAGE IMPAIRMENT AND SOCIAL-EMOTIONAL DISORDER: RESEARCH FINDINGS ON ATYPICAL POPULATIONS OF PRESCHOOLERS

Children With Language Impairment Who Are Rejected by Peers

Problematic peer relationships in childhood foreshadow later difficulties that can include social-emotional disorder, dropping out of school, delinquency, and criminality (Parker & Asher, 1987). The social development of preschoolers has been examined for some time, but until recently, children who were reluctant to engage in social interaction and who spoke little were described variously as "shy," "withdrawn," "reticent," or "inhibited" (Rubin, Hymel, & Mills, 1989). A competing explanation, which has now been confirmed empirically, is that these children have problems in structural language and communication that continue into the school years and interfere with social relationships (Evans, 1996; Fujiki, Brinton, Morgan, & Hart, 1999). Problems occur both in specific interactional skills and in maintaining friendships. A transactional cycle is established whereby children with LI are excluded by peers and therefore have less opportunity to learn and practice the social skills they need for peer interaction (Fujiki et al., 1996). When observed directly, preschoolers with LI have fewer of the conventional gestures and uses of language to enter into peer groups than children with normal language. For instance, they do not respond to requests for clarification by peers or address all participants when they join a group (Brinton, Fujiki, Winkler, & Loeb, 1986). Not only are children with LI less likely to initiate interactions, but they are less or inappropriately responsive to social bids (Brinton & Fujiki, 1982; Gallagher, 1999). When children with LI do initiate interaction with peers, they are more likely than children with normal language to be ignored. They participate in fewer interactions with other children and are addressed less frequently (Hadley & Rice, 1991). Peer rejection is not related to a history of low achievement or poor structural language skills but, rather, inadequate processing of social information. For instance, in kindergarten, peers reject learning-disabled children prior to their being identified in Grade 1. Moreover, children with LI are rejected more often than children who speak English as a second language (Hadley & Rice, 1991).

Adults are also more likely to assign negative attributes to children with LI. In one study, adults were given the task of teaching a game to dyads of preschool girls and then asked to rate their personality. After only a brief interaction, the adults were more likely to rate a child with expressive language problems as less likable and less productive and as having less potential for achievement than her partner (Wood & Valdez-Menchaca, 1996). Moreover, providing adults with a diagnosis did not change their perception.

Children do not outgrow their problems (Evans, 1996). Unsatisfactory peer interactions set into motion processes that undermine social competence for years to come. In their community sample, Beitchman, Brownlie, and Wilson (1996) found that children who met criteria for LI at the age of 5 did more poorly on measures of social competence and adaptive functioning at the age of 12. In another study that followed young children with severe LI, significant deficits in functioning in social relationships continued into adulthood (Clegg, Hollis, & Rutter, 1999; Howlin et al., 2000).

Despite these difficulties, some children with LI do have friends. Moreover, there are some conditions under which children with LI are more socially competent. For instance, they interact better with adults, when the social partner is familiar, and when there have been shared prior experiences with other children (Blank, Gessner, & Esposito, 1979; Rice, Sells, & Hadley, 1991).

Children With Language Impairment
Attending Mental Health Clinics

The preschool years are an important turning point because children are on the cusp of entry into the academic grades where pressures on behavioral regulation and learning increase markedly (Kopp, 1982). There are only a few studies of preschoolers with LI being seen in mental health settings. What findings exist indicate that LI is associated with significant social-emotional disorder in these young children and that treating LI is an important component of early intervention. Cohen and Horodezky (1998) found that approximately half of 4- to 6-year-old children referred for outpatient mental health service had LI. Moreover, among those referred solely for behavioral or emotional problems, approximately one third were found to have LI only after the research assessment was done. These children were rated by parents and teachers as having more externalizing behavior problems than both disturbed children with previously identified LI and those with normal language. For these young children, behavior problems probably overshadowed language difficulties as a reason for referral.

In a more intense day treatment program, Beitchman, Tuckett, and Batth (1987) observed that preschool children who had co-occurring ADHD and expressive LI exhibited more severe receptive and expressive language problems and poorer visual-motor integration skills than children with ADHD who were developing language normally and children with normal language who had another psychiatric disorder. A study by Cohen, Bradley, and Kolers (1987) showed that children with co-occurring LI and social-emotional disorder benefit from this kind of intensive day treatment. They found that children referred for both LI and social-emotional problems made greater gains in treatment than children referred for social-emotional problems alone. Moreover, gains in language functioning preceded behavioral gains, supporting the important contribution of LI to psychopathology.

DEVELOPMENTAL TASKS OF MIDDLE CHILDHOOD:
6 TO 12 YEARS

Case Example

David, aged 9 years, 7 months, was referred because of emotional problems precipitated by his aunt's death. Symptoms included talking about suicide and displaying violent behavior toward peers. Although David's Grade 4 teacher reported achievement below grade level in language arts, mathematics, French, science, and social studies, he had never been assessed. His poor performance was attributed to lack of effort and to conflicts with the teacher and peers, which included temper tantrums, violent behavior, and vandalism. David attributed his poor schoolwork to somatic causes such as fatigue and headaches.

When interviewed, David's parents recalled an unremarkable pregnancy and birth history. David cried excessively at birth but generally was in good health. Development of major milestones was normal. David's mother described a family history of language learning disability related to reading and writing skills, however.

David received diagnoses of Oppositional Defiant Disorder and Attention Deficit Hyperactivity Disorder. His mother rated David in the clinically significant range on the Delinquent subscale of the Child Behavior Checklist. His teacher saw David's problems as more pervasive and rated him in the clinical range on the Anxious/Depressed, Social Problems, Thought Problems, Attention Problems, Delinquent Behavior, and Aggressive Behavior subscales.

David presented as an appealing boy who initially enjoyed the test session. But during tasks that required auditory memory and listening skills, he would look away, lower his head, or cover his face with his hands and knead the skin on his cheeks. Scores on verbal subtests of a test of general intelligence were in the slow learner range and on nonverbal tests in the average range. On tests of cognitive processing and memory, David took a long time to respond, and it was hard for him to remember information long enough to manipulate it in his mind. David also had difficulty recalling a story read to him. On academic achievement tests, his ability to read individual words was at the Grade 2 level. Performance on a task requiring him to read nonwords was even more severely compromised because he could not rely on visual memory for words he already knew. Reading comprehension, spelling, and arithmetic were all below grade level.

Language testing indicated that receptive and expressive vocabulary skills were in the average range. On a test of phonological awareness, David performed at the Grade 1 level. His understanding of grammar was also within average limits. David's ability to express grammatically correct sentences was weak, however. For example, he gave "mens" as the plural response for "man" and made other errors in plural forms and noun possessives, forms that are normally in place for children David's age. Poor performance on tests of grammar is associated with difficulty in oral expression, particularly when sentences need to be planned and produced for conversation, classroom discussion, and written expression. He also did poorly on tests of rote memory for words and sentences and the ability to follow oral directions. Unexpectedly, despite poor language skills, David was able to construct a story. He started with a title, and although the stories were brief, essential components were included.

On a test of the ability to recognize and understand emotions, David made many errors and needed considerable time to label the emotions in pictures of faces. He also made many errors when asked to identify the picture expressing an emotion associated with a brief story read aloud to him. With respect to his capacity to solve social problems involving conflict with a peer, David had difficulty identifying the problem to be solved, labeling the feelings of the participants in conflict, choosing strategies to solve the problem, overcoming obstacles if the strategies did not work (i.e., repair), and knowing when the problem was solved. He gave many "I don't know" answers and seemed to have genuine difficulty understanding what was expected of him. For instance, when asked how the characters felt, David offered a solution. These solutions involved changing his partner's thoughts and behavior rather than altering his own or arriving at a compromise. David's overall score placed him at the Grade 1 level.

On the Children's Depression Inventory, David's responses put him within a range for concern. On a measure of self-esteem, David's responses indicated that he did not feel good about himself with respect to his behavior and unpopularity.

It was concluded that problems in language processing and expression had been overlooked and were a source of anxiety, shame, and frustration to David. Since David's vocabulary was age appropriate and his speech clear, it was understandable that language difficulties had been overlooked. At least some of his academic problems that were attributed to lack of effort could more accurately be explained by difficulty following instructions, poor memory, slow processing, and problems putting ideas into words. The long pauses in responding most likely hindered him in the classroom environment. These problems extended to processing social information necessary for effective social interactions.

David's parents and therapist were told of his genuine difficulties processing information and expressing himself and how this might make it seem as if he was not cooperating. Not to minimize David's sorrow following his aunt's death, this event was considered as the trigger following a long period of chronic stress, anxiety, and depression that David masked by acting out. But David's parents rejected the assessment feedback even though (or perhaps because) there was a family history of language learning problems. They thought he would outgrow his problems ("break out of his shell"). His father often said, "David refuses to work," even after David's low effort was explained as a reflection of his struggles with academic work and the need for repeated exposure before skills and knowledge could be firmly consolidated in long-term memory. David looked relieved when the examiner empathized with the difficulties he was having in the classroom and how upset that must make him feel.

Once feedback was given to the school, support was provided through a language arts program on a withdrawal basis. David was also excused from

French class. Both David's parents and his teacher were encouraged to help him identify his own and others' emotions and to learn words for those emotions and the language to more effectively solve interpersonal problems.

Language, Cognition, and Achievement

In normally developing children, vocabulary continues to grow, and by age 8 years, syntactical and morphological structures are fully mature. There is more variety in language, and children can use difficult constructions such as the passive voice (e.g., "The boy was chased by the dog"). As children move through the primary grades, language gains in sophistication. They come to appreciate that words can have different meanings, are able to play with words, understand and tell riddles and jokes, and use and understand figures of speech and metaphors. From 6 years onward, children also gradually increase their ability to put thoughts and feelings into words. School-aged children's narratives are more coherent and detailed, and they can tell a story that has a logical beginning, middle, and end and multiple episodes. Stories include a protagonist and a problem for which resolution is attempted. Narratives of school-aged children also include affective responses and consideration of others' consciousness. Children with LI typically exhibit problems in more than one of these areas.

Learning to read and write are among the most important tasks of middle childhood. Phonological processing is especially important in the beginning stages of reading when children learn to decode words (e.g., Stanovich, 1988). Even children who are taught using a whole word approach have difficulties in consistently recognizing what words look like and eventually must be able to decode new words. David's poor phonological awareness no doubt contributed to problems with reading achievement. It is notable that he did not exhibit impairments in vocabulary knowledge. In fact, many children with LI do not show difficulties with vocabulary early on. There is, however, a reciprocal relation between language and reading such that vocabulary and grammatical knowledge decline from 3 to 11 years of age in children who have reading disabilities (Stanovich, 1988).

Shifts in cognitive development also contribute to children's communicative competence. To an even greater extent than preschoolers, school-aged children can manipulate objects mentally and apply logic and reasoning. As well, a number of specific cognitive developments contribute to both learning and social relationships. For instance, understanding reversibility facilitates learning arithmetic operations and analyzing perceptions of cognitive, social, and emotional experiences by thinking back over them (i.e., reversing them). Around the age of 7 years, spatial and visual organizational ability, time perception, the capacity to distinguish between parts and wholes, and seriation improve. Mastery of language contributes to the effectiveness of these processes and also provides a means for children to both organize and express their accomplishments. Children with LI encounter problems with a wide range of cognitive processes, which further constrains learning and social relationships (Johnston, 1988).

Memory also improves in middle childhood, and language plays a role here too because information that can be encoded verbally is more likely to be remembered (Kagan, 1984). School-aged children have more sophisticated means of remembering because they can sort and categorize information in multiple ways. This advanced cognitive capacity is translated into active strategies for remembering (e.g., verbal rehearsal, clustering, and verbal association), something that children with LI generally do not do spontaneously. Additionally, children acquire new metacognitive or executive processing skills that continue to become more refined as they move into adolescence. They can think about problem solving as well as actually do it and can sustain attention to cognitive tasks for increasingly long periods of time. As illustrated in the case of David, the stress of having to organize and recall information in class or on tests leads to considerable anxiety.

A major developmental transition occurs at around 6 to 7 years when children in most cultures begin formal full-day schooling. Although it is an exciting milestone for most children, for children with LI it is a time when learning and social-emotional difficulties emerge or intensify. Whereas the early grades are devoted to acquiring basic skills, from Grade 3 onward there is a shift from learning how to read and write to using reading and writing for learning. A number of essential skills are required for this advance, including competent structural and figurative language, memory, and working memory. To understand a paragraph or larger piece of text, a child must keep in mind an accumulation of information from which both literal and figurative conclusions are drawn. Children begin to use writing to summarize information and express themselves. Moreover, in later grades children are expected to take notes, a skill that relies on good auditory processing and memory.

Language and Social-Emotional Development

A relationship with attachment figures continues to be important in middle childhood, but this is less obvious as children move toward independence and form close relationships with peers. Children with friends are better adjusted to school (Ladd, 1990). In normally developing children, the first signs of reciprocal friendships emerge early in this period. Friendships rely increasingly on qualities of mutual affection, commitment, loyalty, and support. Children are more capable of reflecting on and talking about feelings and can both differentiate emotions and recognize that they can have more than one feeling at the same time. They also understand that there are multiple ways to see a situation, realize how their own viewpoints and intentions may be perceived by another, and appreciate that peer relationships rely on coordinating these perspectives and responding to social expectations and cues (Selman & Schultz, 1990). Immature social-cognitive skills contribute to misinterpreting the intentions and motives of other children, leading some children with LI to initiate and elicit negative interactions (Cohen, Menna, et al., 1998). As well, during middle childhood, children's play increasingly takes place in the context of games and sports with rules and strategies and interest in hobbies that require classification and sorting. Children with LI are at a disadvantage in these respects, which often prevents sharing age-appropriate activities. As discussed earlier, even before they enter school, children with LI are rejected by peers. As well as the feelings that this engenders, it means that they have fewer opportunities to have peer role models, to practice negotiating conflicts, and to see that others are not always perfect or confident. In middle childhood, children are even more adept than preschoolers at masking their true feelings. Like David, they may give a false impression of not caring, becoming loners or getting into fights. Children with LI may also have difficulty developing a coherent sense of self because of both their problems representing experiences symbolically and the frequent negative feedback from their environment regarding achievement and social relationships.

Language, Executive Functions, and Affect and Behavior Regulation

In middle childhood, self-control is related to understanding and later retrieving, organizing, and verbalizing rules and internalization of rule-governed language (Luria, 1961; Vygotsky, 1962). In this way, language development is intertwined with metacognitive or executive control skills. Strategies for self-control are based on logical problem solving, the ability to represent reality, conscious control of arousal and anxiety, the capacity to use thinking to delay acting impulsively, and conscious intent to achieve goals. Self-regulation skills also contribute to pragmatic or communicative competence, for instance, helping children organize coherent conversations and inhibit responding prematurely so they can achieve communicative goals (Tannock & Schachar, 1996). During the course of normal development, aggression in school-aged children, when it occurs, is oriented toward verbal hostility in the form of derogation, threats, and teasing. In unstructured play situations, children with LI, who are less facile with language, are more likely to resort to physical aggression instead, as was the case for David.

LANGUAGE IMPAIRMENT AND SOCIAL-EMOTIONAL DISORDER: RESEARCH FINDINGS ON ATYPICAL POPULATIONS IN MIDDLE CHILDHOOD

Children With Language Impairment Attending Mental Health Clinics

Structural Language Skills, Cognition, and Achievement

In middle childhood, referrals for speech-language problems occur less frequently than in late infancy and the preschool years. Rather, when children perform poorly in school, an assessment for learning disabilities is done, which sometimes reveals the presence of LI. When children's behavior is disruptive or otherwise distressing to adults, they are referred for mental health services. Considerable research now attests to the large proportion of school-aged children referred to mental health settings and for special classroom placements because of behavioral or emotional problems who have LI and associated learning problems (Baltaxe & Simmons, 1990; Camarata, Hughes, & Ruhl, 1988; Cohen, Barwick, et al., 1998; Cohen et al., 1993; Gualtieri et al., 1983; Kotsopoulos & Boodoosingh, 1987; Love & Thompson, 1988; Warr-Leeper et al., 1994). Because for some of these children LI was unsuspected until a routine systematic research assessment was done, an important question for practice is whether these children are distinctive in a clinically meaningful way. To answer this question, children with unsuspected LI had to be compared to disturbed children whose LI had been identified (i.e., at school or in a speech-language clinic) and to disturbed children with normally developing language. Using this group comparison design, Cohen and colleagues undertook two studies that systematically screened consecutive referrals of 399, 4- to 12-year-old children referred for outpatient mental health services (Cohen et al., 1993) and 380, 7- to 14-year-old referred children (Cohen, Barwick, et al., 1998;

Cohen, Menna, et al., 1998). The methodology involved administering a comprehensive battery of standardized measures of language structure, narrative discourse, and pragmatics. Standardized behavioral rating scales and a structured psychiatric interview were used to assess parents' and teachers' perceptions of the children's behavior. In the older sample, measures of cognition, achievement, and social cognition were added. This latter study was unique in that the multiple areas of functioning discussed in Chapter 2 were measured simultaneously.

In terms of prevalence, the results of systematic comprehensive screening indicated that of children referred *only* for a social-emotional problem, 34% of 4- to 12-year-olds had LI (Cohen et al., 1993) as did 40% of the 7- to 14-year-olds (Cohen, Barwick, et al., 1998). Combining children with previously identified and unsuspected LI indicated that altogether 58% of children referred for social-emotional problems had LI. This is an underestimate of LI in families, since assessment of siblings indicated an elevated rate of LI in these children as well (Cohen, Barwick, Horodezky, & Isaacson, 1996). Furthermore, the relatively high prevalence of unsuspected LI was not characteristic of children at any particular age. When subgroups of children aged 4 to 6, 7 to 9, 10 to 12, and 13 to 14 years were compared, the prevalence of both previously identified and unsuspected LI was similar at all age levels (Cohen & Horodezky, 1998).

A possible reason why some children's language problems were overlooked emerged when the patterns of language functioning, learning, and social-emotional disturbance were examined in children with previously identified and unsuspected LI. In the 4- to 12-year-old sample, the two groups of children with LI were similar in the severity of receptive language problems. Although children with both previously identified and unsuspected LI had problems with expressive language and social communication, these were more severe in the children whose LI had been previously identified. It is reasonable to assume that it was these children's obvious problems in verbal expression that attracted adults' attention. Children with more subtle receptive language problems were overlooked, a serious oversight given the poor long-term outcomes for children with difficulties in language comprehension. In the sample of 7- to 14-year-olds, the children with previously identified and unsuspected LI did not differ in the pattern of language functioning; they were impaired in both receptive and expressive language. Children with previously identified LI were more likely to meet criterion for reading disability than children with unsuspected LI, however. Therefore, having unsuspected LI in the older sample was associated with relatively milder problems with reading, a possible reason why some of these children's language problems were overlooked. It is important to note that problems were not limited to reading; children with both previously identified and unsuspected LI also performed more poorly than children with normal language on measures of intelligence, verbal and nonverbal working memory, arithmetic, and visual-motor skills (Cohen, Barwick, et al., 1998), something observed by investigators studying children with LI in the community (Beitchman, Nair, Clegg, & Patel, 1986) and in speech-language clinic samples (Bishop & Edmundson, 1987b; Stark & Tallal, 1981). Although teachers rated the school competence of children with un-suspected LI as lower than that of children with normal language, this was attributed to psychosocial factors, such as family dysfunction, rather than to cognitive or learning difficulties (Barwick, Im, & Cohen, 1995).

When social-emotional characteristics were examined, the results were also similar to other studies in that children who had LI exhibited a het-erogeneous pattern of psychopathology, with symptoms associated with ADHD being the most common (Cohen et al., 1993; Cohen, Menna, et al., 1998). In the younger, 4- to 12-year-old sample, however, compared with children with previously identified LI, children with unsuspected LI had more severe externalizing behavior problems. These problems were more noticeable and thus more likely to lead to referral. In contrast, the pattern of social-emotional disturbance was similar in children with previously iden-tified and unsuspected language problems in the 7- to 14-year-old sample (Cohen, Menna, et al., 1998). Although this was not a longitudinal study, the increased similarity in the social-emotional problems of the older clinic-referred children is consistent with studies that have shown that school entry is a point where a dramatic increase in psychopathology is observed (Hinshaw, 1992; Moffitt, 1993).

In these studies, it also was observed that children with LI experienced greater psychosocial disadvantage than children with normal language. They came from homes of lower socioeconomic status and their moth-ers had less education, a frequent finding in studies of children with LI (Cantwell & Baker, 1991). Furthermore, children with unsuspected LI were more likely to come from single-parent households. These stresses may contribute directly to the development of social-emotional problems, as it has been shown repeatedly that environmental adversity contributes to a negative outcome (Werner, 1989). They also may be associated with cir-cumstances that can make families less attentive to their children's lan-guage and learning development and problems.

Taken together, the results of these two studies indicate that children with unsuspected LI meet criteria for LI but have more subtle problems with language and language-related achievement. Elsewhere it has been suggested that when the clinical implications are considered, it may be more productive to think about whether children are impaired rather than whether they meet an operational research definition for reading or other disabilities (Dunn, Flax, Sliwinski, & Aram, 1996).

Social-Emotional Disorder and
Specific Aspects of Language and Communication

The research described above has elucidated the high prevalence of LI in mental health clinic populations. To consider how LI and social-emotional disorder may be linked, the majority of studies have focused on specific aspects of language structure (e.g., Kotsopoulos & Boodoosingh, 1987; Warr-Leeper et al., 1994). The most consistent association of social-emotional disorder has been with receptive LI generally (Cantwell & Baker, 1991; Cohen et al., 1993) and with language problems that are pervasive (Beitchman, Hood, Rochon, & Peterson, 1989).

The social-communicative aspect of language has been increasingly emphasized (Bishop, 2000; Gallagher, 1999). Social communication relies not only on language structures but on cognitive processes that mediate the relationship between language and social-emotional disturbance as represented in social discourse, pragmatic skills, and social-cognitive competence (Prutting, 1982; Westby & Cutler, 1994). School-aged children with LI continue to have problems with conventional communicative skills required for peer relationships. There is a close relationship between structural language, pragmatics, discourse, and social-cognitive skills. Only rarely, however, have they been studied simultaneously in clinical samples and then primarily in children with severe language and social-emotional disorders diagnosed as autistic (e.g., Tager-Flusberg, 1999). The risk of not having a comprehensive language and communication assessment for children with less severe social-emotional problems is that certain aspects of functioning that are important to integrate into a treatment plan will be overlooked. Recently, language, narrative discourse, pragmatic competence, and social cognition have been examined in children with social-emotional disorder (Cohen, Menna, et al., 1998; Vallance et al., 1999), and the findings are summarized in the next sections.

Discourse Deficits and Social-Emotional Disturbance

Mental health professionals often perceive children's problems with communication as a consequence of social-emotional disturbance. Such problems include difficulties formulating and expressing thoughts; sounding incoherent due to the unclear and ambiguous way that people, objects, and events are referred to; and struggling to answer or providing only minimal answers to direct questions. As mentioned earlier, these same symptoms are likely to be considered indicators of a language or communication impairment by a communication specialist. To disentangle discourse deficits associated with LI from those associated with social-emotional disorders, Vallance et al. (1999) examined the narratives of groups of 7- to 12-year-old children from mental health clinics and from normative school settings using stories on the Story Construction subtest of the Detroit Test of Learning Aptitudes-3 (Hammill, 1998). These narratives were analyzed in terms of (a) productivity, (b) language structure (i.e., lexical complexity, syntactic complexity, and linguistic cohesion), (c) information structure (i.e., setting, events, mental states, emotion states, and resolution), and (d) flow of discourse (i.e., efficiency, repetitions, unintelligible utterances, and self-initiated repairs).

Results indicated that disruptions in the *flow of discourse* characterized children with social-emotional disturbance regardless of whether they had LI, whereas discourse deficits in *language and information structure* characterized children with LI regardless of whether they had a social-emotional problem. Regardless of whether or not LI was found, children referred to mental health clinics were less efficient communicators. They used more fillers, repetitions, and repairs than nonreferred children (e.g., "Okay, well, they're like playing basketball. Um, a player broke his foot or something, broke his foot, taking a shot for the last point. Mmm. Um. That's it"). They also were more likely to describe mental states rather than emotional states (e.g., "I know they want to win but there are only 12 minutes left" vs. "They were really happy because they were going to win"). As noted in Chapter 3, maltreated infants also use more repetitions in their speech than nonmaltreated children (McFadyen & Kitson, 1996), a finding supported by clinical anecdotal evidence of adult discourse (Main, 1995). Thus it appears that anxiety or preoccupation with emotional issues may affect fluency and efficiency of language on narrative tasks. Vallance et al. (1999) suggested that clinic-referred children are vigilant about monitoring the effects of what they say, as indicated by the use of self-initiated repair, and that they use less emotion language in favor of mental state language, which represents the thoughts, desires, beliefs, and intentions of characters rather than their feelings.

The deficits of children with LI were different. These children used simpler, shorter sentences and there was poorer cohesion within sentences than in children with normal language. These qualities of discourse were related to poor structural language skills, poor narrative coherence, and failure to explain reasons for a character's actions and outcomes of events (e.g., "Many people have entered and one person hurt theirself"). These attributes characterized both children with LI presenting to a mental health clinic and children with LI in the community who did not have social-emotional problems. Such findings are consistent with other research on children with LI (e.g., Liles, 1985a, 1985b; Liles, Duffy, Merritt, & Purcell, 1995; Ripich & Griffith, 1988; Roth, 1986).

Children with co-occurring LI and social-emotional disorder were at the greatest disadvantage. Not only did these children exhibit the deficits of children with social-emotional problems and children with LI described above, but they also demonstrated some distinct discourse problems, including difficulties with pronominal reference. Pronominal reference allows the listener to understand that who is being spoken about in one context is consistent with who is being spoken about in another context (Liles, 1985a) (e.g., "Rob and John were playing basketball. He fell down."). This has been suggested as reflecting difficulty with understanding the system of *person* (Halliday & Hasan, 1976). Children with both LI and social-emotional disorder also had more difficulty making causal connections across events and relationships, an important task for interpreting the world (van den Broek, 1997) (e.g., "The rocket ship was attacked by asteroids because the men were very scared"). Liles (1985b) suggests that this is important for understanding the role that characters play in events and how their emotions, motives, and goals direct their participation. Difficulty making causal connections may be related to problems observed on social problem solving tasks. In this context, it is notable that impaired use of linguistic cohesion has also been observed in children diagnosed as schizophrenic, independent of measures of formal thought disorder (Caplan, 1996).

In another study, Vallance and Wintre (1997) found that in 8- to 12-year-old children with language learning disabilities, social discourse skills, and particularly understanding of figurative language, mediated the relation between children's language learning disability and their social competence. Children with language learning disabilities were prone to understand and interpret only the literal and concrete meaning of words in a metaphor. Thus it was not structural language problems but the difficulty using language for communication in a social context that posed challenges to establishing social relationships.

Social Cognition, Language Impairment, and Social-Emotional Disorder

Understanding language in social context requires comprehending the thoughts, feelings, and intentions of others, a social-cognitive skill. Recently, Cohen, Menna, et al. (1998) made a detailed examination of a range of social-cognitive skills, including emotion recognition, social problem solving, and self-cognition, in 7- to 14-year-old children referred for outpatient mental health services. With respect to emotion recognition, they found that children with LI had no trouble when they simply had to label facial expressions on photos. When they had to identify the emotion in a social context represented in a brief story, however, difficulties emerged. Moreover, information regarding emotions was processed more slowly; although all of the mental health clinic referred children's responses were slower than expected based on normative data, children with LI took the longest to respond. Thus children with LI were compromised in both speed and accuracy of processing emotional information.

The latter tasks involved identifying one emotion that suited a particular situation. Vallance and Cohen (1998) also evaluated the ability of children with LI and with normal language to understand and predict multiple emotions. Children referred to a mental health clinic who had LI were approximately one developmental level behind children with normal language in their ability to conceptualize the integration of multiple emotions of varying degrees of intensity. Although the literature on children's understanding of emotions in relation to language and behavior is sparse, Cook, Greenberg, and Kusche (1994) reported that the relation between understanding complex aspects of emotion and behavior was eliminated when children's vocabulary was taken into account statistically. In contrast, the association between understanding more basic emotions (e.g., happy, sad) and behavior was still related to vocabulary but not to the extent as when complex emotions were involved. Thus language may be more integral to understanding complex emotions than more basic ones.

Another aspect of social cognition, social problem solving, requires coordination of a number of abilities, including not only identifying the feelings of each participant in a conflict but also generating and evaluating strategies to resolve the conflict and knowing when a conflict is resolved. These steps in the social problem solving process require verbal explanations and repair and rely on cognitive processes such as working memory. In particular, children need to list alternative strategies and also simultaneously process and evaluate each alternative and predict the outcome. Using Selman's developmental model, Cohen, Menna, et al. (1998) found that children with LI referred for mental health service exhibited less mature social problem solving strategies. They did not have difficulty listing alternative strategies, which may be a relatively simpler task (Dale, 1996). Differences could not be attributed solely to children's ability to express themselves in interviews, since covarying for expressive language did not change the results. Other investigators have also shown that when Grade 3 to Grade 7 children with both receptive and expressive language impairments participated in a role-playing situation, they performed more poorly than children with predominantly expressive LI (Stevens & Bliss, 1995), thus confirming that problems in social cognition include but go beyond language expression and are based in difficulties processing social and emotional information.

Although there has been considerable attention paid to theory of mind in autistic children, only minimal evidence is available on the association of milder forms of LI with theory of mind in clinical samples. Moreover, there is little information beyond the preschool years, although theory of mind continues to develop (Freeman, 2000). In a study comparing 6- to 12-year-old children diagnosed as conduct disordered with children diagnosed as autistic, Happé and Frith (1996) found that children with conduct disorder exhibited impairments in social behaviors that presuppose a mature theory of mind and in this regard did not differ from children with autism, although they obviously did not show the stereotyped or bizarre behaviors of autistic children. These authors suggest that most likely some items were failed by these clinical groups for different reasons. For instance, an item such as "weighs consequences of action" might be failed by a child diagnosed as conduct disordered because of impulsive and inattentive behavior, whereas for children with autism social-cognitive processing deficits may be more important. Preliminary findings of a study of theory of mind in mental health clinic and nonclinic samples indicate that the ability to explain the discrepancy between felt and displayed emotions was associated with language competence in a clinic sample but not in a nonclinic sample (Cohen, Im-Bolter, & Vallance, 2000). Although there is dispute regarding whether language is a prerequisite for theory of mind (Bishop, 1997), there is evidence of both temporal (Astington & Jenkins, 1999) and concurrent (Farmer, 2000) associations. The most parsimonious conclusion to draw is that regardless of whether LI is a precursor to problems with theory of mind (and other aspects of social cognition) or vice versa or whether some third factor is involved, performance on social-cognitive and language tasks co-occur at a level greater than chance and therefore should be measured together.

To turn finally to self-cognition, self-perceptions and attributions for success and failure have been studied both as an outcome of poor academic achievement and as a mediator of academic failure (Bryan & Bryan, 1990). For instance, McGee, Williams, Share, Anderson, and Silva (1986) speculated that continuing experience of educational failure may lead to lower self-esteem, which in turn predisposes children toward antisocial behavior in early adolescence. Deficits in self-cognition are not consistent across samples, however. Research comparing children with previously identified and unsuspected LI and children with normal language indicated that children with LI scored within normal limits, with the exception that children with previously identified LI had lower self-esteem about achievement (Cohen, Menna, et al., 1998). This puzzling result may find some explanation from evidence that children with social-emotional problems sometimes inflate ratings of their self-esteem and thus standardized rating scales do not provide a valid estimate of children's actual feelings (Shedler, Mayman, & Manis, 1993). This is a critical issue because it is assumed that self-esteem partially determines whether children will act on the social-cognitive knowledge that they have (Crick & Dodge, 1994).

The above research clearly shows that children with LI who were referred for social-emotional disorder were impaired with respect to social-cognitive skills. Moreover, deficits in social-cognitive skills were not related to whether or not children's LI had been identified or unsuspected. This is important in light of longitudinal research showing the poor long-term social and emotional outcomes for children with LI (Beitchman et al., 1994; Beitchman, Brownlie, & Wilson, 1996; Beitchman, Wilson, et al., 1996a, 1996b; Beitchman et al., 2001; Cantwell & Baker, 1991; Rutter & Mawhood, 1991). It is also important in light of the widespread use of language-based social intervention programs, which may be less effective for some children because of the failure to recognize whether they have the requisite language skills necessary for treatment.

Social-Emotional Disorder and
Language and Communication Impairment:
The Interface of Language Impairment and ADHD

In the previous sections, there was an extensive discussion of the association of language and communication impairments with a broad range of social-emotional disorders. There has been increasing interest in the high prevalence of LI in one particular group of children with social-emotional disorder, those diagnosed as ADHD. As mentioned earlier, although a range of psychiatric disorders is represented among children with LI, the most frequent is ADHD. In my own research, for instance, 63.6% of 7- to 14-year-old children presenting as child psychiatric outpatients reached criteria for LI (Cohen, Menna, et al., 1998). ADHD was the most common psychiatric diagnosis and was given to 46% of these children. This is not surprising in that many of the characteristics that enter into the diagnosis of ADHD overlap with those that would earn a diagnosis of LI (see Table 1.2). determine which deficits are associated with ADHD alone, which are associated with LI alone, and which are associated with both conditions together.

Review of the literatures on ADHD and on LI suggest some potential areas of commonality but also some limitations because the overlap between ADHD and LI has not been considered directly. Of course, children with LI have numerous problems with structural language and communication, such as problems with narrative discourse and pragmatics (e.g., Bishop, 1998; Hayden & Pukonen, 1996; Johnston, 1988). Studies of language functioning in children with ADHD are limited. Structural language and communication problems have been observed in children with ADHD (see review by Tannock & Schachar, 1996), but few studies have separated the effects of ADHD and LI. Where this has been done, it has been suggested that problems with language structure are characteristic only of those children with concurrent reading disabilities (Felton & Wood, 1989; Pennington, Groisser, & Welsh, 1993; Tannock & Schachar, 1996) and that only aspects of language that are likely to come under the influence of inhibitory control, such as narrative discourse and pragmatics, are deficient in children with ADHD generally (Tannock & Schachar, 1996).

Most consistently, children with ADHD have been observed to show deficiencies on cognitive measures of executive functions; those that tap inhibitory control have been emphasized (Barkley, 1997; Tannock, 1998). Children with LI have been shown to be substantially impaired across many domains of cognitive functioning, including but not limited to those requiring inhibitory control (Johnston, 1988). Working memory, one aspect of executive functions, has been acknowledged as integral in the literatures on both ADHD (Mariani & Barkley, 1997) and LI (Weismer, Evans, & Hesketh, 1999). Although the importance of working memory in children with ADHD has been highlighted (Eslinger, 1996), in fact it has rarely been studied in this population. Moreover, the range of structural language problems examined in the literature on ADHD has largely been limited to those underlying reading disability, namely phonological (Pennington et al., 1993; Tannock & Schachar, 1996) and semantic processing (Purvis & Tannock, 1997, 2000) skills. Implications for clinical practice of the available findings from these studies where deficits have been observed also remain problematic because children with ADHD have been compared to normal controls (Purvis & Tannock, 1997; Tannock, Purvis, & Schachar, 1993), to children with reading disabilities without psychiatric disorder (Purvis & Tannock, 1997), and to children with other psychiatric diagnoses than ADHD who have normal language (Beitchman et al., 1987). Children with other psychiatric disorders who have LI had not been included as a comparison group.

To try to understand the relationship between LI and ADHD more fully, Cohen, Vallance, et al. (2000) examined children with ADHD and those with other psychiatric diagnoses who did and did not have LI on measures of language, achievement, and cognition (including intelligence, executive functions, and visual-motor integration). Results indicated that regardless of psychiatric diagnosis, clinically referred children with LI were at a greater disadvantage in all areas of language functioning, including narrative discourse and achievement, and on working memory measures used to tap executive functions. Children with ADHD did have problems with working memory, as reflected in their below-average scores on working memory tasks, but LI was more strongly associated with poor performance on this task than was ADHD.

There was no support for the hypothesis that ADHD would be associated with specific aspects of language (i.e., narrative discourse and pragmatics). As noted earlier, Tannock and Schachar (1996) have hypothesized that children with ADHD have problems in pragmatic and narrative discourse skills because these are tied to executive function capacities, and it is only children with ADHD and co-occurring language-based reading disabilities who exhibit structural language deficits. Cohen et al. (2000) found that the poorest pragmatic skills were not associated with ADHD but with having three co-occurring conditions: ADHD, LI, and reading disability. Narrative discourse was associated with LI, regardless of whether a reading disability was present.

In relation to theoretical considerations, there is an impetus to make a detailed examination of language functioning in children with ADHD in light of recent theoretical work suggesting the potential role that language deficits may play in explaining some of the basic underpinnings of this disorder. For instance, Barkley (1997) suggested that beyond its role in communication and achievement, language may play a central role in this syndrome.

Following from earlier investigators such as Luria (1961) and Vygotsky (1962), he postulated that a developmental impairment in core elements of ADHD is associated with problems in self-directed speech and in internalization of language and its use for self-regulation and mental representation. Because of this, children with ADHD encounter more difficulties in higher-order executive functioning, which includes verbal mediation and planful, goal-directed behavior guidance, than in spontaneous speech (Zentall, 1988). This is particularly interesting in light of suggestions that self-directed speech is important to the development of working memory (Denckla, 1996). Although in early childhood self-directed speech need not be relevant to the task at hand to be effective, by the time children enter school, task-relevant and prescriptive forms of self-directed speech are essential for mental representation of plans and goals and responses to rules and instruction. Not only must children understand rules but they also must retrieve, organize, and express them (Westby & Cutler, 1994). In this way, language structure may take on an increasingly greater guidance function with age such that development of internalized language for self-regulation comes to depend on adequate receptive and expressive language skills. Phonological processing skills may be especially important in helping children decode directives accurately. Other aspects of language structure may also be important. For instance, an adequate vocabulary is necessary to represent the content of events accurately, and an adequate grammar is required for planning, organizing, and sequencing and also sets the context for actions. In this way, language contributes to the efficiency of executive functions and also is a means by which executive function deficits are expressed (Vygotsky, 1962). Of most importance in this context, this is not limited to children who receive a diagnosis of ADHD but contributes to problems in emotion regulation for children with a range of psychiatric diagnoses. We need to be cautious about attributing to children with ADHD what might be a reflection of problems with behavioral and affect regulation generally.

DEVELOPMENTAL TASKS OF ADOLESCENCE:
13 TO 18 YEARS

Case Example

Carlos, aged 14 years, 2 months, was referred for concerns thought to be related to physical and sexual abuse by a security guard the previous summer and a history of physical and verbal abuse by a bus driver. He was very close to his mother and refused to stay at home without her, saying that it depressed him. His teacher complained about Carlos's aggressive behavior in the class-room and on the school grounds and about his poor motivation. Carlos missed many days of school because of illness.

Carlos's mother had emigrated alone from Ecuador with her three children. Contact with Carlos's father was lost when he remarried, and Carlos had not seen his father for 10 years. Carlos's mother attributed Carlos's problems to his experiences of abuse, the lack of a male role model, and her difficulty setting limits.

Carlos's mother reported a number of stresses during her pregnancy, including high blood pressure and emotional strain. Carlos was born at term and weighed 8.5 pounds. He cried excessively and was difficult to soothe. Milestones were recalled as being within normal limits, and Carlos started to use words at age 1 year. He did not put words together until 3 years of age and was late in learning to write, however.

Several psychiatric disorders were diagnosed, including Conduct Disorder, ADHD, Encopresis, and Enuresis. On the Child Behavior Checklist, Carlos's mother rated him in the clinical range with respect to Somatic Complaints, Social Problems, Delinquent Behavior, and Aggressive Behavior. Carlos's teacher rated him within the clinical range on the Attention Problems, Social Problems, Aggressive Behavior, and Delinquent Behavior subscales.

During testing, Carlos was confrontational and argumentative and complained about the length of the assessment. Once he decided to stay, he seemed to enjoy most of the tasks and with praise and encouragement tried his best. Despite the shift in mood during testing, Carlos was difficult to engage in conversation.

On the intelligence test, Carlos scored lower on verbal (low average) than nonverbal (average) subtests. Language testing showed that Carlos had good phonological awareness. Receptive and expressive vocabulary were below average for his age, however, and more consistent with that of a 10-year-old than a 14-year-old. On tests of receptive grammar, scores were within normal limits, but Carlos had difficulty expressing grammatically correct sentences. He also performed well below average on a test of figurative language that tapped his capacity to draw inferences and understand figures of speech. In some instances, he looked blankly at the examiner when a question was asked. Carlos showed a strength in following directions, suggesting that poor performance in the classroom may have been related to weak memory skills rather than attention problems. In line with this, Carlos exhibited problems with processing verbal, spatial, and numeric information on working memory tasks. He took a long time to respond and had difficulty identifying information he had been exposed to at different times. Finally, Carlos found story construction very difficult. His stories comprised a set of descriptions with little sequencing of ideas.

In terms of achievement, although Carlos was able to decode words at grade level, reading comprehension was 2 years below grade, and oral reading was very slow. Problems were observed in extracting both literal and inferential information from text, and he was slow to respond to questions. Spelling was also one year below grade.

Carlos's responses to the social problem solving interview were more appropriate to a younger child of 9 to 11 years. There was little evidence of a capacity to see both partners' positions in a conflict or concern about the relationship or the unfairness of an imbalance. Also notable was that one character in the story had to take full responsibility for the project rather than trying to negotiate the merits of a compromise.

It was concluded that difficulties in language and communication accounted for many of Carlos's problems in both academic and social-emotional contexts. When feedback was given, the examiner noticed that the first time Carlos smiled was when he nodded agreement to conclusions from the assessment. Subsequently, Carlos received remedial help for language and communication problems on a withdrawal basis at school. The family continued to be seen together to help Carlos's mother understand the implications of his language and communication problems, set limits on his behavior, and consider resuming contact with his father. The question was raised as to whether some of the abuse perpetrated on Carlos was a function of his poor verbal skills, which would have made it difficult for him to defend himself or express his experience to adults. Carlos was also seen in individual therapy to help him develop adaptive means of protecting himself in the future. Recommendations were made to the psychotherapist by the speech-language pathologist on how to facilitate Carlos's expression of his thoughts and feelings.

Language and Cognitive Development

Despite ample evidence that for many children early-identified LI persists into adulthood (Cohen, in press), there is relatively little known about adolescent language and the overlap between LI and social-emotional disturbance in this age group. During adolescence, demands on language and cognitive skills for verbal comprehension, reasoning, and expression grow in complexity and abstractness. In normally developing adolescents, vocabulary and the capacity to use figurative language increase, and discourse skills become more refined. Most adolescents do not have difficulty with basic vocabulary, but those with LI, such as Carlos, may struggle with words that have subtle meanings—for instance, "although" and "unless," which link phrases that relate information. They also may have difficulty with words that require keeping more than one referent in mind, such as terms having to do with family kinship or that express spatial or temporal dimensions (e.g., before, next, last) (Wiig & Semel, 1973). Although Carlos exhibited some problems with grammar, adolescents with LI rarely perform poorly on tests of grammar because most grammatic forms are established by the age of 8 years. Often, however, there is little variety in vocabulary and sentence structure and difficulties relating ideas within and across sentences using linguistic devices (Montgomery, 1992), something observed in Carlos's narratives and conversation. Therefore identification of LI turns to subtle difficulties with verbal expression and understanding, such as problems with word finding, narrative discourse, and figurative language (i.e., metaphors, similes, idioms, jokes, and inferences).

Early adolescence gives rise to further shifts in cognitive development with increasing capacity for systematic problem solving. Thought processes become more logical and abstract and adolescents have the capacity for hypothetical thinking. Normally developing adolescents are capable of symbolizing experiences and manipulating symbols to solve increasingly more complex problems. Flexibility and reversibility of thinking allows them to follow arguments from premises to conclusions and back again. Adolescents are famous for their argumentative natures. In the most benign light, these arguments can be seen as a means of exercising newfound language and cognitive skills. Language impairment robs adolescents of the opportunity to practice and refine these skills.

Both language and cognitive development in adolescence are also marked by the capacity for conscious control of thinking about language and cognitive strategies for problem solving. As children get older, they not only show increasing memory span and information-processing capabilities but also greater insight into how their language, cognitive processing, and memory work, that is, *metalanguage, metacognition, metamemory* (Kail, 1984). Moreover, they can retrieve information more effectively than younger children because of the greater sophistication of metamemory skills (Stern, 1985) and consequently are able to invent and use strategies for remembering. The importance of metalinguistic, metacognitive, and metamemory skills for academic success in adolescence cannot be underestimated.

For children with LI, adolescence is a difficult time because academic demands for inferential thinking, understanding abstract concepts, and independent learning increase. These skills require more sophisticated reasoning and problem solving and also memory and working memory skills. Furthermore, academic achievement during adolescence is heavily reliant on reading and writing skills and the capacity for self-guided study. From the fifth grade, reading comprehension is used as an essential tool for learning, and this reaches a peak in adolescence when work on independent projects is a priority. Although Carlos could decode words, in other children with reading problems, longitudinal studies have shown that on average adolescents with LI exhibit problems with phonological awareness just as do their younger counterparts (Bruck, 1992). To circumvent difficulties with decoding, adolescents with LI or language-related reading disabilities often use context to recognize words (Kamhi & Catts, 1999). Unfortunately, this is not very effective in decoding content words (Gough & Wren, 1998), and in fact reliance on context may actually decrease comprehension. Bruck (1990) suggested that this is because working memory resources are applied to predicting words from text, which robs the student of an important resource for comprehension.

Written language also becomes more important. This involves integration of a number of skills that are related to vocabulary, sentence structure, discourse, punctuation, capitalization, and spelling. As well, writing requires executive function skills such as planning, monitoring, evaluation, and revision. The writing of adolescents with LI is sparse, often because of poor memory and organizational skills, and comprises a string of unrelated thoughts (Graham & Harris, 1999), as was the case for Carlos.

Language and Social-Emotional Development

By adolescence, most students have learned how to talk to teachers and peers, participate in the classroom, and debate ideas. Positive social relationships can buffer the stress associated with academic achievement, whereas negative relationships exacerbate the challenge. Early adolescence is a time when friendships become more intense and demanding. Normally developing adolescents have increased capacity to appreciate the reciprocal nature of relationships. This may become apparent when there is a demand for working cooperatively in the classroom. The risk for social-emotional problems emerging or intensifying is considerable for adolescents, especially for those who have had a history of poor achievement and inadequate capacity for engaging in reciprocal relations with peers. Problems with figurative language also may interfere with participating in banter and joking with peers. The verbal social repertoire of adolescent peer relationships is heavily reliant on figurative language, and adolescents with LI can sometimes function at the 7- to 9-year level (Wiig, 1984). At the same time, some adolescents with poor figurative language may have good peer relationships because they have learned the implicit social scripts of peer relationships and dating. Thus adolescents' LI may be overlooked because some of their language is highly scripted from repeated exposure to peer models. Problems emerge, however, in more complex or new situations where the overlearned scripts cannot be applied.

Although in middle childhood self-definition and self-esteem are focused on concrete external traits such as grades, appearance, and success in sports, in adolescence abstract internal personality characteristics take on a larger role in development of self. Normally developing adolescents have a clearer understanding of themselves and see their personal characteristics as enduring qualities. Adolescents with LI, who struggle to keep up with increasingly more difficult schoolwork, are likely to suffer in terms of self-esteem and become more isolated in an attempt to hide their difficulties from peers.

Although social-emotional problems may be particularly severe for adolescents with long-standing language, communication, and achievement problems, in some cases, LI is first identified in adolescence when demands on language increase.

Case Example

Twelve-year-old Paula did not complete her homework; had difficulty organizing her ideas, taking notes, and preparing written work; and was disruptive in class. Difficulties were emerging in her social relationships because she always wanted her own way. She seemed to have problems following peers' banter and jokes and often was teased. Paula's teacher and mother attributed the problems to her preoccupation with her social life, poor attitude, and low motivation. Academic achievement was at the appropriate grade level, but testing showed Paula had problems with memory and formulating her ideas. She also had trouble telling a story and finding the words she wanted to use and scored below grade level on a test of figurative language. Since Paula had not experienced problems previously, it was concluded that due to the higher demands of Grade 7 her language problems were just beginning to interfere with her schoolwork and social relationships. Paula's problems were not associated with academic content but with organization and information processing.

The test results helped Paula's teacher and mother understand how problems with language and social understanding affected her behavior. Paula's teacher recalled that Paula's difficulties expressing herself irritated peers, who would often say "Just come to the point." Subsequently, Paula's teacher began to use more repetition in teaching, made sure Paula understood the material, and helped her use a daytimer. Paula's mother helped her structure activities at home. The feedback was a relief to Paula, as she realized that she was not "stupid." After gaining the support of her teacher and mother and their understanding of her limitations, she began to show improvements in academic functioning and social relationships. At referral, Paula's problems with peers were just emerging, and without intervention they likely would have become more serious.

Language and Affect and Behavior Regulation

Continuing from middle childhood, language is a means of analysis and self-control through the use of internal language for emotion regulation and relationships and for planning and completing work. Metacognitive skills applied to academic tasks also apply to self-control in social situations. The outcome for adolescents who cannot use language to hold their ground, present a point of view, or negotiate outcomes is either withdrawal from social interactions or use of negative behaviors to make their point.

LANGUAGE IMPAIRMENT
AND SOCIAL-EMOTIONAL DISORDER:
RESEARCH FINDINGS ON ATYPICAL
POPULATIONS OF ADOLESCENTS

Children With Language Impairment
Attending Mental Health Clinics

Common reasons for referral during adolescence are similar to those in middle childhood. These include problems with academic work, motivation, cooperation, attention, concentration, emotions, and behavior. Adolescents are unlikely to be referred for assessment of language per se. Thus it is highly pertinent that my research has shown that just as many adolescents have unsuspected LI and associated problems with learning, achievement, and social cognition as do younger children (Cohen, Barwick, et al., 1998; Cohen & Horodezky, 1998; Cohen, Menna, et al., 1998). Although problems associated with ADHD continue into adolescence, two other sets of symptoms become more prominent as reasons for referral: depression and conduct disorders. Early learning difficulties, many of which presumably have a language base, have been shown to be related to depression in adolescence (Kellam, Brown, Rubin, & Ensminger, 1983) as well as to anxiety (Huntington & Bender, 1993). In their follow-up study of children presenting to a speech-language clinic, Baker and Cantwell (1987) observed that the prevalence of psychiatric disorder increased with age among children with LI, an observation also made by Beitchman et al. (2001) in a community sample.

Longitudinal Studies Following Children With Language Impairment Into Adolescence

The implications of having LI for adolescents can perhaps best be understood by examining the outcomes of longitudinal studies that have followed the trajectory of co-occurring LI and social-emotional disorders from infancy or early childhood into adolescence and adulthood. Longitudinal studies have used various samples, including children seen in speech-language clinics and children identified through communitywide screening.

The largest speech-language clinic sample was followed by Cantwell and Baker (1991), who examined 300 of 600 consecutive referrals of children initially assessed at 2 to 15 years of age and reassessed 5 years later. The results of their study indicated an increase in the prevalence of disorders in language usage and auditory processing; 25% of children had developed learning disorders since the initial assessment, especially those with receptive LI (Baker & Cantwell, 1987). Follow-up results also indicated that the prevalence of diagnosable psychiatric disorders increased from the initial assessment 5 years previously, with 60% of the sample receiving some psychiatric diagnosis at follow-up, in comparison to 44% when seen initially. Moreover, approximately 25% of the sample who at first testing did not have a psychiatric diagnosis had one at follow-up. The pattern of diagnosis also changed. The diagnosis of ADHD doubled in prevalence and anxiety disorders more than doubled.

Although studies of clinic samples provide useful information, to fully understand the outcomes of a childhood history of LI, it is necessary to use a community epidemiological sample. Three prospective studies have followed children into adolescence and early adulthood, one in Sweden, the second in New Zealand, and a third in Canada.

In the Swedish study, psychologists rated the amount of vocalization (noncrying) at 3, 6, and 9 months on a five-point scale (Klackenberg, 1980; Stattin & Klackenberg-Larsson, 1993). Vocal communicativeness was rated again by different psychologists at 12 and 18 months and at 2 and 3 years on a similar scale. The ratings of vocalization in infancy were associated with the length and complexity of children's sentence formation, vocabulary use, success of communicating ideas verbally at 3 and 5 years, intelligence at 17 years, and educational level at 20 years. Moreover, a low level of vocalization at as early as 6 months of age was related to registered criminality at 15 years.

In New Zealand, Silva and colleagues sampled 1,037 infants born over a one-year period (Silva, 1980). At 3 years of age, 3% of the sample examined was delayed in verbal comprehension only, 2.5% in verbal expression only, and 3% in both. When followed into the school years, the children with language problems were more likely to have reading disabilities (Silva, Justin, McGee, & Williams, 1984). Adolescents and young adults continued to have reading problems, some of which were related to early language difficulties, and performed poorly on examinations (Williams & McGee, 1994, 1996). Moreover, in adolescence, language-related reading problems were associated with psychopathology (Williams & McGee, 1994, 1996). Some investigators maintain that behavioral difficulties are primary and that these contribute to academic failure (Patterson, DeBaryshe, & Ramsey, 1989). In contrast, others hold the view that early cognitive factors, including verbal ability, are related to later achievement and antisocial behavior (e.g., Moffitt, 1993). Using results from structural equation modeling techniques, a developmental pathway has been traced whereby LI led to psychiatric disorder via reading problems, low achievement, poor verbal self-regulation, and school failure, including poor literacy, with low socioeconomic status and attention problems heightening risk (Fergusson & Lynskey, 1997; McGee, Share, Moffitt, Williams, & Silva, 1988). Transactional effects were such that early reading ability predicted later conduct disorder while at the same time antisocial behavior exerted a detrimental influence on later reading (Williams & McGee, 1994, 1996). This finding suggests that early language problems are compounded when youths become alienated from the mainstream. They are less likely to be motivated to continue in their attempts to achieve given the unrewarding outcome. In this context, it is pertinent that there is strong evidence of a higher than expected prevalence of LI and language-related learning disabilities among incarcerated youths (Myers & Mutch, 1992), runaway and homeless youths (Barwick & Siegel, 1996), school-refusing adolescents (Naylor, Staskowski, Kenney, & King, 1994), and adult female offenders (Wagner, Gray, & Potter, 1983). Teachers and parents are less likely to be supportive of youths who run afoul of societal norms.

The Canadian epidemiology study (Beitchman, Nair, Clegg, Ferguson, & Patel, 1986; Beitchman, Nair, Clegg, & Patel, 1986) provides prospective data on language, cognition, achievement, and psychiatric disorder at 5, 12, and 19 years. Sampling of 1,655 children in the Ottawa-Carleton region of Ontario revealed that, using a relatively liberal criterion for diagnosis, 6.4% of 5-year-olds had only speech impairments and 12.6% had LI (Beitchman, Nair, Clegg, & Patel, 1986). When followed at the ages of both 12 and 19 years, approximately 72% classified as LI at the age of 5 years remained impaired, especially children with pervasive receptive and expressive language problems. Moreover, a small percentage of children not identified as LI at the first assessment were so classified at age 12 and 19 years (Beitchman et al., 1994; Beitchman, Wilson, et al., 1996b; Johnson et al., 1999). The results did not change appreciably when a more stringent criterion for diagnosis of LI was applied to the original sample. This latter finding once again raises the possibility that young children with mild LI may not encounter problems until language demands on academic tasks and social life increase in adolescence. Moreover, at age 19 years those children with a diagnosis of LI at age 5 years still lagged behind non-language-impaired controls in academic achievement regardless of intelligence and were more likely to be classified as learning disabled (Young et al., 2000). LI status at age 5 years was associated with an overall higher rate of psychiatric diagnosis, in particular with anxiety disorders, the most common of which was social phobia. Beitchman et al. (2001) suggest that this may reflect persisting social difficulties related to poor pragmatic skills and inferior school performance. These investigators also examined the risk for substance abuse in the 19-year-old sample. Although those diagnosed as having LI at the age of 5 years were not at greater risk for substance abuse than controls (Beitchman et al., 1999), those who developed learning disabilities at age 12 and 19 did have significantly increased risk of substance abuse disorder at age 19 years (Beitchman, Wilson, Douglas, Young, & Adlaf, in press). Moreover, substance abusers with LI had a higher rate of comorbid psychiatric disorders, particularly antisocial personality disorder and internalizing disorders such as anxiety.

On the more positive side, in a review of long-term effects of reading disability into adolescence and adulthood, Maughan (1995) found that childhood behavioral problems did not necessarily lead to high rates of antisocial behavior or low self-esteem. Although factors such as the severity of difficulties and the context in which they emerged were critical influences on academic and vocational outcomes, those children who received support and encouragement at home and specialized attention in school and who selected environments as adults that were consistent with their personal strengths and limitations fared better (Maughan, 1995). Although Maughan's review concerns children with reading disabilities, presumably the majority also had language impairments.

KEY POINTS

- In the preschool years, language begins to overtake action as children's primary means of communication. Increased capacity for symbolization and language impacts on interactive play with peers. This serves to hone both learning skills and social relationships.

- It is now apparent that many preschoolers who were once regarded as shy or reticent actually have problems in language, pragmatics, and social-cognitive development. These children do not have the skills to initiate and maintain conversations with peers and consequently are rejected.

- Language increasingly becomes a means of self-control from the preschool years onward. Limited language skills in children with LI contribute to problems in behavioral and emotional functioning.

- From middle childhood through adolescence, children are better able to put thoughts and feelings into words and understand the nuances of meaning. Memory improves, partly as a result of the language-based capacity to categorize information and master strategies for recall. Moreover, executive function skills increase such that children can think about problem solving and sustain attention to tasks sufficient to achieve goals. Cognitive, social-cognitive, and language maturity also contribute to strategies for self-regulation and logical thinking and to development of reciprocal friendships.

- Adolescents with LI have a difficult time because academic achievement is heavily reliant on reading and writing skills and the capacity for independent work. They also suffer socially when they do not have a grasp of figurative in language or the social-cognitive maturity for engaging in reciprocal relationships with peers.

- Research spanning the years from preschool through adolescence indicates that language and communication impairments are consistently related to social-emotional disorder. Moreover, a large proportion of children presenting for mental health services and placed in classes for children with social-emotional problems have LI left unsuspected unless a formal assessment is done. These children are as much at risk for language, communication, cognitive, and social-cognitive problems as children whose LI gets identified at school.

- In a mental health clinic setting, on the surface there are many similarities in children's presenting problems. These may be associated with markedly different underlying conditions, however, some of which are related to problems language and communication and associated impairments.

- Findings regarding social-cognitive, pragmatic, and discourse skills in children with LI and social-emotional disorders offer an alternative explanation for difficulties of children in the classroom, at play with peers, at home, and in treatment, such as having difficulties processing social and emotional information, expressing thoughts concisely, and communicating logically.

- Assessments for children with social-emotional problems do not routinely evaluate language skills. Consequently, there are likely to be many children for whom language-based interventions are recommended who lack the basic skills to benefit from them.

5

IDENTIFICATION AND ASSESSMENT

No psychiatric diagnosis is appropriate . . . until a thorough developmental assessment is in hand. Language assessment is an essential part of this because the information provided by this evaluation has a profound impact on one's understanding of behavioral symptoms, the treatment thereof, and the interpretation of the child's problems to parents, teachers, and other caretakers. (Gualtieri et al., 1983, p. 168)

This chapter describes elements of assessment of children with LI and social-emotional disorder from the perspective of developmental psychopathology. It discusses how associated developmental functions can be described with an eye toward gaining a fuller understanding of children who present with concurrent LI and social-emotional disorder that will inform their education and treatment.

There are a number of principles reflecting the perspective of developmental psychopathology that guide assessment (e.g., Hoagwood, Jensen, Petti, & Burns, 1996; Meisels & Fenichel, 1996; Prizant, 1999; Rock, Fessler, & Church, 1997).

1. Information regarding developmental competence and impairment should be collected across contexts and over time from various perspectives with respect to adaptation to demands of home, school, peer relationships, and the community.

2. A range of strategies should be used to obtain information. Typically, standardized tests and questionnaires and observations are used to make a diagnosis or determine eligibility for service. For many of the developmental functions described in Chapters 3 and 4, standardized measures are not available. Use of other types of measures can enhance understanding of children's functioning.

3. Both conventional and unconventional communicative behavior must be considered to understand the language demands of problematic situations along with *what* children are trying to communicate and the *means* by which they are trying to communicate.
4. The characteristics and stability of the child's environment and availability of resources in the family and in the external environment should be ascertained.
5. The outcome of an assessment should be more than a diagnostic label. Assessment findings should provide specific recommendations for intervention, acknowledging that the impact of these will need to be monitored, and possibly revised, over time because the nature of LI and other developmental functions changes with age and treatment.

CONTENTS OF ASSESSMENT

A comprehensive multidimensional assessment for children from preschool through adolescence includes

1. Interviews with family/parents, teachers, and child or youth
2. Hearing screening or assessment
3. Assessment of language and communicative competence
4. Assessment of cognition
5. Assessment of achievement
6. Assessment of social cognition
7. Assessment of play
8. Assessment of caregiver-child interaction
9. Assessment of social-emotional functioning

Interviews With Parents, Teachers, and Child or Youth

Symptoms and Developmental History

The parent and teacher interview includes a description of the child's symptoms in a range of settings and the chronology of the child's development, with special attention paid to communicative and social-emotional functioning. In this context, turning points in the child's history, when problems emerged, worsened, or improved should be identified.

Early in the assessment process, it is useful to have parents, teachers, and the child (aged 11 or older) complete language and communication checklists, such as the *Clinical Evaluation of Language Fundamentals–3* (CELF-3) *Observational Rating Scales* (Semel, Wiig, & Secord, 1996).

For parents of infants, the *Infant/Toddler Checklist for Communication and Language Development* can be used (Wetherby & Prizant, 1998; checklist available on the Internet at www.symbolix.com). Responses to these checklists can be used as a jumping-off point for the assessment. These checklists also ensure a comprehensive screen for difficulties and provide a guide for more in-depth questions about areas of strength and concern. In addition, the perceptions of family members and teachers should be solicited regarding (a) expectations for the child, (b) attributions assigned to social-emotional difficulties, (c) strategies used to help the child (both those that have and those that have not worked), (d) the child's role in the family (especially whether the child is targeted as a cause of family problems), (e) cultural issues and the language environment of the child (e.g., the amount that parents read or talk with their child), (f) the level of family stress and capacity for organization around treatment, and, where relevant, (g) family members' past and current coping with their own language and learning difficulties. Whenever possible, the children themselves should be considered as a valuable source of information.

School Performance

The history of a child's school performance is typically obtained from parent, teacher, and child interviews, report cards, and results of previous assessments. Optimally, children should be observed directly in their classroom, although this is often not an option. A vivid picture of the child's behavior and functioning can be evoked through an interview, however. This helps in understanding the function of inappropriate behavior and the situations in which children function well.

Constitutional Factors

Because development is determined by multiple influences, the model of developmental psychopathology pays less attention to identifying a primary cause of disability and more to understanding the developmental pathway to problematic behavior and relationships. Although constitutional factors can contribute directly to a child's development and disorder, more often the influence is indirect. Children born with even a mild medical or developmental condition, difficult temperament, or other handicap evoke different responses from caregivers, setting the stage for a series of transactions that shape development. Inquiries should always be made as to factors related to social-emotional communication. For instance, parents may recall that their infant was "hard to read," "difficult to soothe," or had frequent tantrums when frustrated in efforts to communicate. Some constitutional factors and medical conditions obviously do contribute directly to children's development (e.g., thyroid deficiency, visual or hearing impairment), and information concerning such conditions can help parents and children appreciate some of the basis for the children's struggles. Important information includes details of the birth history (e.g., prematurity, respiratory problems, feeding problems), temperament, developmental progress, and any syndromes that might be associated with LI (e.g., fetal alcohol syndrome).

Family History

A family history that includes details regarding language, communication, learning, and other developmental disorders should be obtained. Although being diagnosed as having LI or a language learning disability per se may not be recalled by parents, they can describe details of their education, areas of strength and weakness in school, truancy, and school dropout. Answers to these questions provides information about a potential genetic contribution and also a window into the context in which the child has been raised. Just as for constitutional factors, the way that genetic endowment influences social-emotional functioning for children with LI is probably indirect. There is a bidirectional transactional process between genetic and environmental influences such that genetic factors contribute to children's experiences, making them susceptible to or protecting them from environmental influence and shaping the way that others act toward them (Ge et al., 1996). Information on family history is also important so that the parents' own struggles, along with those of the child, can be acknowledged when results of an assessment are discussed.

Environmental Factors

The literature has highlighted the importance of environmental factors for child performance. Numerous risk factors for both social-emotional disorder (Rutter, 1985) and for dual language and social-emotional disorder (Cantwell & Baker, 1991) have been identified. These contextual factors also contribute to whether children with LI encounter problems in social-emotional adjustment. Factors associated with development of communication and social-emotional disorders in children include adverse family conditions such as low socioeconomic status, psychosocial stress such as marital discord, child abuse, and parental mental illness or criminal conviction. The risk associated with these factors is cumulative and increases sharply when more than one risk factor is present (Rutter, 1979). The language and relational environment of the home is also critical and shown to be more important than psychosocial factors such as socioeconomic status (Hart & Risley, 1995; NICHD Early Child Care Research Network, 1999). Children raised in homes where parents talk and read with them are at an advantage. Furthermore, it has been shown that children with reading disabilities who come from supportive homes and who receive appropriate special services have a better outcome (Maughan, 1995).

Sociocultural Environment

Expanding numbers of families have emigrated from a nondominant culture to North America and Europe. Beyond second-language learning issues, cultures vary in their expectations, values, and beliefs about children's behavior and communication. Whereas in many North American homes children's verbal input is valued and desirable, in other cultures children are not expected to speak unless spoken to or to ask a question with an obvious answer. These children do communicate but may rely on nonverbal rather than verbal means of communication. As a consequence, they may be perceived as reticent or withholding. At a minimum, the assessor should obtain information about three dimensions of sociocultural context (Barrera, 1994): (a) rules for communications that are valued and appropriate for the culture—for instance, the usage of particular words; (b) rules for expressing one's own identity and for interacting with others—for instance, where a child is expected to stand or sit in relation to an adult or whether eye contact is appropriate; and (c) preferred and valued styles of identifying and processing information about the world—for instance, the best way to learn. In most instances, parents know that to participate in the dominant culture children must be bilingual and learn not only the language structures of the dominant culture but also the social preferences and pragmatic rules. Obviously, the more usual definition of bilingualism must be brought to bear in deciding whether and how standardized tests should be used with children who do not speak the language in which the tests are written.

Hearing Screening and Assessment

Inquiry should always be made regarding a child's hearing, any history of ear infections, and whether hearing has been tested. Moreover, a hearing screening should be a routine part of a language and communication assessment. Although repeated ear infections (otitis media) do not always affect language development, there is growing evidence that early recurrent otitis media with hearing loss in the first 2 years is associated with speech and language problems at 3 years of age (Shriberg, Friel-Patti, Flipsen, & Brown, 2000). Even children with hearing loss in only one ear are at a significant disadvantage (English & Church, 1999). Furthermore, hearing difficulties often are associated with problems in attention, noncompliance, and overactivity; children who appear to be *not listening* might actually be *not hearing.* When a screening test is failed, a full audiological assessment should be arranged.

ASSESSMENT TOOLS

In this section, tools for assessing language and communication and associated developmental functions are described. It is beyond the scope of this book to comprehensively list or describe these tools. Further information can be obtained from specialized texts (e.g., Lezak, 1995; Meisels & Fenichel, 1996; Paul, 1995; Sattler, 1992). Although both standardized and nonstandardized instruments are described, standardized tests are most commonly used for diagnosis and decision making. Because of the reliance on these measures, it is important to acknowledge both their strengths and their limitations (Crais, 1993; Wetherby & Prizant, 1992).

1. Although a developmental perspective has been promoted in this book, most assessment tools are not developmental in nature. Standardized tests have as their strength the capacity to relate children's abilities to normative expectations for their age. Many psychological and language tests provide developmental scores such as *mental age* or *grade equivalent, age equivalents,* or *percentile for age.* Caution is required in interpreting these scores literally because the units of measurement are not equivalent across development, and in fact developmental scales systematically shrink with age (Halperin & McKay, 1998). For instance, a 4-year-old functioning at the level of a 2-year-old would be very impaired, whereas a 15-year-old functioning at the level of a 13-year-old would be less so. There has been increased interest in criterion-referenced tests. These assess development of a skill in relation to established levels of mastery for a particular developmental level rather than in relation to a comparison sample, but few are available (e.g., *Infant-Toddler Language Scale* by Rossetti, 1990; *Ages and Stages Questionnaire* by Bricker, Squires, & Mounts, 1995). Such tests can be useful for planning and monitoring intervention or education and can be linked to instructional objectives.

2. Standardized tests do not consistently discuss the actual linguistic and cognitive demands of tests.

3. Standardized tests offer few opportunities for children to initiate interactions.

4. Except in the case of infants, parents do not observe the assessment directly or on videotape, although they are a valid source of information concerning their child's strengths and limitations.

5. The sample of children used to norm tests may not be an appropriate comparison group.

6. Formal test situations are decontextualized; that is, children cannot gain cues to help them guess what is expected. The benefit of this is that it permits children's struggles to communicate to become clearer. In naturalistic settings, children may appear to understand or follow instructions but are actually relying on cues from the environmental context. For instance, adults often use gestures and exaggerated intonation to facilitate children's comprehension and expression and provide subtle cues that indicate whether or not a child has responded correctly. Children also draw meaning from context on reading comprehension tasks, although those with language-based reading problems do not benefit from this as much as normal readers (Nation & Snowling, 1998). In interpreting test scores, it is important to revisit children's performance on tests with parents, teachers, and the children themselves to understand how the pattern of test performance relates to functioning in naturalistic settings.

7. Along similar lines, because tests are administered under laboratory conditions, it is difficult to obtain a valid picture of the abilities of children whose behavior is difficult to manage in the classroom.

The bottom line is that in reading the descriptions of the following tests it is important to keep in mind that although standardized tests are currently the primary means to make a diagnostic decision, the scores cannot be relied on alone to understand the nature and extent of a child's language and communication impairments or to plan intervention. It is essential that examiners be familiar with descriptions of the processes being assessed provided in manuals and with developmental demands at particular ages, some of which were described in Chapters 3 and 4. For instance, phonological processing skills are particularly important in the early grades when awareness of language sounds and the ability to match these with visual symbols are essential skills in learning to decode words, the first step in learning to read. In middle childhood and adolescence, when comprehension becomes critical, reading skills depend on multiple processes, including language structures, memory, working memory, and figurative language. Each of these processes must be examined separately to determine where difficulties in comprehension lie. It is also important that what is reported goes beyond scores to include observation of children's quality of performance in relation to these processes in terms of attention, self-correction (repair), and motivation. Assessment can be enhanced further by using dynamic assessment techniques. Dynamic assessment uses a test-teach-retest approach and guided learning (Rock et al., 1997). These techniques involve first testing the child, then teaching compensatory problem-solving strategies, and then reassessing whether the child is able to use them and whether this improves the child's performance. Whenever possible, information should be obtained directly from the child that will help interpret assessment findings. For instance, when children do not answer a question, I ask whether more time is needed or whether the child does not know the answer. I have found that if children say that more time is needed, then a correct answer is often given. Similarly, when children cannot answer correctly, questions can be asked about what they found to be difficult. When a correct answer is given to a question with which children have struggled, they can be asked what helped them get the answer. Not only does this provide useful information to the examiner, but research has shown that asking children to explain both correct and incorrect answers led them to adopt new strategies that had wider applicability both on the current problem and on ones that were not initially presented (Siegler, 2000).

Screening for Language Impairment

Decisions regarding which children require a comprehensive assessment are difficult to make because the social-emotional problems that children display, such as negative behavior or withdrawal, reflect attempts to mask problems associated with LI. Children who do not have language by the age of 2 years are always of concern, but the majority of children presenting to mental health clinics do have some language. With infants, the *MacArthur Communicative Development Inventory* (Fenson et al., 1993) can be used with parents to obtain information on children's verbal and gestural expression and understanding. The *Infant/Toddler Checklist for Communication and Language Development,* mentioned earlier, also can be used. In older children, screening interviews such as the CELF-3 mentioned earlier can be used. The *Denver Developmental Screening Test* is also often used as a brief screening test (Frankenburg, Dodds, & Archer, 1990); it is administered in the presence of the parent, who can provide insight into the child's performance. As well, some longer tests have a screening version that can be administered to the child, such as the *Clinical Evaluation of Language Fundamentals–3 Screening Test* (Semel, Wiig, & Secord, 1996b). Although vocabulary tests such as the *Peabody Picture Vocabulary Test–III* (Dunn & Dunn, 1997) have been used to screen for language difficulties, these are not adequate. As mentioned earlier, children with LI may have age-appropriate vocabulary but be impaired in other language functions.

Assessment of Language and Communicative Competence

Structural Language

Diagnosis of LI typically depends on scores obtained from individually administered standardized tests. Assessment of infants' preverbal communication has been facilitated by development of the *Communication and Symbolic Behavior Scales* (CSBS; Wetherby & Prizant, 1993a). The CSBS, developed for infants aged 0 to 2 years, provides a profile of functioning in 22 areas and broad groupings of (a) communicative functions; (b) gestural, vocal, and verbal communication; (c) reciprocity; (d) social-affective signaling; and (e) symbolic behavior (verbal and play). Important functions such as regulation of others' behavior, attracting attention for social interaction, and joint attention can be observed. Of most importance, this measure permits identification of delays in communication before the infant is able to talk. It also allows for dynamic assessment by manipulating verbal and gestural cues and observing the effect on infants' performance. Since the parents remain in the room when the infant is examined, there is an opportunity to validate what is observed, to point out to the parents their infant's competencies that might not have been reported previously, and to observe parent-infant interaction. The recent completion of a quick scoring procedure (*CSBS Quick-Score;* Wetherby & Prizant, 1997) makes this instrument more accessible to clinicians. Other tests for infants and preschool children, such as the *Preschool Language Scale–3* (PLS-3) for children from birth to age 6 years (Zimmerman, Steiner, & Pond, 1992) and the *CELF–Preschool* for children aged 3 to 7 years (Wiig, Secord, & Semel, 1992), are designed like tests for older children. They have subtests to assess receptive and expressive structural language skills, including semantics and syntax along with auditory verbal memory. The PLS-3 has supplementary scales to assess articulation and a checklist to use for scoring language samples.

In preschool- and school-aged children, structural language functions must be assessed in their expressive and receptive form, including semantics, morphology, syntax, and phonology. Two of the most commonly used test batteries are the *Clinical Evaluation of Language Fundamentals–3* (CELF-3; Semel, Wiig, & Secord, 1996) and the *Test of Language Development–3* Primary and Intermediate forms (TOLD-3; Newcomer & Hammill, 1997). The CELF-3 is used with children between the ages of 6 and 21 years and comprises subtests that measure the expressive and receptive components of semantics and morphosyntax as well as auditory verbal memory. This test extends understanding of some of the processes that may underlie problems with semantics, such as the capacity to group associated words and perceive relationships in the meaning of words. A somewhat different set of subtests is used for children aged 6 to 8 years and children aged 9 years and older. Supplementary tests permit testing of memory for paragraphs (Listening to Paragraphs) and rapid and efficient word finding (Word Associations). Some subtests tap more than one function. For instance, on the Formulated Sentences subtest of the CELF-3, the child is required to create a sentence using a key word provided by the examiner. The primary goal is to measure the ability to express a syntactically correct sentence. Working memory also is important, however, because children must hold in mind the word given by the examiner while at the same time constructing a sentence. The TOLD-3 measures expressive and receptive syntax and semantics on both the primary (4 to 8 years) and intermediate (8 to 12 years) forms. A test of phonology is included in the primary but not the intermediate version of the measure.

A more focused assessment of morphology and syntax can be done with the *Test for Auditory Comprehension of Language–3* (Carrow-Woolfolk, 1998) for children aged 3 to 10 years, which assesses meaning of grammatical morphemes (e.g., prepositions, noun and number, pronouns) and elaborated sentence structures (e.g., negative sentences, active and passive voice, embedded sentences).

Assessment of vocabulary almost invariably includes the *Peabody Picture Vocabulary Test–3* (PPVT-3; Dunn & Dunn, 1997). This multiple-choice test of receptive semantics can be used for individuals from the age of 2 years to adulthood. Comprehension is assessed by their pointing to one of the four picture stimuli that best fits a word or phrase read aloud by the examiner. Expressive semantics is typically measured by asking children to supply a word that best fits a pictorially represented object, grouping, or concept (e.g., *Gardner Expressive One-Word Picture Vocabulary Test–Revised;* Gardner, 2000). The Gardner test is constructed for children aged

2 to 19 years. Using a somewhat different format, the *Expressive Vocabulary Test* (Williams, 1997), constructed for use with individuals spanning from 2.5 to 85 years in age, requires children to supply an alternate word (synonym) for the word describing the picture provided by the examiner. Assessment of phonological processing often begins with a screening tool such as the *Rosner Test of Auditory Analysis Skills* (TAAS; Rosner, 1975), which can be used for children in kindergarten through Grade 8. This test measures awareness of phonological rules to segment words (e.g., cowboy into cow and boy). More comprehensive assessments of elements of phonological processing that can be used to guide intervention require multi-subtest batteries such as the *Phonological Awareness Test* (Robertson & Salter, 1997) for children aged 5 to 9 years and the *Test of Phonological Awareness* (Torgesen & Bryant, 1994), which has separate forms for children in kindergarten and for children in Grades 1 and 2.

The importance of assessing higher-order figurative language in older children and adolescents has been emphasized. The *Test of Language Competence–Expanded Edition* (Wiig & Secord, 1989) evaluates higher-order language that is involved in understanding ambiguous information, making inferences when only partial information is given, recreating sentences, and understanding and expressing figurative language in one's own words. It can be used for children aged 5 to 18 years and measures the capacity to understand ambiguous sentences, make inferences from pieces of conversation overheard, recreate sentences from a set of words, and express figures of speech in their own words.

Narrative and Narrative Discourse Skills

Narrating a story or participating in conversation requires mastery of language structure (vocabulary, grammar) and the ability to make event sequences coherent, to take the viewpoint of others in a story or of a conversational partner, and to take into account the listener's knowledge and perspective. Analysis of narrative and narrative discourse is important for understanding the interface between language and social-emotional disorder because it moves beyond examining language out of context, which is the task of standardized tests, to appreciation of the use of language embedded in a social milieu. In formal assessments, it is usually narrative rather than conversation (narrative discourse) that is examined. Although narrative discourse samples could be obtained for most children in a formal test situation, obtaining sufficient narrative discourse can be a challenge with some children. Children with ADHD, for instance, have been found to have difficulty producing language on demand, although, paradoxically, they are often talkative in other situations (Zentall, 1988). Narrative skills are not usually assessed in children under the age of 6 years. Preschoolers' narratives do not comprise connected sequences; rather, they include descriptions of characters involved in a series of actions or scripted interactions.

Measurement of receptive narrative skills is typically done by assessing children's capacity to remember passages of text read aloud to them and to either repeat the information or to answer questions about content. This is a common element of language test batteries such as CELF-3 and the memory tests discussed below.

There are a number of standardized measures of expressive discourse, such as the *Detroit Test of Learning Aptitudes–4* Story Construction subtest (Hammill, 1998). To measure expressive narrative, 6- to 17-year-old children are required to tell a story about a picture, and the response is scored according to criteria including whether the child gives the story a title, relates a definite sequence of events, mentions an object shown in the picture, attempts humor, expresses some philosophic or moral theme, explains the role of a character, has the character(s) speak, sets a time for the story, uses appropriate terminology, uses proper names, includes drama, and describes relationships. A similar approach is taken with the *Test of Adolescent and Adult Language–3* (Hammill, Brown, Larsen, & Wiederholt, 1994), on which adolescents aged 12 years and older are asked to retell a fictional story. This test can also be used to measure a range of skills related to listening, speaking, reading, and writing. *Evaluating Communicative Competence–Revised* (Simon, 1994) uses language samples to assess functional communication skills; it is especially useful for adolescents. Observations of performance are made on 21 tasks that simulate everyday communicative interactions based on language samples involving such tasks as understanding absurdities, paragraph and story inference comprehension, explanation of relationships, and situational analysis.

The above tests examine qualities of basic story structure, content, and sequencing of events but do not fully capture the difficulties that children with LI have in formulating and expressing thoughts coherently and unambiguously. In discussions of narrative discourse, Grice's (1975) four maxims of qualities underlying competent cooperative conversations are also often brought to bear in analyzing narrative and narrative discourse samples. These are (a) providing sufficient information (not too much or too little), (b) being truthful and not providing information that is either not true or for which there is inadequate evidence, (c) being relevant to the immediate topic or context, and (d) being brief and clear without obscuring meaning

TABLE 5.1   Categories of Discourse Analysis

Language Structure

- Productivity - Provides adequate information for the listener.
- Lexical Complexity - Uses specific words rather than vague words, uses modifier words (e.g., very, really) and evaluative words such as adverbs and adjectives
- Syntactic Complexity - Uses grammatically correct language in relation to total length of communication
- Linguistic Cohesion - Linguistic devices that tie together meaning across sentences
  - Referential Cohesion - Personal and passive pronouns or demonstratives (e.g., this, that) to refer back to people or objects in the preceding text
  - Conjunctive Cohesion to tie together contiguous clauses using relationships that are additive (e.g., and, further), adversative (e.g., yet, although), temporal (e.g., while, then), and causal (e.g., because, for this reason)

Information Structure

- Identifies a setting in terms of characters, action, goals, time and place, and salient features
- Gives information that is accurate
- Introduces event sequences, including cause-and-effect relationships
- Includes internal mental and emotional states
- Resolves the story

Flow of Information

- Efficiency (e.g., minimal repetitions, long pauses, unintelligible utterances) or self-initiated repairs

---

with ambiguity or digressions, repetitions, and so on. Researchers have applied a number of scoring schemes to evaluate narrative samples. Stimuli such as wordless picture books or videotapes with probes from the examiner, narration of a personal event, or response to projective tests can be scored to examine children's understanding of narrative along with their social-cognitive awareness. Although they are more often used for research than for clinical practice, it is worthwhile to become familiar with even broad qualities of disordered discourse. The categories used by Vallance et al. (1999) in their study of narrative discourse of an outpatient mental health clinic sample, which were drawn from a number of sources in the literature on language development (e.g., Halliday & Hasan, 1976; Liles, 1985a, 1985b), are listed in Table 5.1. These can be used as a guide to evaluate narrative discourse along the lines of productivity, language structure, information structure, and flow of information.

The following narrative comes from a 12-year-old girl with good language skills. Her narrative includes an example of repair, as she persists until she can correctly say the word "deteriorating." She conveys enough information to make a story that has a goal, and language structure and flow are good.

Case Example

"The astronauts' project was to fix the deteri . . . deteriate . . . deterior . . . ating satellites because . . . there was need of shots of the earth from space. The astronauts . . . left their shuttle and tried to fix it, but one of the astronaut's strings broke and she was disconnected from the shuttle. After the remaining astronauts saved her, they took a piece of metal and fixed the satellite so it was . . . able to be used for shots of earth again."

The next example comes from an 8-year-old girl with severe LI. She uses exaggerated inflection to help convey meaning, and this is often effective. She easily becomes lost in her narrative and cannot remember what she has already said. At one point, the examiner reminds the child of what she was saying. She uses fillers to buy time when she cannot think of what to say and, unlike the girl in the above narrative, never makes a repair. Productivity, language and information structure, and flow are all very poor.

Case Example

"One day . . . one night . . . Um . . . these space creatures came down from this airplane and shoot rocks at the earth, and earth is . . . is . . . [whispers is—is—is] is . . . they want the earth to craaack into pieces and where nobody can live in it and then'll they die! All the people, they want people to die except them and then they can go back to earth and, and, then, then, then, then, then. Ahm . . . [pause] ahmmm . . . [long silence]—and . . . [Examiner: Then they should go back to earth?] And they can be theirself and they can . . . they can drop dead . . . like the petals that are just shooting out of the sky and then as soon as they come out they shoot . . . Baam! . . . and they, they dead and they are poisonous. That's the end of the story."

The language sample obtained from projective tests can also be analyzed in terms of the quality of narrative discourse under conditions where stimuli are ambiguous, recognizing that linguistic and pragmatic difficulties influence the content of responses (Webster, Brown-Triolo, & Griffith, 1999). The following case example comes from a 6-year-old girl with an expressive language impairment being seen because of sleep difficulties associated with separation anxiety, difficulty focusing, and concerns regarding the past witnessing of abuse of her mother by her father. Her response to a picture from a projective test can be interpreted in terms of both content and narrative quality.

Case Example

"Mmm. Okay. This is about the kids want to go somewhere, but the . . . parents are talkin' about something, they do. The mom said, 'I have nothing to do, what I do?' And the dad says 'You're not going anywhere. Okay, stay home. And no food children.' Then, they raun *[sic]* . . . they rewn *[sic]* how much money they got to go . . . somewhere. 'I have . . . one,' said the girl, 'I got one,' said the boy. Which we have? 'Two together,' says . . . one [pause]. And the mom an dad don't have any money. Many of them didn't get to the somewhere to play good [slurred, almost unintelligible]. [Then whispers:] That's it."

Pragmatics

From the preschool years onward, pragmatic skills rely on four underlying components: structural language skills, knowledge of social rules, social cognition, and executive function skills (Bishop, 1997; Westby, 1999). These are important because children need to plan and organize their social interactions and, within interactions, monitor social interchanges online, which requires working memory skills.

For infants, the CSBS described earlier is an important measure of children's capacity to communicate socially. For many years, the *Prutting and Kirchner Pragmatics Checklist* (Prutting & Kirchner, 1987) has been widely used to assess children's pragmatic skills during and following a period of direct observation in natural settings with family and peers in open-ended conversation. Cohen, Barwick, et al. (1998) also have found that children with and without LI can be distinguished when this checklist is applied in structured test situations, although not all behaviors can be observed. Broad pragmatic parameters are scored as appropriate or inappropriate for children from age 5 years onward, including (a) verbal aspects (e.g., topic selection and maintenance, turn taking, specificity on choice of words), (b) paralinguistic (e.g., intelligibility, fluency), and (c) nonverbal aspects (e.g., body posture, facial expression, eye gaze).

Recently, a new measure, the *Children's Communication Checklist,* has been described (Bishop, 1998; Bishop et al., 2000). This checklist is to be completed by an adult familiar with the child. Items from the checklist are rated on a 3-point scale and have been divided into nine areas of pragmatic knowledge: (a) speech output/intelligibility and fluency, (b) syntax, (c) inappropriate initiation, (d) coherence, (e) stereotyped conversation, (f) use of conversational context, (g) conversational rapport, (h) social relationships, and (i) interests. The checklist is not intended to identify children with LI in the general population but to be used as an adjunct to assessment of children who have already been identified. Although still being developed, it holds promise as a useful tool in assessment of pragmatic communication.

Criteria for Diagnosis of Language Impairment

Diagnosis of LI continues to be a controversial topic (Bishop, 1996). The term LI is used to refer to children with otherwise normal development who experience problems with language acquisition. Research has shown, however, that there is not a fundamental difference between children with LI who exhibit a significant discrepancy between cognitive ability, as measured by intelligence tests and language functioning, and those who do not (Bishop, 1996; Shaywitz, 1996). Moreover, relying on a discrepancy definition creates difficulties in diagnosing children at both ends of the IQ spectrum. Children with superior intelligence may be overidentified as LI, whereas children at the lower end of the spectrum are underidentified. Similarly, in the past there were restrictions in the definition of LI to exclude children with neurological impairment, sensory or physical impairment, deafness, environmental privation, or psychiatric disorder, but this too is being questioned (Bishop, 1997). At least for the time being, any children whose language skills are below the norm for their age should be considered for treatment of LI.

There are also differences in the literature in the exact criteria for diagnosis of LI, that is, the statistical cutoff in deviations from the age-normative mean (standard deviation or SD) on standardized tests (Bishop, 1997). Currently, there is no universal agreement of the numerical cutoff for disorder. For instance, Bishop and Edmundson (1987a, 1987b) used a criterion of 1.5 SD on two or more measures or 2 SD or more below the mean on a single measure. Cohen and colleagues used as a criterion a child having a score of 1 SD below the mean on two measures or 2 SD below the mean on one measure to allow for the possibility that a child may have a severe but specific deficit (Cohen et al., 1993; Cohen, Barwick, et al., 1998). The exception in these studies is that children were not diagnosed solely on the basis of a low score on measures of auditory verbal memory because there is overlap between poor performance on such measures with ADHD (Gascon, Johnson, & Burd, 1986). A less stringent criterion of 1 SD on one test has also been applied and shown to differentiate children in learning and social-emotional characteristics (e.g., Beitchman, Nair, Clegg, & Patel, 1986).

To complicate matters, although the literature has emphasized the importance of a broader definition of communication impairment, diagnosis is often made solely on the basis of structural language skills. Furthermore, there is not a single set of measures to make a diagnosis. This may account for inconsistency in findings in the literature (Bishop, 1997). An understanding of the underlying nature of LI will ultimately permit devising better measures and diagnostic criteria to delineate groups and subgroups of children with LI. For the time being, it is important to be aware of the implications of using different criteria and different tests for diagnosis.

Comparing formal diagnostic schemes, Bishop (1997) noted that classification based solely on a statistical definition of specific LI is inadequate (e.g., *ICD-10;* World Health Organization, 1993) and that some criteria to judge impairment must be included (*DSM-IV;* APA, 1994). The American Speech-Language-Hearing Association (ASHA) Committee on Language, Speech and Hearing (1982) definition is broader, referring to any deviation or impairment of comprehension or use of spoken, written, or other symbol system, which can involve form, content, and function in any combination. Although one person's notion of what is impairment may be different from another's, this criterion is important because relatively mild LI have been shown to be associated with functional impairments as reflected in social-emotional and reading problems (Cohen, Barwick, et al., 1998). The same holds true for psychiatric disorders; children may be impaired even though they do not quite meet criteria for a psychiatric diagnosis (Angold et al., 1999).

Assessment of Cognitive Ability

General Cognitive Ability

For infants and toddlers, the most commonly used measure of infant cognitive development is the *Bayley Scales of Infant Development–2* (Bayley, 1993). Used with children aged 1 to 42 months, the Bayley scales also include a systematic means of rating the child's behavior during testing by the examiner on three scales: (a) Orientation-Engagement (i.e., the infant's approach or avoidance to task-related social interaction), (b) Emotion Regulation (i.e., infant activity, adaptation, affect, cooperation, persistence, and frustration tolerance), and (c) Motor Quality (i.e., fine and gross motor control, and quality of movement) (Bayley, 1993). Selected items from the Bayley scales correlate with the *Reynell Developmental Language Scale* (Reynell, 1985) and can be used to estimate verbal abilities (Siegel, Cooper, Fitzhardinge, & Ash, 1995).

The Wechsler intelligence scales are the most commonly used measures of overall cognitive ability for children from preschool through adolescence. The *Wechsler Preschool and Primary Scale of Intelligence–R* is used for children aged 3 to 7.25 years (WPPSI-R; Wechsler, 1989), *Wechsler Intelligence Scale for Children–III* (WISC-III) for children aged 6 to 17 (Wechsler, 1991), and the *Wechsler Adult Intelligence Scale–III* (WAIS-III) for adolescents aged 16 years and older (Wechsler, 1997). Each consists of subtests that tap verbal and nonverbal (performance) skills. Although some subtests are intended to be nonverbal, verbal skills are still demanded. For instance, the Picture Arrangement subtest requires children to arrange pictures in correct order to tell a story, which obviously relies on more than visual perceptual skills. Moreover, all tests are verbally administered and rely on the instructions being understood by the child.

Traditionally, psychological assessment has begun with administration of one of the Wechsler scales, with the pattern of discrepancy or scatter on verbal and nonverbal subtests used to determine whether a more thorough language assessment should be done. In fact, this is not a good guide. Although some children with LI exhibit a large verbal-nonverbal IQ discrepancy, on average this is not the case (Cohen et al., 1993). Verbal subtests of intelligence tests do not measure the kinds of language functions measured by specialized language tests. For instance, on the Wechsler scales, a child can earn full points on the Vocabulary subscale with a one-word answer or a lengthier answer with many agrammaticisms and mispronunciations. Moreover, scores from verbal subscales of an intelligence test generally measure acquired knowledge rather than language functions. A child can have a low verbal IQ score and not have LI and can also have normal verbal intelligence and still have LI. Therefore the Wechsler scales alone cannot be used to diagnose LI.

Another commonly used measure of cognitive ability is the *Stanford-Binet Intelligence Scale* (Thorndike, Hagen, & Sattler, 1986), which is appropriate for a wide age range of 2 years through adulthood. It also comprises a number of subscales, although unlike the Wechsler scales the specific subscales differ at different age levels. This obviously limits the use of this measure to monitor children's development. Finally, the *Kaufman Assessment Battery for Children* (Kaufman & Kaufman, 1993), designed on the basis of a theory that information is processed either simultaneously or sequentially, is used with children aged 5 to 23 years. Because the processes are tapped by different tasks (i.e., simultaneous by visual tasks and sequential by verbal and memory tasks), the theoretical underpinnings are somewhat misleading. With this kept in mind, this test can be useful in assessing the kinds of processing difficulties that children with LI encounter.

Memory

Strains on memory become increasingly apparent as children progress through school. Short-term memory and working memory are critical to a range of capacities in learning, achievement, and social relationships that require that new information be stored, recalled, and manipulated. For children to learn, they must be able to hold information in short-term memory for a long enough period to consolidate it in long-term or permanent memory. Therefore assessment of memory is often a component of language tests (e.g., CELF-3, DTLA-3), cognitive assessments (e.g., Wechsler scales), and neuropsychological test batteries (e.g., NEPSY; Korkman, Kirk, & Kemp, 1997). There are also specialized instruments that measure various aspects of memory.

The *Wide Range Assessment of Memory and Learning* (WRAML; Sheslow & Adams, 1990), for children aged 5 to 17 years, yields a memory index for three aspects of short-term memory: visual and verbal memory and new learning (repeated trials). The *Children's Memory Scale* (Cohen, 1997), for children aged 5 to 16 years, measures similar skills as the WRAML but includes a test of working memory. A virtue of the latter scale is that it was developed in concert with the WISC-III and thus memory abilities can be examined in relation to both general cognitive ability and achievement on the *Wechsler Individual Achievement Test* (Wechsler, 1992).

Executive Functions

Although executive functions contribute to performance on all tasks, they are not specifically measured by most standardized intelligence tests. Working memory is increasingly used as an index of executive functions (Eslinger, 1996). The Backward Digit Span subtest of the WISC-III, in relation to Forward Digit Span, is often used as an index of working memory. The most recent editions of the WAIS-III and the Children's Memory Scale each measure working memory. Frequently, an assessment of executive functions is made on the basis of observation and interview concerning attention and work habits (Levine, 1994). As well, performance tasks that require the ability to shift from one task or concept to another; to plan and organize discourse or written products; and to manage simultaneously sources of information, such as is required on working memory tasks are examined. Dynamic assessment has a role in assessing executive functions. Problem-solving strategies such as self-talk and reflective pausing are taught, and then the child's performance is reassessed when these techniques are used. Neuropsychological test batteries such as the NEPSY also always include measures of executive functions (Korkman et al., 1997). The NEPSY has a form for children aged 3 to 4 years and another for children aged 5 to 12 years.

Visual-Motor Integration

Many children diagnosed as LI also have been found to have difficulties in nonverbal areas of functioning such as visual-motor integration. Copying tests such as the *Developmental Test of Visual-Motor Integration* (Beery & Buktenica, 1997) follow a developmental sequence of geometric forms and can be used for screening. A comprehensive assessment of children can be done with the *Wide Range Assessment of Visual Motor Abilities* (Adams & Sheslow, 1995), which assesses copying (visual-motor), perceptual matching (visual-spatial), and pegboard performance (fine-motor) abilities.

Assessment of Achievement

Assessments of school-aged children include measures of achievement in reading decoding, reading comprehension, spelling, and mathematical reasoning and computation. The *Wechsler Individual Achievement Test* (WIAT; Wechsler, 1992), used to assess children aged 5 to 16 years, includes subtests to measure reading decoding and comprehension, listening comprehension, spelling, oral expression, mathematics reasoning and computation and, for children 8 years of age and older, a writing sample. The WIAT and WISC-III were developed and normed together, which facilitates comparisons between a child's intellectual and academic functioning. A more comprehensive measure is the *Woodcock-Johnson Psychoeducational Battery–Revised* (Woodcock, Johnson, Mather, McGrew, & Werder,

1991). This measure, suited for a wide age range from 2 to 95 years, includes eight tests of achievement along with subtests that measure long- and short-term memory, auditory and visual processing, processing speed, comprehension, and reasoning. Moreover, on the test of achievement, underlying processes such as word attack skills and vocabulary are measured along with level of achievement. Although the test is lengthy to administer, evaluation of underlying component skills means that this measure can provide useful information for developing remedial plans.

Children who exhibit reading difficulties often require more specialized assessment. The *Gray Oral Reading Test* (Wiederholt & Bryant, 1992), used when a measure of oral reading is required, can be administered to children aged 7 to 19 years. The *Stanford Diagnostic Reading Test* (Karlsen & Gardner, 1995), constructed for children in four age groups ranging from 7 to 19 years, is especially useful for measuring silent reading and reading speed.

Assessment of Social Cognition

Although there is evidence that it is important to measure social-cognitive skills, these are not routinely included in clinical assessments, because instruments to measure social cognition are less well developed than measures of language and cognition.

Emotion Recognition and Understanding

Developmental milestones for emotion recognition and understanding are provided in Table 5.2. The *Diagnostic Analysis of Nonverbal Accuracy Scale* (DANVA; Nowicki & Duke, 1994), designed to measure individual differences in accuracy of expressive and receptive nonverbal social information, was originally developed on children in Grades 1 through 5. Children are asked to identify emotions associated with facial expressions and to create the appropriate emotion to fit a situational description. They also are asked to listen to audiotaped sentences and indicate how the person is feeling (happy, sad, angry, or fearful). Both child and adult pictures and voices are used. A benefit of this measure is that it requires minimal verbal expression. The *Denham Affective Perspective Taking Task* (Denham, 1986) can be used with infants aged 2 and 3 years. It presents two unambiguous and two ambiguous stories for each of four basic emotions (happy, sad, angry, and scared) and can be used with puppets.

TABLE 5.2 Development of Theory of Mind and Understanding Emotions

Age	Theory of Mind	Understanding Emotions		
		Recognizing Emotions	Using and Manipulating Emotions	
8–17 months	Follow line of regard Joint attention on objects	Exhibit emotions of happy, mad, sad, surprised, disgusted, afraid Respond to emotional reactions of others Use emotional expression of caregivers as social reference for approach-avoidance	Seek to change affect of another by direct contact	
18 months–2 years	Engage in pretend Understand physical relation between a person's line of sight and behavior Understand goal-directed action Understand mental words by conceptualizing internal states as being directed at objects (understands desires)	Understand link between desires, outcomes, and emotions Predict that receipt of broken toy will make child unhappy	Use words happy, sad, mad, and scared Change doll's affect by bringing suitable object	
3 years	Understand that other people see the world differently from themselves Understand that imaginary objects are different from real objects Understand that people's actions can be determined by their desires, intentions, and thoughts Understand that perceptual activity (seeing, being told) is in some way connected to knowing	Match emotion words happy, sad, mad, and afraid to faces Know that comforting is right and hurting is wrong Recognize there can be a variety of reasons for an emotional response Ask for reasons for emotional reactions Predict that receipt of toy that is not what was desired will result in negative affect	Talk about causes and consequences of emotions (e.g., "Santa will be happy if I pee in the potty") Use object and "friend" to change affect	

Age			
4-5 years	Words such as remember, now, and think appear in spontaneous speech Conceptualize internal states as representing states in the world (understand desires and beliefs) Recognize that different perceptual viewpoints can lead persons to different interpretations Understand how access to information by seeing or hearing is causally related to knowledge and how knowledge and belief can be causally related to actions in the world (beliefs cause people to act in certain ways)	Know the situation that will provoke primary emotions (match emotion word to picture)	Object and friends used to comfort baby, to make father happy Can describe a personal situation in which they are happy, sad, mad, scared, or surprised
6-8 years	Make appropriate judgments of situations in which one knows, remembers, forgets, or guesses	Can offer appropriate situations for emotions such as jealousy, worry, pride, shame, and guilt Understand concept or personal responsibility and role of social standards understand that one can have first one emotion and then a second emotion in response to a situation	Use words "proud," "jealous," "worried" Can intentionally use facial expressions to mislead
8-10 years	Understand strategies to hide deceit and to detect deceit	Understand that one can have two concurrent emotions of opposite type in response to a situation	Use of words "relieved" and "disappointed" emerges at preadolescence

SOURCE: Westby (1999, pp. 198-199). From *Communication Disorders and Children With Psychiatric and Behavioral Disorders, 1st edition*, by D. Rogers-Adkinson and P. Griffith (Eds.). © 1999. Reprinted with permission of Delmar, a division of Thomson Learning. Fax 800-730-2215.

Social Problem Solving

The *Test of Problem Solving–Revised Elementary* (Bowers, Huisingh, Barrett, Orman, & LoGiudice, 1994) and *Adolescent* versions (Bowers, Huisingh, Barrett, Orman, & LoGiudice, 1991) were designed to measure students' language-based critical-thinking skills but provide some information relevant to both pragmatics and social problem solving. The Elementary version of the scale is intended for children aged 6 to 12 years, and the Adolescent version for children aged 12 to 18 years. Questions cover a broad range of critical-thinking skills, including clarifying, analyzing, generating solutions, evaluating, and affective thinking. The child responds verbally to questions that deal with photo stimuli presented simultaneously with the examiner's questions. For example, "The boy is unconscious and no one knows him. Why do the paramedics want to know his name?" Although this measure has age norms, it does not provide a sense of the social problem solving process.

The *Interpersonal Negotiating Strategies Interview* (INS; Yeates & Selman, 1989; Yeates et al., 1990) can be used with children from the preschool years through adolescence to measure strategies that children use to meet interpersonal needs in a variety of contexts. A rating scale also is available to measure these strategies in action. Strategies are scored from the child's responses to hypothetical conflictual interactions with another person with regard to achieving a goal, such as the following:

> Randy and Tom are friends. They have just been assigned to work together on a project in school and only have two days to finish the project. They meet after school and Randy says he wants to start working on the project right away, but Tom wants to play softball first. (Schultz, Yeates, & Selman, 1989, p. 18)

The scoring describes how children coordinate their understanding of others' thoughts, feelings, and motives in conjunction with their own in attempting to balance inner and interpersonal conflicts. *Structurally,* development of interpersonal negotiating skills is seen as moving through four developmental levels from an egocentric stage to a level in which there is a capacity to view oneself in the broader social context involving multiple differentiable perspectives (Selman, 1980; Schultz et al., 1989; Table 5.3). Strategies can be characterized as impulsive at the least mature level and collaborative at the most mature. Strategies are further classified as self-transforming and other-transforming to reflect individual differences in the priority given to one's own goals or those of the other and the capacity to strive for balance. The *functional* aspect of the model involves four sequential problem-solving steps: (a) defining the problem, which reflects accuracy in understanding the problem and an appreciation that the individuals in the problem-solving situation have different perspectives; (b) generating alternative strategies, which reflects the capacity to think of alternate social problem solving strategies; (c) selecting and implementing a specific strategy, which requires the capacity to anticipate consequences as well as to repair or revise strategies that do not work; and (d) evaluating outcomes. Because the process of social problem solving also includes understanding that interactions depend on several contextual factors, including the age and relative familiarity of the interactive partner, stories vary along the dimensions of child versus adult and familiar versus unfamiliar character. A detailed scoring manual is available (Schultz et al., 1989). A questionnaire also has been used with teachers to assess social problem solving in action (Schultz & Selman, 1989). There is evidence of both the reliability and the validity of the INS scoring procedure (Schultz & Selman, 1989), and scores have been shown to be consistent with social perspective taking when applied to how young adolescents dealt with stressful dilemmas in their own lives (Menna & Keating, 1993, cited in Menna & Cohen, 1997; Schultz & Selman, 1989).

Theory of Mind

Theory of mind has been examined primarily in developmental research with preschoolers. These experimental tasks all include an element of deception, for instance, around an unexpected location or identity (Cutting & Dunn, 1999). Recently, tasks have been devised for older children (e.g., Dennis, Barnes, Wilkinson, & Humphreys, 1998) that involve concealment of true feelings (deception). Because of the paucity of measures, Table 5.2 summarizes development of theory of mind that can guide observation.

Self-Cognition

Questionnaires such as the *Piers-Harris Children's Self-Concept Scale–Revised* (Piers & Harris, 1984) or the *Offer Self-Image Questionnaire–Revised* (Offer, Ostrov, Howard, & Dolan, 1992) can be completed by children on their own. Obvious caution must be raised in their use with children and adolescents with LI who may have difficulty understanding specific questions or inflate ratings of their self-esteem.

TABLE 5.3   Social Perspective Coordination and Interpersonal Negotiation

---

Developmental Levels of Social Perspective Coordination

Level 0: *Egocentric and Undifferentiated (before 6 years of age).* At Level 0, physical and psychological characteristics of persons are not clearly differentiated. This confusion between objective/physical and subjective/psychological features is seen in the failure to distinguish between acts and feelings and unintentional and intentional behavior. Subjective perspectives are not differentiated, so that the possibility that another person may interpret the same behavior differently is not recognized.

Level 1: *Subjective and Unilateral (by 6 years of age).* The key conceptual advance from Level 0 to Level 1 is the clear differentiation of physical and psychological characteristics of persons. Each person is acknowledged to have a unique, subjective, and covert psychological life. Subjective states of others, however, are thought to be directly observable. The relating of perspectives, moreover, is accomplished in one-way, unilateral fashion, in terms of the perspective of and impact on one actor.

Level 2: *Self-Reflective and Reciprocal (by 11 years of age).* The major conceptual progression as compared to Level 1 is the ability to step outside oneself mentally and take a second-person perspective on one's thoughts and actions, along with the realization that others can do so as well. People are understood to be capable of acting in opposition to their thoughts and feelings. Differences between perspectives are seen relativistically. A reciprocity occurs wherein the perspectives of self and other are both appreciated, although not in relationship to one another.

Level 3: *Third-Person and Mutual (by 15 years of age).* Level 3 reflects an advance over Level 2 in that children are able to step outside not only their own immediate perspective but indeed outside the self as a system. They can begin to take a truly third-person perspective. The self is seen as both actor and object, as are others. The perspective on relationships simultaneously includes and coordinates the perspectives of self and other(s), and the system is seen from a generalized perspective. Reciprocal perspectives are not only acknowledged but seen to be in need of mutual coordination.

(Continued)

Assessment of Play

There are a variety of formats for play assessments, and each serves a particular purpose. Children can be assessed alone in free play or when being directed, while playing with a parent or other caregiver, and during play with a peer. Moreover, play can be observed in naturalistic settings of classroom, day care, or home and in the clinic. Play assessments are most typically done with infants and preschoolers, although they are useful to include in assessments of older children.

TABLE 5.3   (Continued)

Four Levels of Interpersonal Negotiation Strategies

Level 0: Impulsive. Strategies at the first level involve primarily impulsive and physical behavior to get what one wants or to avoid harm. They are based on egocentric and undifferentiated perspective-taking skills, which do not differentiate subjective perspectives or distinguish between actions and feelings. Other-transforming strategies at this level use unreflective force to achieve a goal (e.g., hitting or grabbing); self-transforming strategies rely on unreflective obedience or withdrawal to protect oneself (e.g., fleeing or hiding).

Level 1: Unilateral. Strategies at the next level consist primarily of unilateral attempts to either control or appease the other person. They depend on subjective perspective-taking skills, which differentiate subjective perspectives but do not allow them to be considered simultaneously. Thus other-transforming strategies at this level involve willful one-way orders to assert power, control the other person, and satisfy oneself (e.g., ordering or telling); self-transforming strategies involve unwilling submission to the power, control, and wishes of the other person (e.g., obeying or giving in).

Level 2: Reciprocal. Strategies at this level involve attempts to satisfy the needs of both participants in reciprocal fashion through trades, exchanges, and deals. They rely on self-reflective perspective taking, which not only differentiates between subjective perspectives but also allows those perspectives to be considered simultaneously. Other-transforming reciprocal strategies consciously use psychological influence to change the other person's mind (e.g., giving reasons or going first when taking turns); self-transforming strategies use psychological compliance to protect one's own interests by making them secondary to the other person's (e.g., bartering or going second).

Level 3: Collaborative. Strategies at the highest level involve attempts to collaboratively change both one's own and the other person's wishes in order to develop mutual goals. These strategies rest on third-person perspective-taking skills, which permit the ability to coordinate the self's and the other's perspectives in terms of the relationship between them or from a third-person viewpoint. At this level, strategies are neither self- nor other-transforming but instead mutualistic, using self-reflection and shared reflection to facilitate the process of dialogue that leads to compromise and the construction of mutually satisfactory resolutions. They demonstrate concerns for a relationship's continuity and the understanding that solutions to immediate problems have a bearing in that regard.

SOURCE: Adapted from Schultz, Yeates, and Selman (1989, pp. 7-8). Reprinted with permission.

Most measures of play simply chart the developmental sequence of play. The *Belsky and Most Play Scale* (Belsky & Most, 1981) and the *Symbolic Play Scale* (Patterson & Westby, 1994) chart the sequence of exploratory and pretend play in infants aged 5 to 24 months. McCune-Nicolich (1977) also has developed a brief scale that describes pretence and language and provides a framework for evaluating an individual child in both language and play. A summary of the development of symbolic play is provided in Table 5.4.

TABLE 5.4 Summary of Symbolic Play Development

Age	Props	Themes	Organization	Roles	Language Use in Play
By 18 months	Uses one realistic object at a time	Familiar everyday activities in which child is active participant (e.g., eating, sleeping)	Short, isolated pretend actions	Autosymbolic pretend (e.g., child feeds self pretend food)	Language used to get and maintain toys and seek assistance operating toys (e.g., "baby," "mine," "help")
By 22 months	Uses two realistic objects at a time	Familiar everyday activities that caregivers do (e.g., cooking, reading)	Combines two related toys or performs actions on two people (e.g., uses spoon to eat from plate; feeds mother, then doll)	Child acts on dolls and others (e.g., feeds doll or caregivers)	Uses word combinations to comment on toy or action; uses word for intents, needs, feelings, ("want that," "mad," "hungry")
By 24 months	Uses several realistic objects		Multischeme combinations of steps (e.g., put doll in tub, apply soap, take doll out and dry)		Talks to doll briefly; describes some of the doll's actions (e.g., "baby sleeping"); uses phrases and markers for -*ing* and plurals/possessives
By 30 months		Common but less frequently experienced or especially traumatic experiences (e.g., shopping, doctor)		Emerging limited doll actions (e.g., doll cries)	Talking to doll and commenting on doll's actions increase in frequency

Age	Symbolic/Theme	Props	Sequences	Roles	Language
By 3 years	Observed but not personally experienced activities (e.g., police, firefighter); compensatory play—reenacts experienced events but modifies original outcomes		Temporal sequences of multischeme events (e.g., prepare food, set table, eat food, clear table, wash dishes)	Child talks to doll in response to doll's actions (e.g., "Don't cry now," "I'll get you a cookie"); brief complementary role play with peers (e.g., mother and child; doctor and patient)	Uses complete sentences with past tense and future aspect: children may comment on what they have just completed or what they will do next (e.g., "Dolly ate the cake." "I'm gonna wash dishes.")
By 3.5 years		Miniature props, small figures, and object substitutions		Attributes emotions and desires to dolls; reciprocal role taking with dolls (child treats doll as partner—talks for doll and as caregiver)	Uses dialogue for dolls and metalinguistic markers (e.g., "he said"); uses words to refer to emotions and thoughts
By 4 years	Familiar fantasy themes (e.g., Batman, Wonder Woman, Cinderella); violent themes common	Imaginary props (language and gesture help set the scene)	Planned play events with cause-effect sequences (e.g., child decides to play a birthday party and gathers necessary props and assigns roles)	Child or doll has multiple roles (mother, wife, doctor; firefighter, husband, father); child can handle two or more dolls in complementary roles (dolls are doctor and patient); attributes thoughts and plans to doll	Uses language to plan and narrate the story line; uses connecting words "so," "because," "but"
By 6 years	Creates novel fantasy characters and plots	Language and gesture can carry the play without props	Multiple planned sequences (plans for self and other players)	More than one role per doll (doll is mother, wife, doctor)	Elaboration of planning and narrative story line; uses sentences with temporal markers, "then," "when," "while," "before," "first," "next"

SOURCE: Patterson and Westby (1994, pp. 135-161). From *Communication Development: Foundations, Processes, and Clinical Application*, by E. Haynes & B. Shulman (Eds.). © 1994. Reprinted with permission of Allyn and Bacon.

The *Home Observation for the Measurement of the Environment Scale* (HOME; Bradley & Caldwell, 1984) comprises both interview and observational formats completed during a home visit. The HOME Scale assesses not only the child's play but the quality of the learning environment (e.g., toys, books) and responsivity of a parent. This instrument has been adapted for use with infants, preschoolers, and elementary school age children. An even more comprehensive measure of play is the *Transdisciplinary Play-Based Assessment* (Linder, 1993). This assessment tool provides the context for observations of play to be made by a multidisciplinary team regarding social-emotional, cognitive, language, communication, and sensorimotor skills. Information is first obtained from caregivers regarding a child's development. Subsequently, a play session is observed with the child alone and then with parents, a peer, and a play facilitator.

Assessment of Caregiver-Infant Interaction

It is important to observe how parents interact with their young children to foster or detract from both communicative and social-emotional functioning. Most commonly, the precursors of attachment security, as reflected by indices of sensitive, responsive, and nonintrusive caregiver interactions, are measured. The CSBS, described earlier, also provides a context in which to observe play in children from birth to age 2 years. As well, some clinicians may have the option of videotaping interactions under structured and unstructured situations. Reviewing these tapes collaboratively with parents helps them identify how the child may be communicating albeit in an inappropriate fashion and also to consider strengths the child has displayed.

There are a number of scales that can be used as a guide in assessing caregivers with their infants. The *Nursing Child Assessment Satellite Training Teaching Scale* (NCAST; Barnard, Eyres, Lobo, & Snyder, 1983) can be used to observe parent responsivity and sensitivity to the infant and the infant's ability to signal needs in a structured play setting. The *Mother/Infant/Toddler Play and Feeding Scales* (Chatoor, 1986; Chatoor, Menville, Getson, & O'Donnell, 1988) assess interactive play in a free play or feeding setting and includes scales to code dyadic reciprocity, mother-infant conflict, maternal intrusiveness, and maternal unresponsiveness. Although most observational tools tapping behaviors associated with attachment security have been developed for infants, attempts have been made to adapt these for relationships in middle childhood (Kerns, Tomich, Aspelmeier, & Contreras, 2000). Because these scales require training to code, a table

TABLE 5.5   Socioemotional Dimension in Communication Assessment for Young Children

I. SOCIAL RELATEDNESS

A. *Social and communicative motivation*
   1. Does child typically prefer to be in proximity of others, or alone?
   2. Does child bring attention to self for social engagement?
   3. Does child respond to and initiate social games and routines?
   4. Does child visually orient to others (face-to-face gaze)?
   5. Does child regularly use gaze shifts to reference the attention of others?
   6. What is the frequency of communicative acts directed to adults and other children?

B. *Joint attention*
   1. Does child follow adults' visual line of regard or observe adults' or other children's activities?
   2. Does child communicate to establish joint attention verbally or preverbally by commenting, requesting information, or providing information?
   3. Is child able to respond to the preverbal or verbal signals of others to establish shared attention?
   4. Is child able to maintain and follow up on topics introduced by others (for older preschoolers)?

C. *Social imitation*
   1. Does child imitate actions, vocalization, and/or verbalizations with some evidence of social orientation (e.g., gaze checks, sharing of affect, verbal communication)?

II. EMOTIONAL EXPRESSION AND RELATEDNESS

A. *Attachment*
   1. Does child use caregivers as a base for security and emotional "refueling"?
   2. After a reasonable period of time, does older preschool child see other adults (e.g., preschool teacher, grandparents) as a base of security?

B. *Emotional expression*
   1. Does child express different emotions through facial expression, vocalization, and/or verbalization that are appropriate to the situational and interpersonal context?
   2. Does child share emotional states by directing affect display to others?
   3. Does the child understand and respond appropriately to the emotional expressions of others?

C. *Empathy*
   1. Does older preschool child demonstrate concern for or actively attempt to soothe another child who has been hurt or is otherwise in distress?

(Continued)

summarizing social-emotional relational dimensions that can be observed in assessment of young children and their parents is provided (Prizant, 1999; Table 5.5).

TABLE 5.5   (Continued)

III. SOCIABILITY IN COMMUNICATION

Does child communicate for the functions of:
1. Behavioral regulation (i.e., requesting objects/actions, protesting)?
2. Social interaction (i.e., greeting, calling, requesting social routine, requesting comfort)?
3. Joint attention (i.e., commenting, requesting and providing information)?
4. Does child communicate for all three general functions or primarily for behavioral regulation, which may be indicative of a limited sociability in communication?

IV. EMOTION REGULATION AND COMMUNICATIVE COMPETENCE
1. Does communicative competence vary significantly with different communicative partners?
2. Does communicative competence vary significantly in comfortable, familiar contexts as opposed to unfamiliar, emotionally arousing contexts?
3. How does degree of emotional arousal (positive or negative) influence communicative competence (e.g., child withdraws, speech becomes disorganized, child uses developmentally less sophisticated means)?
4. Does child demonstrate self-regulatory strategies to modulate arousal?
5. Does child demonstrate mutual regulatory strategies?
6. What are the most effective means others can use to help the child to modulate extreme states of arousal?

V. EXPRESSION OF EMOTION IN LANGUAGE AND PLAY
1. Does child use vocabulary to talk about emotional states (self or other)?
2. Do emotional themes emerge consistently in play, and are they an attempt to understand stressful life events?

VI. CLINICIAN'S SUBJECTIVE REACTIONS
1. Was the child fun to be with?
2. Did the clinician have to do most of the work to keep the interaction going?
3. Did the clinician find the child's communicative signals and affective displays easy to read?
4. Is it possible to develop a positive relationship with the child in a reasonable period of time?

SOURCE: Prizant (1999, pp. 313-314). From *Communication Disorders and Children With Psychiatric and Behavioral Disorders, 1st edition,* by D. Rogers-Adkinson and P. Griffith (Eds.). © 1999. Reprinted with permission of Delmar, a division of Thomson Learning. Fax 800-730-2215.

Assessment of Social-Emotional Functioning

Standardized Behavioral Checklists

For descriptive and diagnostic purposes, standardized behavioral checklists normed for children of different ages can be completed by parents, teachers, and, in some cases, children themselves. The most commonly used of these are the Achenbach scales, including the *Child Behavior Checklist* for children aged 4 to 16 (Achenbach, 1991a), the *Teacher Report Form* for the same age range (Achenbach & Edelbrock, 1986), and the *Youth Self Report* for youths aged 11 years and older (Achenbach, 1991b). A form is also available for parents to complete on their 2- to 3-year-old infants (*Child Behavior Checklist 2-3;* Achenbach, 1992). Items reflect both broad internalizing and externalizing dimensions of behavior as well as symptom subscales, including Withdrawal, Somatic Complaints, Anxious/ Depressed, Social Problems, Thought Problems, Attention Problems, De- linquent Behavior, and Aggressive Behavior. Questions concerning activi- ties, social relationships, and school performance make up the Social Competence Scale. Having different informants complete the scales and comparing the symptom profiles is often a useful tool in the process of pro- viding feedback about children to their families.

More specialized instruments also are often administered, such as the *Conners Rating Scales–Revised* (Conners, 1997), particularly for symp- toms associated with ADHD. Scales also may be administered directly to children to examine anxiety and depression such as the *Children's Manifest Anxiety Scale* (Reynolds & Richmond, 1985) and the *Children's Depres- sion Inventory* (Kovacs, 1992). These latter scales are self-administered and care needs to be taken to ensure that the child understands the questions.

Structured Psychiatric Interviews

A number of psychiatric diagnostic schemes provide categorical diagno- ses, including the *Diagnostic Interview Schedule for Children,* the *Schedule for Affective Disorders and Schizophrenia for School-Age Children,* and the *Diagnostic Interview for Children and Adolescents* (see special section ed- ited by McClellan & Werry, 2000). There are also some interviews that pro- vide both categorical and dimensional information. The *Child Assessment Schedule* (CAS; Hodges, 1991) has the advantage of being a standardized interview that generates psychiatric diagnoses based on the *Diagnostic and Statistical Manual of Mental Disorders* (APA, 1994) and at the same time yields continuous symptom scores for scales containing diagnostically re- lated items and information on child functioning. This interview is themati- cally organized around topical areas, including school, friends, activities, hobbies, family, fears, worries and anxieties, self-image, mood, physical complaints, expression of anger, and reality testing. Both parent and child versions of this interview are available, although interviews with children under 10 years of age have questionable reliability. Dimensional and categorical scaling have also been combined in the *Diagnostic and Statistical Manual for Primary Care–Child and Adolescent Version* (DSM-PC; Wolraich, Felice, & Drotar, 1997).

INTEGRATING AND SUMMARIZING ASSESSMENT RESULTS

The value of assessing how language and communication problems and social-emotional disorders interact with concomitant domains of development and with environmental factors in the home, school, and community has been promoted in this book. Although integrative developmental assessment has begun to be designed for infants (Meisels & Fenichel, 1996), for school-aged children and adolescents translating a transactional view of developmental psychopathology to assessment and treatment is relatively new; work still needs to be done to determine the best way to serve the needs of children with multiple co-occurring problems (e.g., Hoagwood et al., 1996; Prizant, 1999; Rock et al., 1997). Some brief examples of such integration were illustrated in case examples presented in earlier chapters. Integration of assessment information can best be provided by a well-functioning multidisciplinary team that can formulate ways in which functional domains overlap and interact with one another, use developmental information to consider alternate explanations for problem behaviors, and make specific recommendations for treatment. This is more difficult than it sounds because values differ in terms of what is acceptable or normal functioning. Also, when there are problems in multiple domains a broad array of services and interventions may be required and it will be necessary to set priorities and sometimes to sequence interventions. As well, it is important to consider how interventions may be modified to address more than one need. The struggle of assessment teams to plan and coordinate services for children with co-occurring language and communication impairments and social-emotional problems cannot be underestimated. The decision about where and how to deliver services optimally should be undertaken only after the range, type, and severity of a child's symptoms; the capacity of the family to participate in intervention; and the systemic supports and resources are considered. It also must be recognized that a certain amount of trial and error is needed, something that is difficult to tolerate when there are time-limited services and scarce resources. But the alternative of offering fragmented services or reporting only findings that fit existing services is not a productive route to take. As conceptions of developmental problems evolve so too must the services that are provided.

GIVING FEEDBACK

Giving accurate and sensitive feedback from an integrative assessment is not only is the beginning of a treatment plan but is an intervention in itself. Feedback provides children with LI and their family with a better understanding of the reasons for difficulties in learning in social contexts and sets the stage for intervention. The feedback session is an opportunity to correct misattributions and acknowledge a child's genuine difficulties with communication. That is, rather than being unwilling to cooperate or lacking interest in relationships, children may be struggling with auditory verbal memory problems, slow processing, or difficulties with pragmatics. Older children often feel validated when their genuine difficulties are brought to light. Although not all children and parents will accept assessment findings, in the majority of cases they are relieved to have a rational explanation for the child's behavior. Moreover, it can provide an immediate boost to children's self-esteem when they know that they are not "dumb" or "weird." It is especially important to highlight children's strengths, and in fact the feedback should always begin with these.

It is also critically important to enlist children, parents, and teachers in the validation of specific findings and their interpretation. Clinicians see children in a constrained setting and must rely on external sources for important information regarding the full range of a child's behaviors. The feedback also provides an explanation for all parties for why a child who may have performed superbly in the early grades, when demands on language processing were minimal, falters when demands increased. Obviously, collaboration needs to go beyond sharing assessment findings and single conversations during a feedback interview. Rather, professionals must work together to arrive at a diagnosis, determine the resources and strategies and the capacity of children and their families to use these, and maintain communication about the children's needs and responses to intervention over time.

Both in written reports and in verbal feedback, it is important to illustrate how specific language-processing problems are linked to specific difficulties in school, at home, and with peers such as in the following excerpt from a report.

Case Example

On *Clinical Evaluation of Language Fundamentals–3,* Alice's performance was significantly lower than average for her age on a test that required her to follow a sequence of steps read aloud to her and on a test of her understanding grammatical structures. Problems with understanding grammar as well as difficulties remembering sequences of information are likely to contribute to Alice's difficulty remembering classroom instructions and explanations, participating in extended conversations, and remembering what she has read. For instance, while she is still working to understand the beginning of an explanation, the teacher has communicated several additional ideas that Alice may miss. As a consequence, Alice often acquires an incomplete understanding of the subject matter. Moreover, as Alice struggles to keep up, she is likely to experience tremendous mental fatigue and loss of focus. Thus it is not surprising that Alice seems to "tune out" during classroom discussion. Deficits in processing sentences can also impede writing grammatically correct sentences and punctuating them, as is the case with Alice. The rules associated with writing make less sense to children with limited appreciation of how sentences work.

Case Example

Examiner [to parents]: Johnny seems to have difficulty on a task where he has to remember more than two things at a time. Does that fit with what you have observed at home? For instance, what happens when you ask Johnny to do something?

Wherever possible, the child's input should be enlisted in the feedback session.

Case Example

Examiner: Some kids need extra time to understand what their teacher says. I wonder if this ever happens to you? Sometimes the teacher starts to say something and you start to think about that. But in the meantime the teacher talks about new things. Then you miss those new things and it's really hard to catch up. Has that ever happened to you?

Child: Yeah. All the time.

Examiner: That must really be frustrating.

Giving feedback to families is often an important meeting point of mental health and communication specialists because, as was seen in the case examples presented throughout this book, parents' responses to feedback can vary and indicate that further work with the family is required before they can be enlisted in interventions for their child.

KEY POINTS

- An assessment is undertaken for diagnosis, determination of eligibility for services, and planning and monitoring intervention.

- Applying the model of developmental psychopathology to assessment means that information about language and communication and associated conditions must be examined over time, from different perspectives, and in different contexts. The child's language environment must also be considered.

- Standardized tests are most commonly used to arrive at a diagnosis of LI. It is important to be aware of the limitations of these instruments in understanding children's language and communicative functioning and in treatment planning.

- There are no well-standardized measures for many of the areas of functioning important to understanding communication problems, such as pragmatics and social cognition. Unlike standardized tests, which can be scored and interpreted fairly easily, most existing measures of pragmatics and social cognition require a great degree of practice. Gaining familiarity with such measures will enrich research and clinical work that seeks to understand the functioning of children with co-occurring communication and social-emotional problems.

- Through observation and interview, examiners attempt to understand how children communicate and whether they are impaired in this respect.

- There is still no single criterion for diagnosis of LI. Moreover, even children who do not meet a typical criterion may be impaired. Similarly, children with social and emotional problems who do not meet criteria for a psychiatric disorder may be impaired.

- Giving feedback from an assessment is an important endeavor and is often an intervention in itself. Understanding the source of difficulties helps parents, teachers, and clinicians make accurate attributions for the children's behavior, and this facilitates treatment planning.

- Assessment findings should be validated by parents, teachers, and children and reports written to reflect how language and communication impairments impact on children's daily life.

6

TREATMENT

As the child learns speech, he can begin to express in a "cooler" medium . . . what before could be expressed only in action, image, or affectivity. Speech and cognition permit higher levels of learning, of social sharing, and new forms of displacement that assist in the developing control process. (Pine, 1985, p. 163)

Professionals from a range of disciplines have become increasingly sensitive to how developmental issues inform treatment (Giddan, Bade, Rickenberg, & Ryley, 1995; Kazdin, 1995; Russ, 1998). Applying a developmental perspective optimally means that one would be sufficiently informed by theoretical foundations and research findings regarding the course of development and the processes that are critically related to adaptive and maladaptive functioning. The intent of treatment would then be to interrupt maladaptive developmental processes in favor of those that promote learning and social-emotional growth. Treatment planning also would integrate information about various areas of development and influences on the developmental process. Progress has been made in applying a developmental model to treatment (e.g., Eyberg, Schuhmann, & Rey, 1998; Vernberg, 1998). At this point, however, there is not the precise knowledge of developmental processes, the means to analyze developmental change, or the understanding of what constitutes adequate functioning required to apply this model consistently. As seen in Chapter 5, the range of assessment tools is limited, and this in turn limits the precision of the assessment process in informing treatment plans. Some of the reasons for these gaps lie in understanding of development itself as well as limitations in measurement. It is also true that research on treatment often poses contradictory findings. For

137

instance, although this book has promoted an integrative model that incorporates multiple domains of development, research on treatment efficacy more typically has examined discrete treatments for a particular problem, often only under laboratory conditions (Weisz & Weiss, 1993). Multifocused interventions have been more likely to be evaluated in community-based programs (e.g., Conduct Problems Prevention Research Group, 1999a, 1999b). Moreover, it has been shown that change in one domain of functioning does not necessarily result in change in other domains and that change in one situation does not generalize to others (Vernberg, Routh, & Koocher, 1992). Even where social and emotional problems and problems of language and learning have been identified, the trend has been to institute parallel treatments through case management or intervention in specialized treatment facilities. Consequently, most of the interventions discussed in this chapter were not designed specifically to treat children with co-occurring LI and social-emotional disorder. They do, however, meet some of the requirements of an integrative developmental approach for treating these children or have the potential to do so with adaptations.

INTERVENTIONS TO IMPROVE COMMUNICATIVE AND SOCIAL-EMOTIONAL COMPETENCE: INFANTS AND TODDLERS

As we now know, the early signs of difficulties communicating and relating to others are detectable long before a child learns to speak and are evidenced in nonverbal communications such as eye gaze or shared visual focus (joint attention). Because of the critical role of early relationships for learning and social-emotional adjustment and the openness of these relationships to change (Waters, Merrick, Treboux, Crowell, & Albersheim, 2000), improving communicative competence in infants may serve a dual purpose of enhancing both the development and the quality of interpersonal relationships. As we shall see below, working the other way around, that is, enhancing the relationship, can also have positive effects on language and cognitive development.

Over the past 10 to 15 years, there has been a shift in intervention away from therapist-guided infant stimulation programs to interventions that build on the mutuality of communicative and social-emotional development with the goal of fostering development in both arenas. These interventions are also consistent with current views regarding the critical role of social interaction in language development (Chapman, 2000). Since sensitive, responsive, and nonintrusive parenting are considered essential to both communication and secure attachment, parents are often involved as the primary agents of change in interventions that emphasize following their child's communicative lead. These child-directed approaches are also important in light of Vygotsky's (1962) contention that in the process of learning both to communicate and to control their own behavior, children must recognize that they have the capacity to regulate their external environment (Tronick, 1989).

For instance, the Hanen Early Language Parent Program (Girolametto, Verbey, & Tannock, 1994; Manolson, 1985, 1992) promotes joint engagement in reciprocal social interactions between parent(s) or other caregivers with infants and preschoolers. At the beginning of the program, a videotape is made of each parent interacting with his or her child. When the tape is viewed jointly with the program facilitator, parents often see for themselves or are shown that they are directive and intrusive. This is particularly the case for children who exhibit delays in language and communicative development. Subsequently, parents are taught interactional techniques by a specially trained facilitator, the core of which is to follow their child's communicative lead and respond in a way that fosters engagement in joint activity suited to the child's abilities and interests in naturally occurring situations. This is done by the parent waiting for the child to initiate interaction while showing interest and positive anticipation; following the child's focus of attention and play; and modeling language by labeling, expanding, recasting, and extending child verbalizations or talking in parallel about a child's nonverbal activities. Group meetings of parents allow for further teaching, observation of videotapes, and sharing experiences in implementing the procedure. A program based on the same basic concepts and procedures has also been developed for use by teachers and other caregivers in classroom settings (Weitzman, 1992).

Systematic evaluation of this approach, primarily with children with developmental delays and late talkers who were not explicitly identified as having social-emotional problems, has shown positive effects on qualities of parent-child interaction and improved ability of the parents to engage their child and support communication (Girolametto et al., 1994; Tannock et al., 1992). Improvements in language functioning in this sample required more targeted intervention to develop vocabulary (Girolametto, Pearce, & Weitzman, 1997). In this latter study, although phonological abilities were not targeted, there was evidence of secondary effects on this aspect of language functioning.

Turning now to the field of infant mental health, we find that the use of techniques that require following the child's lead are prominent here too (DeGangi & Greenspan, 1999; Muir, Lojkasek, & Cohen, 1999). One of these, an infant-led psychotherapy delivered through a program called Watch, Wait, and Wonder (Cohen, Muir, et al., 1999; Muir et al., 1999), has been shown to be associated with both enhanced relational and cognitive changes. Watch, Wait, and Wonder is carried out as follows. For half the session, the mother is instructed to get down on the floor with her infant, to observe her infant's self-initiated activity, and to interact only at her infant's initiative, thus acknowledging and accepting her infant's spontaneous behavior. Moreover, it puts mother and infant into a situation that can meet the requirements for secure attachments to form by facilitating maternal sensitivity and responsiveness. This also means that the mother is physically accessible and, if required, psychologically available. It is presumed that in this way both mother and infant modify or revise their mental models of one another to be more in line with their new experiences together in therapy. In the second half of the session, the mother is asked to discuss her observations and experiences. Unlike the interactional language interventions, the mother is not instructed by the therapist to comment on or extend her child's play. Moreover, unlike traditional psychotherapies, the therapist does not interpret the mother's or infant's behavior and does not help the mother make links between current difficulties and past relationships. The primary purpose of the discussion is to make it possible for the mother to follow her infant's lead through enhancing her observations and understanding her relationship with her infant. Another infant-led approach, *floor time* (Greenspan, 1992), focuses on specific developmental and relational goals, also working on the assumption that sensitive and appropriate responsiveness is essential. In floor time, however, the therapist more actively models and guides the mother in ways to interact with her infant in a sensitive and responsive manner than is the case with the approach used by Muir and colleagues (Muir et al., 1999).

Using a sample of 10- to 30-month-old infants, Cohen, Muir, et al. (1999) compared Watch, Wait, and Wonder with a more traditional psychodynamic psychotherapeutic approach with the mother and the infant present (Fraiberg, Adelson, & Shapiro, 1975). Both treatments resulted in reducing infants' presenting problems, increasing mothers' confidence that they could manage these problems, and decreasing stress associated with parenting. When observed playing, mothers were also less intrusive and engaged in less conflict with their infants. These gains were maintained or increased further 6 months later (Cohen, Lojkasek, E. Muir, R. Muir, & Parker, 2000). At the same time, there were differential treatment effects. In particular, in the group receiving Watch, Wait, and Wonder there was a greater shift toward a more organized or secure attachment relationship. Moreover, although both treatment groups showed improved language functioning, the infants receiving Watch, Wait, and Wonder exhibited significantly greater gains in cognitive development and increased capacity to regulate their own emotions and behavior to engage in cognitive tasks. Thus behavioral changes in the infant and the mother were related to significant improvement in cognitive performance. As well, at the end of treatment mothers of children in the Watch, Wait, and Wonder group were significantly less depressed and psychologically distressed and reported more satisfaction and efficacy in parenting than mothers in the psychotherapy group. Gains made by the Watch, Wait, and Wonder group were maintained at 6-month follow-up, and at that point the group receiving psychodynamic psychotherapy caught up to the Watch, Wait, and Wonder group in most respects. Differential effects were still present in that mothers in the Watch, Wait, and Wonder group also showed further gains in parenting confidence and reduced parenting stress. Overall, the findings suggest that different mechanisms were involved in effecting change in the two groups. Cohen and colleagues (Cohen et al., 1999; Cohen, Lojkasek, et al., 2000; Muir et al., 1999) have used attachment theory as a conceptual base and from this suggest several explanations. In Watch, Wait, and Wonder, the mother is uniquely accessible to her infant, creating the potential for psychological connection. Once infants are reassured and less preoccupied with gaining access to their mother, they can feel secure to explore. Indirectly, this may have accounted for the increase in cognitive abilities. Also, once the mother feels more competent in reading her infant's cues and interactions become more pleasurable, the mother may be more likely to gain confidence in her capacity to work things out with her infant on their own rather than relying on the therapist's expertise. The uncovering process in psychodynamic psychotherapy and gaining insight into earlier relational difficulties may have left the mother preoccupied or distressed, temporarily interfering with aspects of the mother-infant relationship and the mother's sense of her own competence (Goldfried & Wolfe, 1998; Seligman, 1995). The treatment results on maternal depression are important in light of the findings reported in the NICHD day care study (NICHD Early Child Care Research Network,

1999) that maternal depression was directly related, over time, to their toddler's language development. These changes bode well for the mother being available to interact with her child.

Case Example

Samantha had been developing normally during the first 2 years of her life. Then, following a series of seizures, she lost her ability to speak and became very active, not settling on one task for very long. Samantha's mother was distressed about the interruption in her daughter's development and her own feelings of helplessness in getting Samantha back on track developmentally. While medical and developmental evaluations were being done, Watch, Wait, and Wonder was recommended to assist with the mother-child relationship. When mother and child were observed during the assessment, Samantha's mother pursued Samantha intrusively and relentlessly in her attempts to settle her infant's behavior and maintain her attention on a task. These efforts were met with resistance by Samantha, who continued to flit from one task to another, showing little regard for her mother's attempts to interact with her. She avoided eye contact, made distressed vocalizations, and pulled away.

In the first Watch, Wait, and Wonder session, Samantha moved around the room, touching objects and furniture. She was aimless in her wandering, picking up toys but not getting involved. She finally settled on the doctor's kit and dumped its contents on the floor. She put the stethoscope in her ears and went over to her mother, who had been watching Samantha's play with interest, and put it in her ears. Samantha alternated between placing the stethoscope in her ears, moving to the other side of the room, and returning to put them back in her mother's ears. As she put them in her mother's ears, the mother made the sound "wa." Although Samantha remained silent, she smiled at her mother.

In the next session, Samantha played with stacking toys and persisted in taking the rings off the base and then fitting them back on again, verbalizing as she played. She explored the room again and found a tiger, placing it on a chair while she continued to play attentively with other small toys taken from a bucket. Finally, she took the tiger to her mother, who said "roar," and Samantha imitated this sound. What ensued was a series of turns in which mother and child said "roar." The communicative turns continued, and the mutual pleasure of both Samantha and her mother were clearly evident during their interaction.

Although Samantha's development obviously was still a concern, she was beginning to communicate both in gesture and vocalization, and the relationship with her mother was more positive and mutually pleasurable than at the outset. Moreover, in later sessions she showed evidence of symbolic play, which had not been observed previously.

INTERVENTIONS TO IMPROVE COMMUNICATIVE AND SOCIAL-EMOTIONAL FUNCTIONING: PRESCHOOL THROUGH ADOLESCENCE

In the preschool through adolescent years, four broad types of interventions are discussed: (a) interventions specifically focused on enhancing social competence (social skills or social-cognitive maturity), particularly with peers, of children with communication impairments and children with social-emotional disorders; (b) interventions focused on behavioral management; (c) psychotherapy, including play therapy; and (d) family therapy.

Interventions Focused on Enhancing Social Competence With Peers

An outcome of the increased focus on pragmatics has been a growth of interventions in the context of social communication with peers. The move toward interventions to improve the peer relationships of children and youths has proceeded in parallel in the field of language and communication disorders and the field of mental health. Communication specialists have developed interventions based on delineation of crucial skills underlying pragmatics and discourse (e.g., Gallagher, 1993,1996). Multiple forms of interventions may be included in a communication intervention program (Gallagher, 1996). Instructional procedures used in these interventions typically involve modeling, role playing, self-instructions, reinforcement, coaching, and problem-solving strategies (Asher, 1985). Mental health professionals have used similar interventions, focusing on the social-cognitive processes necessary for social problem solving with peers and adults. The techniques used in social skills training appear to be similar to those used in interventions aimed to improve pragmatic skills. With few exceptions, however, the research literature on each of these has ignored the other. The literature summarizing research on social skills training does not often mention language and communicative competence and the literature on interventions for pragmatics and social communication does not often mention social-emotional functioning. Because of this, it is uncertain whether the children enrolled in these different programs are comparable. In the following sections, specific interventions designed by communication specialists and mental health specialists that may impact on both pragmatic and social-emotional functioning are described.

Improving Conversational Skills With Peers

Working under the assumption that children's conversational abilities are dependent on qualities of the conversational partner and context (Brinton & Fujiki, 1995), interventions have been directed at developing related skills (Gallagher, 1999; Rice, 1993; Windsor, 1995). Some studies of children with LI have shown promising outcomes, including targeting specific conversational behavior such as entering into an interaction, responding to questions, asking questions, developing appropriate topics, acknowledging the communication of others, and complimenting conversational partners (Brinton & Fujiki, 1995). Instructions, verbal prompting such as reminding children that it is their turn to ask a question, modeling, behavioral rehearsal, and social reinforcement are all used. For instance, a rule taught for entering a conversation might be "When you see someone you want to play with, look at them or gently tap their shoulder and say, 'Hi, do you want to play?'"

A related approach is script training. Script training, more specific than conversational intervention, is geared toward learning the lines for participating in common activities such as going to a restaurant; going to a movie; or, in younger children, playing lemonade stand (Goldstein & Gallagher; Goldstein, Wickstrom, Hoyson, Jamieson, & Odom, 1988). Approaches that use event-based learning and scripts involve teaching children repetitive interactional routines to help them understand the structure of conversation. In the process, children learn the expectations implicit in a given role for conversation. Especially with young children prompts are needed to stay in their roles (Goldstein et al., 1988). Research suggests that children's conversational interactions are improved in situations where they share knowledge of events and have mutual expectations (Gallagher, 1999). For scripting, this might include such activities as preparing a snack in a preschool setting, working on a classroom mural, or planning a dance.

Peer Involvement in Intervention

There is evidence that peer involvement in treatment has a positive impact on peer acceptance and children's self-perceptions of their social efficacy (Bierman & Furman, 1984). Peers have been used in interventions to facilitate improvement in social skills and play in a number of ways. First, in group situations they may be used to model appropriate communicative behaviors in role-play situations that target particular social behaviors for intervention to improve social skills and play. When this is not feasible, peer models can be drawn from videotapes or films. Interventions also have used role play in group situations and group discussions to clarify goals and brainstorm about social and communication skills to provide feedback on these to other group members and to devise scripts for social interaction (Donahue, Szymanski, & Flores, 1999). Input from peers is often solicited in this process so that the important social skills can be targeted for intervention (Cartledge, Frew, & Zaharias, 1985). In older children and adolescents, the need to link social problem solving skills to personal experiences, goals, and self-evaluation is emphasized (Donahue, Szymanski, et al., 1999).

A second way in which peers are used is as confederates (Goldstein & Wickstrom, 1986) who are given a specific role to play in the intervention so that antecedent and consequent events can be manipulated. The goal is to provide increased opportunities for practice of particular language and communication skills. This might include expanding or recasting verbal utterances, asking for clarification, or prompting pragmatic behaviors such as eye contact. In these situations, it is the peers who have a script that includes reinforcing positive social behaviors in the children with LI.

A third way of facilitating positive peer social interactions is through cooperative group activities (Furman & Garvin, 1989). Children are given the task of working together on a common goal, such as a project. Each child has a specific task and whether the group gets a reward depends on the successful contribution of each member to completing the assigned task and reaching the goal. Although each child is competent to complete the specific task assigned, group members are expected to help one another. When this works successfully, there is an opportunity for the child with LI to feel proud and confident and to share in the group's success.

Ostrosky, Kaiser, and Odom (1993) emphasize that the nature and role of peers and their capacity to take their role responsibly must be carefully considered in these interventions. Peers without disabilities should be seen as facilitators rather than as interventionists. As well, all students should be taught strategies for improving social communication. Furthermore, individualized instruction for initiating and responding is necessary, possibly before group activities are undertaken. Finally, attention should be paid to skill maintenance. When popular children are included in the intervention for children with LI, they not only provide examples of skillful social behavior but also improve the social status of children with LI among peers and alter their negative perceptions (Gallagher, 1999).

Teaching Alternate Means of Communication

Observation and identification of the communicative needs that inappropriate behavior is serving (functional assessment) is the first step in approaches that teach alternate modes of communication. Most commonly, such communication needs are requesting, commenting, protesting, and seeking attention. Once the communicative need is identified, alternative means of communication that meet the same communicative need but in a socially appropriate way are taught using instructional techniques to help the child acquire words, phrases, and pragmatic behaviors (e.g., making eye contact, standing at a socially comfortable distance). Observational techniques are used to examine the peer interactions of children with LI and peers, including peers' own descriptions of the child with LI and their interactions together to plan the intervention (Gallagher & Craig, 1984; Goldstein & Gallagher, 1992). For instance, Gallagher and Craig (1984) devised an intervention for a 4-year-old who repeatedly used the phrase "It's gone" even though peers were annoyed when he said this and rejected him when he used the phrase when trying to join a social group. Noting this, they used direct instructional techniques, similar to those often used to increase vocabulary, to substitute "It's gone" with "Let's play."

Identifying and Labeling Emotions in Self and Others

Development of vocabulary for emotion or internal state language is important for children both to express their own emotions and to understand the emotions of others. Children with LI often misjudge others' emotions and are insensitive to cues from facial expression, vocal inflection, and body language. They not only require greater competence in labeling emotions but also need help to reflect on them and understand nuances and degrees of feeling. Dale (1996) has suggested that it would be helpful to teach words that reflect a continuum of feelings and not just broad categories of feelings. For instance, the emotion "afraid" could be further broken down into "nervous," "scared," and "terrified." The responses and the steps that they would take to cope with the various feelings might be quite different. Intervention could begin with looking at pictures or listening to tapes and be supplemented with reading stories or watching films about emotional experiences, observing others or pantomiming emotions, and developing coping strategies. Teachers or parents may label an apparent feeling in the child— "You look mad"—and inquire about the source of the feeling—"What are you mad about?" Strategies for controlling impulsive responses also often are taught. Group therapy experiences help reinforce strategies and comment on the impact on others' feelings and behaviors.

Developmentally, the approach to identifying internal states and their outward expression progresses from a reliance on vocal inflection, which is what is most salient in older infants and preschoolers, to reliance on facial features, which is most salient in older children (Papoušek & Papoušek, 1986). Giddan et al. (1995) have outlined interventions that may be undertaken during different developmental periods. They described a milieu intervention for children with behavior problems, grouping classes according to social-emotional rather than age or grade criteria. A multidisciplinary team helped the children understand what they were feeling, why they felt this way, and how to label and communicate feelings in an acceptable and productive way. Parent training and parent treatment groups also were implemented. Using this developmental approach, for instance, emphasis on vocal rather than visual cues along with modeling were applied with preschoolers. Children were helped to identify expressed feelings by name, alternative nonverbal responses were demonstrated, and appropriate requesting behavior modeled. Acceptable angry behavior also was modeled. Additionally, the teacher demonstrated vocal, facial, and bodily characteristics of an emotion while simultaneously reflecting on and labeling it. To make these activities more concrete, the teacher also shared an experience to illustrate cause and effect between events and emotions. In school-aged children, overt behavior and its impact on others is particularly important. With a focus on developing social and communication skills and the language of feelings, students pantomimed emotions and read stories about emotional experiences. As well as labeling and talking about feelings, they were helped to develop coping strategies. Teaching and modeling of acceptable expressions of negative feelings continued to be a strategy with these older children. Finally, with adolescents there was a greater emphasis on discussion of feelings with peers, role play, and help with anticipating situations that aroused anxiety. Adolescents were also assisted to make choices about ways to react. Regardless of the particular behavior or emotional problem, the goal was to increase awareness of feelings and the capacity to label and talk about feelings in oneself and in others.

*Social-Cognitive Approaches to
Enhancing Social Problem Solving*

Social problem solving interventions rely on enhancing the link between social-cognitive processes and behavior (Asher, 1985; Gallagher, 1996)

They focus on underlying thought processes and teaching children *how* to think rather than *what* to think. It is assumed that, through practice and rewarding outcomes, changes in the way children process social and emotional information will ensue. There is a broad range of interventions that work to improve both the interpersonal thinking and the interpersonal behavior of children. These interventions also have as a goal increasing the children's capacity to identify cues for different emotions in themselves and others. Specific aspects of intervention include modeling, role playing, self-instruction, reinforcement, coaching, teaching problem-solving strategies, and provision of self-reflective feedback (Forness & Kavale, 1996).

Selman and colleagues (Selman & Schultz, 1990; Selman, Watts, & Schultz, 1997; Yeates & Selman, 1989) have applied to intervention what has been learned about the sequential steps in the social problem solving situation measured by the INS interview. This includes defining the problem (perception/theory of mind), generating alternative strategies (which involves memory), selecting and implementing a strategy (social action), and appraisal (evaluating consequences, repair). This model of social problem solving is explicitly developmental and traces a sequence that proceeds from a physicalistic and egocentric orientation to one that takes into consideration interpersonal relationships. Yeates and Selman (1989) suggest that to be most effective, direct instruction must be supplemented by interventions during ongoing negotiations in meaningful relationships, typically with peers, so that children experience the consequences of their successes and failures. Using an intervention called *pair therapy,* two children with contrasting, but equally ineffective, relational approaches to friendship are brought together with a facilitator who helps them develop the capacities in which they are deficient. Friendship knowledge and skills are both promoted in this approach in relation to real-life issues (Selman, Beardslee, Schultz, Krupa, & Podorefsky, 1986; Selman et al., 1997). Because of the developmental nature of the model, unlike other approaches that try to bring a child up to the norm for age or to the highest developmental level on particular skills, this intervention explicitly promotes and encourages social-cognitive conceptualizations that are one step above a child's current level (Selman & Schultz, 1990). Therefore recognition of children's developmental level is crucial. As well, children are encouraged to achieve greater balance with their social partner, so that children who passively comply with other children's demands would be encouraged to negotiate a more balanced solution, even though their needs may still be subsumed under those of other children. Similarly, children who use aggressive means would be encouraged to verbalize demands rather than exhibit them physically. In one study, this model was applied to peer pairs over 10 weekly sessions (Selman & Schultz, 1990). Sessions were divided into two parts. The first part involved discussion of the information-processing steps together with structured discussions about application of the steps. The second part was devoted to the peer dyad choosing and then enacting an age-appropriate activity with the trainer's guidance in negotiating throughout the play period. Ultimately, two dyads (four children) were involved. Although case reports using this approach illustrate positive outcomes (Selman & Schultz, 1988), systematic research has not been undertaken.

Social problem solving interventions specifically for children with LI have not been designed. Based on research findings reported in Chapter 4 (Cohen, Menna, et al., 1998), it is essential that children's capacity to understand and to express themselves be factored into treatment planning. For instance, social-cognitive training may require teaching specific vocabulary words and using some of the interventions to effect changes in conversational competence described earlier. Although these programs offer potential opportunities for integrating language and social-emotional development, to date this kind of integration has only been reported for one program for preschoolers (Spivack, Platt, & Shure, 1976). Although the program was not explicitly developed for children with LI, the necessity of children grasping linguistic concepts such as "and," "same," "different," and "not" was recognized. Consequently, children were first taken through a series of games and exercises to enhance the prerequisite language and cognitive skills. Conceptual words such as "if-then," "happy-sad," or "maybe-might" also were incorporated in exercises to help the children evaluate solutions in light of potential consequences. The intent was for the children to understand the concept implied by the word. Working under the assumption that it is easier to teach new concepts using words already familiar to the child, essential words were identified. Words that dealt with people and interpersonal qualities also were taught. Trainers used scripts to increase the social problem solving ability by applying daily lessons presented in a game format. The script indicated the proper sequencing to teach skills. Daily sessions of 5 to 20 minutes over a 10-week period were used with children in small groups. Once prerequisite skills were acquired, games were introduced to encourage the children to think of alternative solutions to hypothetical problems and consider various consequences. In the process, the children were guided through dialogues. The emphasis was on seeking solutions and evaluating them rather than finding a particular solution to a problem. Research showed training effects that were sustained when the children were followed one year later in kindergarten (Shure & Spivack, 1982).

Current Status of Social-Interactional and Social-Cognitive Approaches

There is evidence of the positive effects of interventions focused on social problem solving (e.g., Kazdin, Siegel, & Bass, 1992). It appears that older children benefit more than younger ones (Durlak, Fuhrman, & Lampman, 1991), which suggests that more advanced cognitive and language development facilitates intervention. Treatment of social skills deficits in children with learning disabilities, many of whom have LI, has produced more modest effects (Forness & Kavale, 1996), probably because of the greater hurdles for children with language and cognitive-processing difficulties. Caution also has been raised about using interventions that involve coaching because they rely on children attending and comprehending (Fey, 1986). This means that modifications to the model are required.

A further difficulty with the above interventions is that generalization to new contexts and long-term effects have not been proved (Guralnick, 1990). As is often the case with model programs, they are relatively short term and therefore their failure to generalize or to produce long-term gains is not surprising. Ongoing or booster sessions are necessary for many interventions (Kazdin, 1997). Moreover, because language needs of children shift with age, reconvening therapy is likely to be required, for instance, when problems with figurative language increase during adolescence.

An example of a program that has been applied universally and that has acknowledged the need for continuity of programming over the long term is the multifocused school-based FAST Track program aimed at preventing conduct problems in high-risk samples (Conduct Problems Prevention Research Group, 1999a, 1999b). Although not designed specifically for children with LI and social-emotional disorder, it has shown an impact on some aspects of both. This program is unique in that whereas most interventions focusing on social problem solving have been brief and used primarily with dyads and small groups, the FAST Track program involves whole classrooms. Taking a comprehensive approach, the curriculum used in the FAST Track program, called the PATHS (Promoting Alternative Thinking Strategies) curriculum, involves parent groups, child social skills training groups, parent-child sharing time, home visiting, child peer pairing, and academic tutoring. It is available to children starting in Grade 1 and continuing through school. With respect to the social-cognitive component, four domains of skills were included: (a) skills for emotional understanding and communication (i.e., recognizing and labeling emotions), (b) friendship skills (i.e., participation, cooperation, fair play, and negotiation), (c) self-control skills (i.e., behavioral inhibition and arousal modulation), and (d) social problem solving skills (i.e., problem identification, response generation, response evaluation, and anticipatory planning). At the end of Grade 1, the high-risk intervention group progressed significantly in acquisition of almost all the skills were considered critical, including emotional and social coping skills, social-cognitive capacity, and peer relationships. Although language was not directly examined, there was significant improvement in word attack skills, which involve phonological awareness and contribute to reading proficiency.

Interventions Focused on Behavioral Management

Behavior Therapy

Behavioral or cognitive-behavioral therapies are often implemented in day care and classroom settings and at home to reduce noncompliant, aggressive, or socially inappropriate behaviors (e.g., Chamberlain & Patterson 1995; Webster-Stratton, 1989). Behavioral techniques include procedures such as reinforcing positive prosocial behavior, removal of reinforcers for problematic behavior (i.e., response cost), ignoring annoying behavior, and time out to remove children from a situation where they are reinforced with attention for inappropriate behavior. Whitehurst and Fischel (1994) reported a study by Laplante, Zelazo, and Kearsley (1991) in which training parents of preschoolers to use behavioral management techniques resulted in a reduction in misbehavior and an increase in vocabulary and verbal interaction in children compared to a group that did not receive this intervention. Since language is typically not examined in studies evaluating behavioral management, these findings are interesting but remain tentative. Nevertheless, therapists must take care in implementing behavioral management techniques in situations where there are rifts in the parent-child relationship. These rifts could be exacerbated in behavioral therapies unless the relationship is attended to first. When the behavior is punished, then it may be communication itself that becomes inadvertently extinguished (Greenberg, Kusche, Cook, & Quamma, 1995). The functional approach, described earlier, is relevant in this context as a way of understanding what purpose behavior problems serve (Wickstrom-Kane & Goldstein, 1999). Given the assumption that children want to communicate for positive social interchange, emotion expression, and curiosity or learning, it is necessary to determine how a problem behavior may serve a communicative function with the goal of helping children to use more appropriate and conventional forms of communication. This is another arena in which collaborative work between communication and mental health specialists could be productive. Undertaking a functional assessment to determine underlying prosocial intentions of problematic behavior can then be used to design interventions.

Parent-Child Interactional (Filial) Therapy

Another way that behavioral techniques have been modified, which has potential for contributing to fostering both language development and parent-child relationships in treatment, is parent-child interactional therapy, sometimes called filial therapy, which integrates two types of treatment (Hembree-Kigin & McNeil, 1995). Parent-child interactional therapy was originally developed to treat children with disruptive and oppositional behavior problems and their families. The treatment is divided into two sequential components, both of which take place in a play environment. The first component is child directed and the second is parent directed. In the child-directed play sessions, parents are taught to adopt a nondirective approach to interacting and playing with their child. This child-led approach is used to build a warm and responsive relationship between parents and their child. Acknowledging that behavioral and language problems co-occur, Hembree-Kigin and McNeil (1995) suggest that when language problems are relatively mild the child-centered play could serve as a means of stimulating language development. Particular aspects of parent-child interactional training that might prove beneficial are fostering parents' engagement with their child around reflecting and elaborating feelings; modeling ways to deal with frustration; and fostering turn taking, eye contact, and vocal expressiveness. Having a special play time with the child is also intended to boost parent and child self-esteem, which in itself stimulates motivation to communicate. The second part of treatment emphasizes teaching behavioral management techniques to parents to improve child compliance. Parents are taught to direct their child's behavior with clear, age-appropriate instructions and application of consistent consequences. The therapist draws on various techniques including modeling, instruction, coaching, role playing between parents and therapist, and giving homework to parents. Since most children engaged in parent-child interactional therapy have disruptive behavioral problems, the fact that many such children referred to mental health settings also have concomitant LI suggests that, prior to undertaking treatment, language should be assessed.

Evaluation of parent-child interactional therapy has shown that parents of preschoolers aged 3 to 6 years changed their interactional style and were more successful in gaining the child's compliance at home, which persisted at 4-month follow-up. This was associated with a decrease in ratings of parenting stress (Schuhmann, Foote, Eyberg, Boggs, & Algina, 1998). There were no findings reported, however, on whether this treatment was as successful for children with LI as for children with normally developing language.

Cognitive Behavior Modification

Cognitive-behavioral techniques involve helping children change dysfunctional beliefs about themselves and others. The assumption is that dysfunctional cognitive-processing schema that have become automatic must be replaced by ones that are functional and adaptive. In both children and adults, the use of self-talk is an essential tool for cognitive mediation and self-regulation. Therefore it is not surprising that children with language-based learning problems have been reported to have more difficulty with cognitive behavior modification (Abikoff, 1985; Kazdin, 1997). Moreover, this approach is less suitable for preschoolers, who, although capable of self-talk, do not have the cognitive maturity to internalize and apply what they have learned (Cohen, Sullivan, Minde, Novack, & Helwig, 1981). Therefore it is necessary to consider how this intervention could be modified to structure the language environment of therapy to compensate for potential communication deficits. One obvious step would be to ensure that children understand the vocabulary to be used in the self-talk procedures and to assess the success of application of this vocabulary. It also may be necessary to use shorter and simpler sentences, group together elements of self-talk, allow for slower pacing, and provide opportunities for extended practice.

Psychotherapy and Play Therapy

Language remediation is typically saved for children with moderate or severe LI. Fewer resources have been allocated to children with relatively mild problems. Nevertheless, children with mild LI have been shown to have social-emotional problems and difficulties in achievement that interfere with functioning (Cohen, Barwick, et al., 1998; Cohen, Menna, et al., 1998), and these are the children who often come to the attention of mental health professionals. There should be interest in the language of these children because of the central role that language plays in the processes of self-regulation and cognitive mediation and the involvement of language in the process of all forms of child psychotherapy.

The capacity to identify and label emotional cues in oneself and others, to verbally interpret and describe behavior, and generally to become more thoughtful about and to articulate and clarify interpersonal processes are important goals of psychotherapeutic interventions. Even in play therapy, reliance on symbolic play and understanding of commentary and interpretations are important. Children and adolescents with LI are likely to be at a disadvantage in psychotherapy and encounter difficulties expressing themselves verbally and understanding syntactically complex, lengthy, and emotionally loaded discussions with a therapist or family members. Formulating answers to "how" and "why" questions, which require procedural knowledge and inferential skills, are particularly difficult for children and adolescents with LI. An answer of "I don't know" may not signal resistance but, rather, difficulty creating a narrative, a task that requires formulating, on demand, cohesive, coherent responses to specific questions on topics often chosen by the therapist. Even simple strategies such as allowing a child with LI more time to respond can be effective.

It might be presumed that improved language functioning would also facilitate other forms of language-based therapy, although there is only minimal evidence for this in young children (Robertson & Weismer, 1999). Interestingly, there is evidence that the converse is true and that psychotherapy can have a salutary effect on language (Russell, Greenwald, & Shirk, 1991). In a meta-analysis of the child psychotherapy literature, Russell et al. (1991) selected studies that had included measures of language functioning as an outcome. Children in these studies were, on average, 9 years of age. Russell et al. found 18 studies comparing an active psychotherapeutic treatment with controls that included at least one measure of language as indicated by expressive-receptive language or reading measures. None of these studies was explicitly intended to change language. They also assessed the type of verbal process likely to have taken place in treatment. One was spontaneous verbal interactions such as those used in psychotherapy. A second involved prescribed task and problem-solving interactions such as in social problem solving or social-cognitive treatments. A third type of verbal interaction characterized behavioral exchanges in which verbal interaction played a secondary role, such as parent management training. Results indicated that therapies that emphasized spontaneous language produced effect sizes that were over 10 times as large as those with explicit goal-oriented formats for language interaction and over 4 times as large as those that emphasized behavioral rather than verbal exchanges. Moreover, length of treatment was correlated with language but not nonlanguage effect sizes. The findings of this study raise questions about scripted interventions and suggest the importance of building opportunities for generalization and practice in real-world settings. Shirk and Russell (1996) propose that increased language proficiency may be promoted in verbal psychotherapies by the patient's participation in focused communicative interactions that clarify and expand on verbalizations. As well, there are some broad parallels in components of remedial interventions for LI and for psychotherapy, such as feedback, monitoring, repetition, and facilitating discourse skills through helping with sequencing, clarifying, expanding, and modeling appropriate ways to communicate, that could facilitate further dialogue. It is important to acknowledge that Russell et al.'s (1991) findings applied primarily to those children who were experiencing peer relationship problems and low self-esteem and not to children with more entrenched emotional and behavioral problems. Since these authors found that language had been measured in only 17% of the 105 outcome studies they reviewed, there is certainly room for more research.

There is also need for more information on the nature of therapist-child language interactions. Russell (1998) has emphasized the need to match both verbal and nonverbal behavior in psychotherapeutic interventions to children's developmental level and suggested that therapists' language is not typically matched to the level of narrative competence of the child. For instance, Russell, van den Broek, Adams, Rosenberger, and Essig (1993) assessed three clinically relevant dimensions of narrative during individual therapy sessions. The first dimension was the structural connectedness of narrative, that is, to what extent events were connected causally and temporally. The second dimension was the degree to which the psychological interior of action was made manifest, that is, the degree to which protagonists in a story showed perspective taking and their own psychological or motivational perspective on the events that were talked about or enacted in play. The third dimension was linguistic complexity, that is, the number of words per segment of the narrative. These authors maintained that for the therapist's narrative to be therapeutic the therapist needs to model or illustrate how events are causally and temporally linked, how events relate to subjective perspectives, and how to achieve repairs through language that is not too dissimilar from that of the child in terms of complexity. Obviously, the child-therapist narrative will depend on the child's developmental level in terms of language structure, discourse, and social-cognitive maturity. Although Shirk and Russell (1996) discuss the importance of language, pragmatics, and narrative structure in therapy and cite findings regarding changes in language functioning as an outcome of psychotherapeutic treatment, their work does not specifically focus on children with co-occurring LI and social-emotional disturbance. Therefore replication of their findings on this sample, with extensions of treatment that involve therapists matching their language to that of their child patients, is needed.

Family Therapy

The family is an important arena in which children practice social-communicative interactions. Optimally, the family environment is responsive to children's needs and developmental capacities and provides adequate opportunities for children to experience successful communicative transactions and emotionally satisfying and secure social relationships. If children experience success in their families and a sense of self as a competent communicator, this becomes internalized. Moreover, under these conditions children perceive social experiences and interactions as enjoyable and intrinsically rewarding rather than as stressful. When family-child relationship disturbances are combined with language and communication impairments, social interactions are likely to be stressful for all parties. For instance, when children cannot communicate clearly, parents may employ a highly controlling or directive style or, in the extreme, neglect or abuse their children. Moreover, in light of evidence of a genetic component to LI (Hohnen & Stevenson, 1999), more than one family member may be struggling with understanding and communicating thoughts and feelings. In all cases, it is important to hear the family's own rendering of how their child's language or communication disorder has influenced family life. Guilt, anger, and misattribution (blaming) are common negative responses. Having children with a disability does not always have a negative impact on family adjustment, and this is important to acknowledge as well.

Childhood language and communication impairments may also disrupt the development of mutual parent-child regulatory strategies that require the ability to clearly communicate tangible needs and emotional states. Children with LI are more likely to have unsuccessful interactions and more frequent communication breakdowns, to fail to repair or exhibit inadequate repair, and to be unsuccessful in resolving communication exchanges. These experiences compromise children's developing sense of confidence and mastery in social exchange, which ultimately may reduce the motivation to communicate.

The importance of involving parents in communication therapy has been mentioned at various junctures in this chapter. Of course, mental health interventions also include parents, and often the family is the focus of therapy. Working with the family system requires being able to integrate perspectives of different family members. Individual family members' roles in the family and the interactional patterns between family members and their influence on the family as a whole need to be acknowledged. Thus when children are first identified as having LI, even that knowledge influences the family system. As said previously, children who may have been labeled as uncooperative, lazy, or withdrawn will now need to be seen as children who are struggling to communicate and to understand what others say to them. This paves the way for establishing realistic expectations and environmental modifications. For some families, adjustment to the new information brings about immediate changes for the better.

Case Example

Assessment of 11-year-old Frankie revealed that he had particular difficulty with grammar and auditory verbal processing. Despite normal overall intelligence, he was performing below the average range for his age on measures of his ability to follow directions and in grammatic expression and understanding. When this feedback was given to the family members, they were helped by the therapist to reconsider the source of some of the behaviors that had been irritating them and interfering with family activities. Frankie himself was able to describe his difficulties for his family and was pleased that his behavior was validated in some way and that a plan was being made to help him in school. In subsequent family therapy sessions, Frankie's mother periodically looked at him to see whether he was following the conversation and checked his understanding by asking whether he understood what was being said or asking him to repeat the gist of what had transpired in the session in his own words. She was able to do this in a calm and supportive way that Frankie could accept. Having had his genuine difficulties with auditory comprehension explained to him and his family, for the first time he felt pleased that he was not being blamed for behaviors that were out of his control.

For other families, time is needed to grieve over the loss of their expectations for children who were thought to be gifted or creative as the parents' need to have their own aspirations realized is undermined.

Case Example

Derek was an 8-year-old boy referred by his parents for assessment for placement in a gifted class. The parents felt that Derek was bored in his current classroom and consequently was acting up in class, not completing his work, and getting only mediocre grades. In the interview, Derek presented as an articulate child who was knowledgeable about films. His father was a film producer who spent considerable time with Derek, took him on film shoots, and talked with him about his work. Formal assessment revealed that Derek was consistently functioning in the average range of ability on cognitive and academic achievement tests. He also had a mild receptive language impairment. Personality testing suggested that, despite a calm demeanor, Derek was an anxious child worried about whether he could meet expectations. Reflecting back on Derek's conversations concerning films, the examiner realized that much of Derek's knowledge was scripted and intended to please and impress adults. When feedback was given to the parents, they remained silent and did not ask questions. The examiner suggested making an appointment one month hence, at which time they would have had an opportunity to see the written report. At that meeting, the parents ignored the initial reasons for referral for giftedness but elaborated on the incompetence of Derek's teacher and how they had dealt with the school around specific assignments. Attempts to discuss the test findings and their implications for Derek were neatly avoided.

The importance of communication and mental health professionals working together to examine family interaction patterns in relation to their child's language and communication problems is clear. Although mental health professionals have considerable experience working with the grieving process, communication specialists may see the family only as uncooperative. A situation such as Derek's may provide an opening for collaboration between communication and mental health specialists with the goal of understanding parents' resistance to accepting the assessment feedback and speculating about the function of a child's behavior in the family. Families such as these often continue to blame others for their child's performance but also, in time, may come to be able to hear the feedback.

For yet other families, where children have been scapegoated or where family members with similar problems do not want to face the fact that their child must endure similar struggles, change occurs more slowly or not at all. Moreover, affected children may become aligned with one parent against another or be scapegoated by both parents as different from siblings or as upsetting the family balance in some way. Such children's behavior can serve to maintain the family system in a predictable, albeit dysfunctional, way.

Case Example

Fifteen-year-old Ashley, a patient in a residential treatment center, was initially referred because of her violent and oppositional behavior. Her parents cited as examples of Ashley's difficult and noncompliant behavior numerous incidents when they would ask her a question and she would not respond, remaining sullenly silent. The language assessment indicated that Ashley had significant expressive language problems. The speech-language pathologist noted that Ashley often had trouble finding words but if given time was able to respond correctly. The feedback session was held with Ashley, her parents, the therapist, and the psychologist and speech-language pathologist who did the assessment. Both parents were surprised about the findings but seemed relieved to hear that there could be an alternate explanation for at least some of Ashley's behavior. At the end of the feedback session, as the family was leaving the room, Ashley's father asked her a question to which there was no immediate response. At that point, he turned to the examiner and said in an angry irritated voice, "You see what I mean?"

Ashley was struggling with academic expectations, on the one hand, and social and familial expectations, on the other. Although her language impairment was significant, this was nevertheless the first time that it had been diagnosed. Thus it was likely that the history of interactions between Ashley, her family, her school, and the community at large was based on erroneous attributions for some of Ashley's behavior, and hence labels such as "unmotivated," "resistant," "rude," and "having an attitude" were common. In reality, her acting-out behavior, delayed responding, withdrawal from school tasks and social engagements, and arguments and misunderstandings with family and peers stemmed at least in part from difficulties with language processing and communication. The feedback had an impact on Ashley's mother but clearly had not changed her father's attributions for Ashley's behavior. Given that the therapist also heard the feedback, it was hoped that, in time, some of Ashley's behavior could be reframed in family therapy sessions as a communication problem and incorporated in suggestions about modifying and adapting family communication. In the meantime, staff members in the residential unit were able to apply some of the examiner's recommendations in treatment for Ashley, including helping her understand that some of her difficulties were not her fault.

When collaborations work well, family members can feel increased motivation to seek goals for communication, language, learning, and social-emotional functioning. Many relatively simple recommendations made to parents can promote both communication and interpersonal growth. Such recommendations include ensuring eye contact before giving a direction; grouping directions into short, manageable units; not giving too many directions at one time; having the child repeat back what is said; asking specific rather than open-ended questions; giving the child extra time to respond; and reflecting back to the child the feelings and ideas that the parent thinks he or she may be experiencing when upset. This is optimal, but unfortunately the two-way interactional process between families and their children can be interrupted when a child or parent has difficulty communicating or when they are not able to accept the feedback and blame external factors such as the school or teacher.

Still other families are disorganized, and when overwhelmed by stresses, parent mental illness, or marital conflict, it may be difficult for them to attend to their children's language needs. Moreover, in these families individuals often do not expect to be listened to and often resort to yelling (Green, 1989). Also, in these families more than one family member might have problems with language processing and expression that contribute to their dysfunctional interactional style. The point here is that it may be difficult to actively engage family members in helping their child with LI. In these situations, a child's difficulties communicating and sustaining attention may actually worsen. Moreover, in cases where the parents do not support the teacher and are uninvolved in their children's school-related activities, the problems will be exacerbated because parents' support and involvement in education (Green, 1989) and in therapeutic interventions (Cohen, Kolers, & Bradley, 1987) is an important contributor to outcome. Although in many cases intervention needs to proceed without active family involvement, the door should be left open for collaboration down the road. Parents need time to think about and digest information, to make their own observations, and to talk with friends and professionals.

Clinicians have a responsibility to discuss and explore with the family situations in which the clinician's and the family's observations and decisions vary significantly, particularly when the child's behavior is ignored, underreported, or exaggerated. The difficulties for children with language and communication impairments in individual therapy can multiply in family therapy settings, where more than one person is often talking at one time and where conversation is often grammatically complex and emotionally loaded. It is often the case that children with LI have difficulty attending for sustained periods of time and some parents have difficulty adjusting their input to accommodate their child's special needs. Among clinicians' many roles is ensuring that adults do not talk about children in such a way as to exclude them from therapeutic conversations (Stacey, 1994). The clinician needs to highlight children's (and parents') stress in communicating and how this is reciprocally related to responses to the child. Optimally, family therapy helps family members to understand the source of some of the child's difficulties in social and emotional situations by exploring various family members' beliefs and attributions about the source of the child's difficulties. With communication assessment information at hand, it is important to work with families to determine what behaviors represent an attempt to communicate and to find more positive ways of dealing with behavior and to ascertain whether a child's symptoms serve a function in the family. It is also important to acknowledge that this may place a heavy responsibility on mental health clinicians who are not well versed in the nature of language and communicative development; this is where active collaboration with communication specialists is essential.

PROFESSIONAL COLLABORATION

The material reviewed in this chapter confirms that there are important overlaps between the work of mental health and of communication professionals. Mental health professionals often are not familiar with the nature of communication impairment and communication specialists are often not familiar with the nature of social-emotional disorders. Although mutual education regarding terminology, symptoms, prognosis, and treatment approaches is a necessary first step, it must be acknowledged that there is still often a gray area in differential diagnosis. Given the multiple needs of children with LI, the transactional interrelationships between a range of abilities, and children's social environmental context, service delivery for children with LI must be provided in a model that emphasizes collaboration of between professionals with one another and with families, active mediation, a functional and developmental orientation, and a systems approach. There is as yet little written regarding how to best collaborate, and the difficulties of such collaborative partnerships must be recognized. A new body of systematic research is required that acknowledges that language and communication impairments are lifelong conditions, that examines how existing knowledge can best be integrated into the assessment and treatment process, and that systematically evaluates treatments for children and adolescents with a history of LI.

For professionals working with children with social-emotional problems, an important first step is simply to be aware of the potential presence and influence of language and communication impairments and to consider alternate explanations for problem behavior and ruptures in learning and therapeutic environments. A second step is to tackle the complex task of understanding the specific contributions of language, communicative, and social-emotional problems to functioning, through comprehensive examination not only of language but of cognitive, social-cognitive, and academic abilities. Moreover, in each of these domains the child's developmental level should be determined and developmental movement facilitated in both specific skills and strategies for learning and affect regulation (Westby & Cutler, 1994). Furthermore, the impact of accurate and sensitive feedback from an integrative assessment concerning the intimate connection between language impairment and social-emotional disorder and social impairments that reach across school, work, and social relationships should not be underestimated as it is an intervention in itself. Such feedback provides children with LI and their families with a better understanding of the reasons for difficulties in learning in social contexts and an opportunity to accurately attribute some behaviors to genuine difficulties in communication rather than to an unwillingness to cooperate or a lack of interest in relationships. Obviously, collaboration must go beyond sharing assessment reports and single conversations during a feedback interview. Professionals need to work together to arrive at a diagnosis and an understanding of a child's problems in adjustment, determine necessary resources and strategies and the capacity of the child and the family to use these, and continue communication over time.

For communication specialists working with children with LI, traditionally, knowledge of social-emotional disorder was limited to autism and pervasive developmental disorders (Baltaxe & Simmons, 1990). It is only relatively recently that other forms of social-emotional problems have been discussed. As a starting point, communication specialists should become familiar with the terminology of social-emotional disorder, including broad terms such as *internalizing* and *externalizing* problems as well as the specific symptoms included in standardized behavioral rating scales. They should also gain familiarity with the specific criteria for psychiatric diagnoses to ascertain where there is an overlap between LI and social-emotional disorder and where there is not.

KEY POINTS

- Applying a developmental perspective means that treatment planning integrates information about various areas of development and influences on the developmental process. The intent of treatment is to interrupt maladaptive developmental processes in favor of those that promote learning and social-emotional growth.

- Adopting a developmental model also means facilitating development in affected domains rather than focusing on elimination of symptoms.

- Interventions to improve the communication and social-emotional functioning of infants and toddlers have shifted away from therapist-guided programs toward interventions that facilitate parents building mutually rewarding communicative and social-emotional development to foster development in both areas simultaneously.

- A number of interventions for children in the preschool period through adolescence have focused on building social relationships by improving pragmatic communication and social-cognitive skills. There is evidence that these need to take place over a long period of time and to be tailored to fit the needs of individual children if effects are to persist and generalize.

- The capacities to identify and label emotional cues, verbally interpret emotional states, and engage in discourse around interpersonal processes are important goals of social skills, behavioral, and psychotherapeutic interventions.

- The need to factor children's communicative impairments and competencies into a range of treatments has become increasingly obvious.

- Children's first and most enduring social communications are practiced in the family context. Consequently, understanding the mutual influences of family and child communicative capacity is essential in the assessment and treatment process.

- Because there are important overlaps in the work of communication specialists and mental health professionals, there is need to find a way of building collaborative partnerships that go beyond sharing assessment reports and single conversations. Professionals need to work together to understand children's problems, determine the resources and strategies and the capacity to use these, and maintain communication about children's needs and responses to intervention over time.

7

EPILOGUE

This book was stimulated by research spanning the years from infancy through adolescence indicating that a large proportion of children who receive mental health services have problems with language and communication and that these are often unsuspected unless a routine assessment is done. Thus, although on the surface there are many similarities in the problems children present to mental health clinics, these may be associated with markedly different underlying conditions, some of which are related to problems with language and communication.

Mounting evidence indicates that a life span approach to understanding the developmental trajectory for the interface of language and communication impairments with social-emotional disorder is essential for theoretical and practical purposes. Communication begins in the first days of life, and ongoing transactions with the physical and interpersonal environment set a course of development that can be interrupted for good or for ill. One hypothetical trajectory, in this case for development of Conduct Disorder, was proposed by Moffitt (1993). It illustrates how even relatively mild deficits in language might interact with environmental events to exert an influence at critical developmental turning points and ultimately have a significant long-term impact. The developmental path that Moffitt proposes starts with an infant who begins life with deficits, even mild ones, that could have arisen from a range of potential early constitutional differences, for instance, prenatal risks, genetic predisposition, and temperamental style. This early vulnerability sets into motion a chain of negative relational transactions that begin in infants' relationships with their parents and that "evoke a chain of failed parent-child encounters" (Moffitt, 1993, p. 139). These failed encounters might contribute to problems even in the earliest attachment relationships and continue as an escalating cycle of coercive parent-child encounters that have wide-ranging implications for both social-emotional relationships and educational attainment. Problems can also come about because the parents themselves have language impairments and emotional problems that limit the amount of verbal input and cognitive stimulation they can provide. Although Moffitt did not discuss pragmatic or discourse deficits, these could be added to the model. Even for parents who can provide adequate stimulation, children with LI show less interest in literacy activities and therefore are difficult to engage (Terrell, 1994). Such children enter school without the cognitive, linguistic, behavioral, or social prerequisites for learning and participating in the school culture. Children who start school who are not prepared to read are at risk for behavioral problems, peer rejection, and poor academic performance (Rutter & Giller, 1983). Moreover, the negative transactions begun at home spread to relationships with teachers and peers. Altogether, negative outcomes are most likely for children who grow up in a high-risk psychosocial environment; have weak verbal skills; and are exposed to an inconsistent, punitive, and insensitive parenting style. It also has been shown that an accumulation of experiences in children with LI can lead to increased anxiety (Beitchman et al., 2001; Cantwell & Baker, 1991). Thus a comparable trajectory might also be traced to anxiety. Research has supported some elements of Moffitt's model (Williams & McGee, 1996) but not others (Aguilar, Sroufe, Egeland, & Carlson, 2000). The point being made here has less to do with validating the details of this specific model than with emphasizing the importance of continuing to test and refine transactional models of development generally. These models are important for assessment and treatment because they potentially indicate not only how problems form but when and how a negative developmental course can be interrupted. In this context, we also need to determine whether there is something specific about language deficits, and this is still open to question. Some frameworks have been proposed for understanding the interrelationship between language and associated impairments (e.g., Bishop, 1992; Vygotsky, 1962), but more work needs to be done.

An important practical implication of the research findings summarized in this book is that there continue to be many children for whom language-based interventions are recommended who lack the basic skills to benefit from them. Currently, most interventions applied to children with social-emotional problems do not make examination of language skills a routine component of pretreatment assessment and posttreatment monitoring. As often as not, low achievement and social-emotional problems are attributed solely to psychosocial factors. Although I promote more routine assessment of language, communication, and associated conditions, I must also acknowledge that there are only a few instruments to assess some of the most important aspects of communication and pragmatic skills and social-cognitive functions that are integral to understanding the interface of language impairment and social-emotional disturbance. Using and improving current instruments along with developing new ones is an important undertaking.

Findings reviewed in this book have a number of implications for treatment. First, it should be recognized that giving feedback from assessment of language and communication skills is an important intervention in and of itself because understanding the source of children's difficulties helps parents, teachers, and clinicians make accurate attributions for children's behavior. Adults can be more empathetic with children whose misbehavior reflects a struggle to understand and communicate. Second, if we take to heart the idea that the goal of treatment is to move children ahead developmentally, then adaptive functioning should be facilitated in affected domains rather than focusing on elimination of symptoms that may be superficial signs of underlying difficulties. Third, understanding developmental processes necessarily involves taking a closer look at the therapeutic process as well as outcome (Russell, 1998; Shirk, 1998). Although there is considerable process research in the field of adult therapies, this is not the case in treatment research on infants and children. Fourth, measures of language and communicative competence must be increasingly included as outcomes in light of Russell et al.'s (1991) findings concerning the unexpected salutary effect of psychotherapy on language for some children and findings that mother-infant psychotherapy results in improved cognitive performance (Cohen et al., 1999).

Because there are important overlaps in the work of communication specialists and mental health professionals, there is a need to systematically evaluate the various ways of building collaborative partnerships that go beyond sharing assessment reports and single conversations. Mental health practitioners may be aware of children's language and communication problems in therapy but do not always have strategies for interweaving this knowledge in the treatment process. Similarly, speech-language pathologists are often at a loss as to how to deal with children's behavior problems so that they can proceed with helping children communicate more effectively. The solution is not to send a child away to the other professional until either the language or the social-emotional problem is fixed. Rather, professionals need to work together to understand the child's problems, determine the resources and strategies and the means of using these, and maintain communication about the child's needs and responses to interventions over time.

REFERENCES

Abikoff, H. (1985). Efficacy of cognitive training interventions in hyperactive children: A critical review. *Clinical Psychology Review, 5,* 479-512.

Achenbach, T. M. (1991a). *Manual for the Child Behavior Checklist/4-18 and 1991 Profile.* Burlington: University of Vermont Press.

Achenbach, T. M. (1991b). *Manual for the Youth Self-Report.* Burlington: University of Vermont Press.

Achenbach, T. M. (1992). *Child Behavior Checklist 2-3.* Burlington: University of Vermont Press.

Achenbach, T. M., & Edelbrock, C. (1986). *Manual for the Teacher's Report Form.* Burlington: University of Vermont, Department of Psychiatry.

Adams, W., & Sheslow, D. (1995). *Wide Range Assessment of Visual Motor Abilities.* Wilmington, DE: Wide Range Inc.

Adamson, L. B., & Bakeman, R. (1985). Affect and attention: Infants observed with mothers and peers. *Child Development, 56,* 582-593.

Adamson, L. B., & Chance, S. E. (1998). Coordinating attention to people, objects, and language. In A. M. Wetherby, S. F. Warren, & J. Reichle (Eds.), *Transitions in prelinguistic communication* (pp. 15-38). Baltimore, MD: Paul H. Brookes.

Aguilar, B., Sroufe, L. A., Egeland, B., & Carlson, E. (2000). Distinguishing the early-onset/persistent and adolescence-onset antisocial behavior types: From birth to 16 years. *Development and Psychopathology, 12,* 109-132.

Ainsworth, M. D. S., Blehar, M. C., Waters, E., & Wall, S. (1978). *Patterns of attachment: A psychological study of the Strange Situation.* Hillsdale, NJ: Lawrence Erlbaum.

American Psychiatric Association. (1994). *Diagnostic and statistical manual of mental disorders* (4th ed.). Washington, DC: Author.

American Speech-Language-Hearing Association Committee on Language, Speech and Hearing Services in the Schools. (1982). Definition: Communicative disorders and variations. *ASHA, 24,* 949-950.

Angold, A., Costello, E. J., Farmer, E. M. Z., Burns, B., & Erkanli, A. (1999). Impaired but undiagnosed. *Journal of the American Academy of Child and Adolescent Psychiatry, 38,* 129-137.

Asher, S. (1985). An evolving paradigm in social skills training research with children. In B. Schneider, K. Rubin, & J. Ledingham (Eds.), *Children's peer relations: Issues in assessment and intervention* (pp. 157-171). New York: Springer-Verlag.

Astington, J. W., & Jenkins, J. M. (1999). A longitudinal study of the relation between language and theory-of-mind development. *Developmental Psychology, 35,* 1311-1329.

Audet, L., & Ripich, D. (1994). Psychiatric disorders and discourse problems. In D. N. Ripich & N. A. Creaghead (Eds.), *School discourse problems* (pp. 191-227). San Diego, CA: Singular Publishing.

Baddeley, A. D. (1986). *Human memory: Theory and practice.* Hove, UK: Lawrence Erlbaum.

Bakeman, R., & Adamson, L. B. (1984). Coordinating attention to people and objects in mother-infant and peer-infant interactions. *Child Development, 55,* 1278-1289.

Baker, L., & Cantwell, D. P. (1987). A prospective psychiatric follow-up of children with speech/language disorders. *Journal of the American Academy of Child and Adolescent Psychiatry, 26,* 546-553.

Baltaxe, C. A. M., & Simmons, J. Q. (1988). Communication deficits in preschool children with psychiatric disorders. *Seminars in Speech and Language, 9,* 81-91.

Baltaxe, C. A. M., & Simmons, J. Q. (1990). The differential diagnosis of communication disorders in child and adolescent psychopathology. *Topics in Language Disorders, 10,* 17-31.

Barkley, R. (1997). Behavioral inhibition, sustained attention, and executive functions: Constructing a unifying theory of ADHD. *Psychological Bulletin, 121,* 65-94.

Barnard, K. E., Eyres, S., Lobo, M., & Snyder, C. (1983). An ecological paradigm for assessment and intervention. In T. B. Brazelton & B. M. Lester (Eds.), *New approaches to developmental screening of infants* (pp. 199-218). New York: Elsevier.

Baron-Cohen, S. (1995). *Mindblindness.* Cambridge: MIT Press.

Barrera, I. (1994). Thoughts on the assessment of young children whose sociocultural background is unfamiliar to the assessor. *Zero to Three, 13,* 9-13.

Barwick, M. A., Cohen, N. J., Horodezky, N. B., & Lojkasek, M. (2000). *Language and communication in relation to the mother-infant attachment relationship in clinic and community infants.* Manuscript submitted for publication.

Barwick, M., Im, N., & Cohen, N. J. (1995, April). *Parent and teacher attributions underlying psychiatric referral for children with unsuspected language and learning impairments.* Poster presented at the meeting of the Society for Research in Child Development, Indianapolis, IN.

Barwick, M. A., & Siegel, L. S. (1996). Learning difficulties in adolescent clients of a shelter for runaway and homeless street youths. *Journal of Research on Adolescence, 6,* 649-670.

Bates, E., Benigni, L., Bretherton, I., Camaioni, L., & Volterra, V. (1979). *The emergence of symbols: Cognition and communication in infancy.* New York: Academic Press.

Bates, E., Bretherton, I., & Snyder, L. (1988). *From first words to grammar.* New York: Cambridge University Press.

Bates, E., O'Connell, B., & Shore, C. (1987). Language and communication in infancy. In J. D. Osofsky (Ed.), *Handbook of infant development* (pp. 149-203). New York: John Wiley.

Bayley, N. (1993). *Bayley Scales of Infant Development–2.* San Antonio, TX: Psychological Corporation.

Beeghly, M., & Cicchetti, D. (1994). Child maltreatment, attachment, and the self system: Emergence of an internal state lexicon in toddlers at high social risk. *Development and Psychopathology, 6,* 5-30.

Beery, K. E., & Buktenica, N. A. (1997). *Developmental Test of Visual-Motor Integration.* Cleveland, OH: Modern Curriculum Press.

Beitchman, J. H., Brownlie, E. B., Inglis, A., Wild, J., Ferguson, B., & Schachter, D. (1996). Seven-year follow-up of speech/language impaired and control children: Psychiatric outcome. *Journal of the American Academy of Child and Adolescent Psychiatry, 37,* 961-970.

Beitchman, J. H., Brownlie, E. B., Inglis, A., Wild, J., Mathews, R., Schachter, D., Kroll, R., Martin, S., Ferguson, B., & Lancee, W. (1994). Seven year follow-up of speech/language impaired and control children: Speech/language stability and outcome. *Journal of the American Academy of Child and Adolescent Psychiatry, 33,* 1322-1330.

Beitchman, J. H., Brownlie, G. B., & Wilson, B. (1996). Linguistic impairment and psychiatric disorder: Pathways to outcome. In J. H. Beitchman, N. J. Cohen, M. M. Konstantareas, & R. Tannock (Eds.), *Language, learning, and behavior disorders: Developmental, biological, and clinical perspectives* (pp. 493-514). New York: Cambridge University Press.

Beitchman, J. H., Cohen, N. J., Konstantareas, M. M., & Tannock, R. (1996). *Language, learning, and behavior disorders: Developmental, biological, and clinical perspectives.* New York: Cambridge University Press.

Beitchman, J. H., Douglas, L., Wilson, B., Johnson, C., Young, A., Atkinson, L., Escobar, M., & Taback, N. (1999). Adolescent substance use disorder: Findings from a 14-year follow-up of speech/language-impaired and control children. *Journal of Clinical Child Psychology, 28,* 312-321.

Beitchman, J. H., Hood, J., Rochon, J., & Peterson, M. (1989). Empirical classification of speech/language impairment in children: II. Behavioral characteristics. *Journal of the American Academy of Child and Adolescent Psychiatry, 28,* 118-123.

Beitchman, J. H., Nair, R., Clegg, M., Ferguson, B., & Patel, P. G. (1986). Prevalence of psychiatric disorders in children with speech and language disorders. *Journal of the American Academy of Child Psychiatry, 25,* 528-535.

Beitchman, J. H., Nair, R., Clegg, M., & Patel, P. G. (1986). Prevalence of speech and language disorders in 5-year-old kindergarten children in the Ottawa-Carleton region. *Journal of Speech and Hearing Disorders, 51,* 98-110.

Beitchman, J. H., Tuckett, M., & Batth, S. (1987). Language delay and hyperactivity in preschoolers: Evidence for a distinct subgroup of hyperactives. *Canadian Journal of Psychiatry, 32,* 683-687.

Beitchman, J. H., Wilson, B., Brownlie, E. B., Walters, H., Inglis, A., & Lancee, W. (1996a). Long-term consistency in speech/language profiles: I. Developmental and academic outcomes. *Journal of the American Academy of Child and Adolescent Psychiatry, 35,* 804-814.

Beitchman, J. H., Wilson, B., Brownlie, E. B., Walters, H., Inglis, A., & Lancee, W. (1996b). Long-term consistency in speech/language profiles: II. Behavioral, emotional, and social outcomes. *Journal of the American Academy of Child and Adolescent Psychiatry, 35,* 815-825.

Beitchman, J. H., Wilson, B., Douglas, L., Young, A., & Adlaf, E. (in press). Substance use disorders in young adults with and without learning disabilities: Predictive and concurrent relationships. *Journal of Learning Disabilities.*

Beitchman, J. H., Wilson, B., Johnson, C. J., Atkinson, L., Young, A., Escobar, M., & Douglas, L. (2001). Fourteen-year follow-up of speech/language impaired and control children: Psychiatric outcome. *Journal of the American Academy of Child and Adolescent Psychiatry, 40,* 75-82.

Belsky, J., & Most, R. K. (1981). From exploration to play: A cross-sectional study of infant free play behavior. *Developmental Psychology, 20,* 630-639.

Benasich, A. A., Curtiss, S., & Tallal, P. (1993). Language, learning, and behavioral disturbances in childhood: A longitudinal perspective. *Journal of the American Academy of Child and Adolescent Psychiatry, 32,* 585-594.

Berk, L. E. (1994). Why children talk to themselves. *Scientific American, 271,* 78-83.

Berk, L. E., & Potts, M. K. (1991). Development and functional significance of private speech among attention-deficit hyperactivity disordered and normal boys. *Journal of Abnormal Psychology, 19,* 357-377.

Bierman, K. L., & Furman, W. (1984). The effects of social skills training and peer involvement on the social adjustment of preadolescents. *Child Development, 55,* 151-162.

Bishop, D. V. M. (1991). Developmental reading disabilities: The role of phonological processing has been overemphasised. *Mind and Language, 6,* 96-101.

Bishop, D. V. M. (1992). The underlying nature of specific language impairment. *Journal of Child Psychology and Psychiatry, 33,* 3-66.

Bishop, D. V. M. (1994). Grammatical errors in specific language impairment: Competence or performance limitations? *Applied Psycholinguistics, 15,* 507-550.

Bishop, D. V. M. (1996). Nonword repetition as a behavioural marker for inherited language impairment: Evidence from a twin study. *Journal of Child Psychology and Psychiatry, 37,* 391-403.

Bishop, D. V. M. (1997). *Uncommon understanding: Development and disorders of language comprehension in children.* Hove, UK: Psychology Press.

Bishop, D. V. M. (1998). Development of the Children's Communication Checklist (CCC): A method for assessing qualitative aspects of communicative impairment in children. *Journal of Child Psychology and Psychiatry, 39,* 879-891.

Bishop, D. V. M. (2000). Pragmatic language impairment: A correlate of SLI, a distinct subgroup, or part of the autistic continuum? In D. V. M. Bishop & L. B. Leonard (Eds.), *Speech and language impairments in children: Causes, characteristics, and outcome* (pp. 99-113). Hove, UK: Psychology Press.

Bishop, D. V. M., Chan, J., Adams, C., Hartley, J., & Weir, F. (2000). Evidence of disproportionate pragmatic difficulties in a subset of children with specific language impairment. *Development and Psychopathology, 12,* 177-200.

Bishop, D. V. M., & Edmundson, A. (1987a). Language-impaired 4-year-olds: Distinguishing transient from persistent impairment. *Journal of Speech and Hearing Disorders, 52,* 156-173.

Bishop, D. V. M., & Edmundson, A. (1987b). Specific language impairment as a maturational lag: Evidence from longitudinal data on language and motor development. *Developmental Medicine and Child Neurology, 29,* 442-459.

Bishop, D. V. M., North, T., & Donlan, C. (1995). Genetic basis of specific language impairment: Evidence from a twin study. *Developmental Medicine and Child Neurology, 37,* 56-71.

Bishop, D. V. M., North, T., & Donlan, C. (1996). Nonword repetition as a behavioural marker for inherited language impairment: Evidence from a twin study. *Journal of Child Psychology and Psychiatry, 37,* 391-403.

Bishop, D. V. M., & Rosenbloom, L. (1987). Classification and overview of child language disorders. In W. Yule & M. Rutter (Eds.), *Language development and disorders* (pp. 16-41). London: MacKeith.

Blager, F., & Martin, H. (1976). Speech and language of abused children. In H. P. Martin (Ed.), *The abused child* (pp. 83-92). Cambridge, MA: Ballinger.

Blake, J., Austin, W., Cannon, M., Lisus, A., & Vaughan, A. (1994). The relationship between memory span and measures of imitative and spontaneous language complexity in preschool children. *International Journal of Behavioral Development, 17,* 91-107.

Blank, M., Gessner, M., & Esposito, A. (1979). Language without communication: A case study. *Journal of Child Language, 6,* 329-352.

Bloom, L. (1993). *The transition from infancy to language.* New York: Cambridge University Press.

Bloom, L., & Beckwith, R. (1989). Talking with feeling: Integrating affective and linguistic expression in early language development. *Cognition and Emotion, 3,* 313-342.

Bloom, L., & Capatides, J. (1987). Expression of affect and the emergence of language. *Child Development, 58,* 1513-1522.

Bloom, L., & Lahey, M. (1978). *Language development and language disorders.* New York: John Wiley.

Bloomquist, M., August, G., Cohen, C., Doyle, A., & Everhart, K. (1997). Social problem solving in hyperactive-aggressive children: How and what they think in conditions of automatic and controlled processing. *Journal of Clinical Child Psychology, 26,* 172-180.

Bornstein, M. H., & Tamis-LeMonda, C. S. (1990). Activities and interactions of mothers and their first born infants in the first six months of life: Covariation, stability, continuity, correspondence, and prediction. *Child Development, 61,* 1206-1217.

Bornstein, M. H., & Tamis-LeMonda, C. S. (1997). Maternal responsiveness and infant mental abilities: Specific predictive relations. *Infant Behavior and Development, 20,* 283-296.

Bowers, L., Huisingh, R., Barrett, M., Orman, J., & LoGiudice, C. (1991). *Test of Problem Solving–Adolescent.* East Moline, IL: LinguiSystems.

Bowers, L., Huisingh, R., Barrett, M., Orman, J., & LoGiudice, C. (1994). *Test of Problem Solving–Revised Elementary.* East Moline, IL: LinguiSystems.

Bowlby, J. (1969). *Attachment and loss: Vol. 1. Attachment.* New York: Basic Books.

Bowlby, J. (1973). *Attachment and loss: Vol. 2. Separation.* New York: Basic Books.

Bradley, R. H., & Caldwell, B. M. (1984). 174 children: A study of the relationship between home environment and cognitive development during the first 5 years. In A. Gottfield (Ed.), *Home environment and early cognition development* (pp. 5-56). Orlando, FL: Academic Press.

Bretherton, I., McNew, S., & Beeghly-Smith, M. (1981). Early person knowledge as expressed in gestural and verbal communication: When do infants acquire a "theory of mind"? In M. Lamb & L. Sherrod (Eds.), *Infant social cognition* (pp. 333-373). Hillsdale, NJ: Lawrence Erlbaum.

Bricker, D., Squires, J., & Mounts, L. (1995). *Ages and Stages Questionnaire.* Chicago: Applied Symbolix.

Brinton, B., & Fujiki, M. (1982). A comparison of request-response sequences in the discourse of normal and language-disordered children. *Journal of Speech and Hearing Disorders, 47,* 57-62.

Brinton, B., & Fujiki, M. (1995). Conversational intervention with children with specific language impairment. In M. E. Fey, J. Windsor, & S. F. Warren (Eds.), *Language intervention: Preschool through the elementary years* (Vol. 5, pp. 183-212). Baltimore, MD: Paul H. Brookes.

Brinton, B., Fujiki, M., Winkler, E., & Loeb, D. (1986). Responses to requests for clarification in linguistically normal and language-impaired children. *Journal of Speech and Hearing Disorders, 51,* 370-378.

Brown, A. L., Bransford, J. D., Ferrara, R. A., & Campione, J. C. (1983). Learning, remembering, and understanding. In J. H. Flavell & E. M. Markman (Eds.), P. Mussen (Series Ed.), *Handbook of child psychology: Vol. 3. Cognitive development* (pp. 77-166). New York: John Wiley.

Brown, J. R., & Dunn, J. (1991). You can cry, mum: The social and developmental implications of talk about internal states. *British Journal of Developmental Psychology, 9,* 237-256.

Brown, J. R., & Dunn, J. (1992). Talk with your mother or your sibling? Developmental changes in early family conversations about feelings. *Child Development, 63,* 336-349.

Bruck, M. (1990). Word recognition skills of adults with childhood diagnoses of dyslexia. *Developmental Psychology, 26,* 439-454.

Bruck, M. (1992). Persistence of dyslexics' phonological awareness deficits. *Developmental Psychology, 28,* 874-886.

Bruner, J. (1975). From communication to language: A psychological perspective. *Cognition, 3,* 17-48.

Bruner, J. (1983). *Child's talk: Learning to use language.* New York: Norton.

Bruner, J. (1984). Interaction, communication, and self. *Journal of the American Academy of Child Psychiatry, 23,* 1-7.

Bryan, J. H., & Bryan, T. (1990). Social factors in learning disabilities: Attitudes and interactions. In G. T. Pavlidis (Ed.), *Perspectives on dyslexia* (Vol. 2, pp. 247-281). New York: John Wiley.

Burke, A. E., Crenshaw, D. A., Green, J., Schlosser, M. A., & Strocchia-Rivera, L. (1989). Influence of verbal ability on the expression of aggression in physically abused children. *Journal of the American Academy of Child and Adolescent Psychiatry, 28,* 215-218.

Bus, A. G., Belsky, J., van IJzendoorn, M. H., & Crnic, K. (1997). Attachment and bookreading patterns: A study of mothers, fathers, and their toddlers. *Early Childhood Research Quarterly, 12,* 81-98.

Bus, A. G., & van IJzendoorn, M. H. (1988). Attachment and early reading: A longitudinal study. *Journal of Genetic Psychology, 149,* 199-210.

Bus, A. G., & van IJzendoorn, M. H. (1992). Patterns of attachment in frequently and infrequently reading mother-child dyads. *Journal of Genetic Psychology, 153,* 395-403.

Camarata, S. M., Hughes, C. A., & Ruhl, K. L. (1988). Mild/moderate behaviorally disordered students: A population at risk for language disorders. *Language, Speech, and Hearing Services in Schools, 19,* 191-200.

Camp, B. W., Blom, G. E., Herbert, F., & vanDoorninck, W. J. (1977). "Think Aloud": A program for developing self-control in young aggressive boys. *Journal of Abnormal Child Psychology, 5,* 157-169.

Cantwell, D. P., & Baker, L. (1987). Clinical significance of children with communication disorders: Perspectives from a longitudinal study. *Journal of Child Neurology, 2,* 257-264.

Cantwell, D. P., & Baker, L. (1991). *Psychiatric and developmental disorders in children with communication disorder.* Washington DC: American Psychiatric Press.

Caplan, R. (1996). Discourse deficits in childhood schizophrenia. In J. Beitchman, N. J. Cohen, M. M. Konstantareas, & R. Tannock (Eds.), *Language, learning, and behavior disorders: Biological, developmental, and clinical perspectives* (pp. 156-177). New York: Cambridge University Press.

Carrow-Woolfolk, E. (1998). *Test for Auditory Comprehension of Language-3.* San Antonio, TX: Psychological Corporation.

Carson, D. K., Klee, T., Perry, C. K., Muskina, G., & Donaghy, T. (1998). Comparison of children with delayed and normal language at 24 months of age on measures of behavioral difficulties, social and cognitive development. *Infant Mental Health Journal, 19,* 59-75.

Cartledge, G., Frew, T., & Zaharias, J. (1985). Social skill needs of mainstreamed students: Peer and teacher perceptions. *Learning Disability Quarterly, 8,* 132-139.

Caulfield, M. B., Fischel, J. E., DeBaryshe, B. D., & Whitehurst, G. J. (1989). Behavioral correlates of developmental expressive language disorder. *Journal of Abnormal Child Psychology, 17,* 187-201.

Chamberlain, P., & Patterson, G. R. (1995). Discipline and child compliance in parenting. In M. Bornstein (Ed.), *Handbook of parenting: Vol. 4. Applied and practical parenting* (pp. 205-225). Mahwah, NJ: Lawrence Erlbaum.

Chapman, R. S. (2000). Children's language learning: An interactionist perspective. *Journal of Child Psychology and Psychiatry, 41,* 33-54.

Chatoor, I. (1986). *Mother/Infant/Toddler Play and Feeding Scales.* Washington, DC: Children's Hospital National Medical Center.

Chatoor, I., Menville, E., Getson, P., & O'Donnell, R. (1988). *Manual for observational scale for mother-infant interaction during feeding.* Unpublished manuscript, Children's Hospital National Medical Center, Washington, DC.

Cicchetti, D. (1993). Developmental psychopathology: Reactions, reflections, projections. *Developmental Review, 13,* 471-502.

Cicchetti, D., & Beeghly, M. (1987). Symbolic development in maltreated youngsters. *New Directions in Child Development, 36,* 47-68.

Cicchetti, D., & Cannon, T. D. (1999). Neurodevelopmental processes in the ontogenesis and epigenesis of psychopathology [Editorial]. *Development and Psychopathology, 11,* 375-394.

Cicchetti, D., Rogosch, F. A., & Toth, S. L. (2000). The efficacy of toddler-parent psychotherapy for fostering cognitive development in offspring of depressed mothers. *Journal of Abnormal Child Psychology, 28,* 135-148.

Cicchetti, D., & Toth, S. (1995). A developmental psychopathology perspective on child abuse and neglect. *Journal of the American Academy of Child and Adolescent Psychiatry, 34,* 541-565.

Clegg, J., Hollis, C., & Rutter, M. (1999, June). *Developmental language disorders: A longitudinal study of cognitive, social and psychiatric functioning.* Poster presented at the biennial meeting of the International Society for Research in Child and Adolescent Psychopathology, Barcelona, Spain.

Cohen, M. (1997). *Children's Memory Scale.* Toronto: Harcourt Brace.

Cohen, N. J. (1996). Psychiatrically disturbed children with unsuspected language impairments: Developmental differences in language and behavior. In J. H. Beitchman, N. J. Cohen, M. M. Konstantareas, & R. Tannock (Eds.), *Language, learning and behavior disorders: Developmental, biological, and clinical perspectives* (pp. 105-127). New York: Cambridge University Press.

Cohen, N. J. (in press). Developmental language disorders. In P. Howlin & O. Udwin (Eds.), *Outcomes in neurodevelopmental and genetic disorders.* Cambridge, UK: Cambridge University Press.

Cohen, N. J., Barwick, M., Horodezky, N. B., & Isaacson, L. (1996). Comorbidity of language and social-emotional disorders: Comparison of psychiatric outpatients and their siblings. *Journal of Clinical Child Psychology, 25,* 192-200.

Cohen, N. J., Barwick, M. A., Horodezky, N., Vallance, D. D., & Im, N. (1998). Language, achievement, and cognitive processing in psychiatrically disturbed children with previously identified and unsuspected language impairments. *Journal of Child Psychology and Psychiatry, 39,* 865-877.

Cohen, N. J., Bradley, S., & Kolers, N. (1987). Outcome evaluation of a therapeutic day treatment program for delayed and disturbed preschoolers. *Journal of the American Academy of Child and Adolescent Psychiatry, 26,* 687-693.

Cohen, N. J., Davine, M., Horodezky, N., Lipsett, L., & Isaacson, L. (1993). Unsuspected language impairment in psychiatrically disturbed children: Prevalence and language and behavioral characteristics. *Journal of the American Academy of Child and Adolescent Psychiatry, 32,* 595-603.

Cohen, N. J., Davine, M., & Meloche-Kelly, M. (1989). Prevalence of unsuspected language disorders in a child psychiatric population. *Journal of the American Academy of Child and Adolescent Psychiatry, 28,* 107-111.

Cohen, N. J., & Horodezky, N. B. (1998). Prevalence of language impairments in psychiatrically referred children at different ages: Preschool to adolescence [Letter to the editor]. *Journal of the American Academy of Child and Adolescent Psychiatry, 35,* 461-462.

Cohen, N. J., Im-Bolter, N., & Vallance, D. D. (2001). *Theory of mind and language functioning in mental health clinic and non-clinic samples.* Poster presented at the Society for Research in Child Development conference, Minneapolis, MN.

Cohen, N. J., Kolers, N., & Bradley, S. (1987). Predictors of the outcome of treatment in a therapeutic preschool. *Journal of the American Academy of Child and Adolescent Psychiatry, 26,* 829-833.

Cohen, N. J., Lojkasek, M., Muir, E., Muir, R., & Parker, C. J. (2000). *Six-month follow-up of two mother-infant psychotherapies: Convergence of therapeutic outcomes.* Manuscript submitted for publication.

Cohen, N. J., Menna, R., Vallance, D., Im, N., & Horodezky, N. (1998). Language, social cognitive processing, and behavioral characteristics of psychiatrically disturbed children with previously identified and unsuspected language impairments. *Journal of Child Psychology and Psychiatry, 39,* 853-864.

Cohen, N. J., Muir, E., Lojkasek, M., Muir, R., Parker, C. J., Barwick, M., & Brown, M. (1999). Watch, Wait, and Wonder: Testing the effectiveness of a new approach to mother-infant psychotherapy. *Infant Mental Health Journal, 20,* 429-451.

Cohen, N. J., Sullivan, J., Minde, K., Novak, C., & Helwig, C. (1981). Evaluation of the relative effectiveness of methylphenidate and cognitive behavior modification in the treatment of hyperactive kindergarten children. *Journal of Abnormal Child Psychology, 9,* 44-64.

Cohen, N. J., Vallance, D. D., Barwick, M., Im, N., Menna, R., Horodezky, N., & Isaacson, L. (2000). The interface between ADHD and language impairment: An examination of language, achievement, and cognitive processing. *Journal of Child Psychology and Psychiatry, 41,* 353-362.

Cohn, J. F., & Tronick, E. Z. (1987). Mother-infant face-to-face interaction: The sequence of dyadic states at 3, 6, and 9 months. *Developmental Psychology, 23,* 68-77.

Cole, P. M., Michel, M. K., & O'Donnell-Teti, L. (1994). The development of emotion regulation and dysregulation: A clinical perspective. *Monographs of the Society for Research in Child Development, 59*(2-3, Serial No. 240).

Conduct Problems Prevention Research Group. (1999a). Initial impact of the Fast Track prevention trial for conduct problems: I. The high-risk sample. *Journal of Consulting and Clinical Psychology, 67,* 631-647.

Conduct Problems Prevention Research Group. (1999b). Initial impact of the Fast Track prevention trial for conduct problems: II. Classroom effects. *Journal of Consulting and Clinical Psychology, 67,* 648-657.

Conners, C. K. (1997). *Conners Rating Scales–R.* Tonawanda, NY: Multi-Health Systems.

Cook, E. T., Greenberg, M. T., & Kusche, C. A. (1994). The relations between emotional understanding, intellectual functioning, and disruptive behavior problems in elementary-school-aged children. *Journal of Abnormal Child Psychology, 22,* 205-219.

Cooper, P. J., & Murray, L. (1997). The impact of psychological treatments of postpartum depression on maternal mood and infant development. In L. Murray & P. J. Cooper (Eds.), *Postpartum depression and child development* (pp. 201-220). New York: Guilford.

Coster, W., & Cicchetti, D. (1993). Research on the communicative development of maltreated children: Clinical implications. *Topics in Language Disorders, 13,* 25-38.

Coster, W. J., Gersten, M. S., Beeghly, M., & Cicchetti, D. (1989). Communicative functioning in maltreated toddlers. *Developmental Psychology, 25,* 1020-1029.

Crais, E. (1993). Families and professionals as collaborators in assessment. *Topics in Language Disorders, 14,* 29-40.

Crick, N. R., & Dodge, K. A. (1994). A review and reformulation of social information-processing mechanisms in children's social adjustment. *Psychological Bulletin, 115,* 74-101.

Crittenden, P. (1996). Language and psychopathology: An attachment perspective. In J. Beitchman, N. J. Cohen, M. M. Konstantareas, & R. Tannock, (Eds.), *Language, learning, and behavior disorders: Developmental, biological, and clinical perspectives* (pp. 59-77). New York: Cambridge University Press.

Cutting, A. L., & Dunn, J. (1999). Theory of mind, emotion understanding, language, and family background: Individual differences and interrelations. *Child Development, 70,* 853-865.

Dale, P. S. (1996). Parent report assessment of language and communication. In K. N. Cole, P. S. Dale, & D. J. Thal (Eds.), *Assessment of communication and language* (Vol. 6, pp. 161-182). Baltimore, MD: Paul H. Brookes.

DeGangi, G. A., Di Pietro, J. A., Greenspan, S. I., & Porges, S. W. (1991). Psychopathological characteristics of the regulatory disordered infant. *Infant Behavior and Development, 14,* 37-50.

DeGangi, J. A., & Greenspan, S. I. (1999). The effectiveness of short-term interventions in the treatment of inattention and irritability in toddlers. *Journal of Developmental and Learning Disorders, 1,* 277-298.

DeLoache, J. S. (1989). The development of representation in young children. In H. W. Reese (Ed.), *Advances in child development and behavior* (Vol. 22, pp. 1-27). San Diego, CA: Academic Press.

Denckla, M. B. (1996). Biological correlates of learning and attention: What is relevant to learning disability and Attention Deficit Hyperactivity Disorder? *Journal of Developmental and Behavioral Pediatrics, 17,* 114-119.

Denham, S. (1986). Social cognition, prosocial behavior, and emotion in preschoolers: Contextual validation. *Child Development, 57,* 194-201.

Dennis, M., Barnes, M. A., Wilkinson, M., & Humphreys, R. P. (1998). How children with head injury represent real and deceptive emotion in short narratives. *Brain and Language, 61,* 450-483.

Dixon, W. E., Jr., & Shore, C. (1997). Temperamental predictors of linguistic style during multiword acquisition. *Infant Behavior and Development, 20,* 99-103.

Dodge, K. A., Pettit, G. S., McClaskey, C. L., & Brown, M. M. (1986). Social competence in children. *Monographs of the Society for Research in Child Development, 51*(2, Serial No. 213).

Donahue, M. L., Hartis, D., & Cole, D. (1999). Research on interactions among oral language and emotional behavioral disorders. In D. L. Rogers-Adkinson & P. L. Griffith (Eds.), *Communication disorders and children with psychiatric and behavioral disorders* (pp. 69-98). San Diego, CA: Singular Publishing.

Donahue, M. L., Szymanski, C. M., & Flores, C. W. (1999). When "Emily Dickinson" met "Steven Spielberg": Assessing social information processing in literacy contexts. *Language, Speech, and Hearing Services in Schools, 30,* 274-284.

Dunn, J. (1996). Children's relationships: Bridging the divide between cognitive and social development. *Journal of Child Psychology and Psychiatry, 37,* 507-518.

Dunn, J., Bretherton, I., & Munn, P. (1987). Conversations about feeling states between mothers and their young children. *Developmental Psychology, 23,* 132-139.

Dunn, J., & Brown, J. (1991). Relationship talk about feelings and the development of affect regulation in early childhood. In J. Garber & K. Dodge (Eds.), *The development of emotion regulation and dysregulation* (pp. 89-110). Cambridge, UK: Cambridge University Press.

Dunn, J., Brown, J., & Beardsall, L. (1991). Family talk about feeling states and children's later understanding of others' emotions. *Developmental Psychology, 27,* 448-455.

Dunn, J., Brown, J., Slomkowski, C., Tesla, C., & Youngblade, L. (1991). Young children's understanding of other people's feelings and beliefs: Individual differences and their antecedents. *Child Development, 62,* 1352-1366.

Dunn, J., & Munn, P. (1987). The development of justification in disputes. *Developmental Psychology, 23,* 791-798.

Dunn, L. M., & Dunn, L. J. (1997). *Peabody Picture Vocabulary Test–Revised (Form L).* Circle Pines, MN: American Guidance Service.

Dunn, M., Flax, J., Sliwinski, M., & Aram, D. (1996). The use of spontaneous language measures as criteria for identifying children with specific language impairment: An attempt to reconcile clinical and research findings. *Journal of Speech and Hearing Research, 39,* 643-654.

Durlak, J. A., Fuhrman, T., & Lampman, C. (1991). Effectiveness of cognitive-behavioral therapy for maladapting children: A meta-analysis. *Psychological Bulletin, 110,* 204-214.

Easterbrooks, M. A., & Goldberg, W. A. (1984). Toddler development in the family: Impact of father involvement and parenting characteristics. *Developmental Psychology, 55,* 740-752.

Engel, S. (1996). The guy who went up the steep nicken: The emergence of story telling during the first three years. *Zero to Three, 17,* 1-9.

English, K., & Church, G. (1999). Unilateral hearing loss in children: An update for the 1990s. *Language, Speech, and Hearing Services in Schools, 30,* 26-31.

Eslinger, P. J. (1996). Conceptualizing, describing, and measuring components of executive function: A summary. In G. R. Lyon & N. A. Krasnegor (Eds.), *Attention, memory, and executive function* (pp. 367-396). Baltimore, MD: Paul H. Brookes.

Evans, M. (1996). Reticent primary grade children and their more talkative peers: Verbal, nonverbal and self concept characteristics. *Journal of Educational Psychology, 88,* 739-749.

Eyberg, S. M., Schuhmann, E. M., & Rey, J. (1998). Child and adolescent psychotherapy research: Developmental issues. *Journal of Abnormal Child Psychology, 26,* 71-82.

Farmer, M. (2000). Language and social cognition in children with specific language impairment. *Journal of Child Psychology and Psychiatry, 41,* 609-626.

Felton, R. H., & Wood, F. B. (1989). Cognitive deficits in reading disability and attention deficit disorder. *Journal of Learning Disabilities, 22,* 3-13.

Fenson, L., Dale, P., Reznick, S., Thal, D., Bates, E., Hartung, J., Pethick, S., & Reilly, J. (1993). *MacArthur Communicative Development Inventory.* San Diego, CA: Singular Publishing.

Fergusson, D. M., & Lynskey, M. T. (1997). Early reading difficulties and later conduct problems. *Journal of Child Psychology and Psychiatry, 38,* 899-907.

Fey, M. B. (1986). *Language intervention with young children.* Needham, MA: Allyn & Bacon.

Fischel, J. E., Whitehurst, G. J., Caulfield, M. B., & DeBaryshe, B. (1989). Language growth in children with expressive language delay. *Pediatrics, 82,* 218-227.

Fisher, L., Ames, E. W., Chisholm, K., & Savoie, L. (1997). Problems reported by parents of Romanian orphans adopted to British Columbia. *International Journal of Behavioral Development, 20,* 67-82.

Fivush, R. (1991). The social construction of personal narratives. *Merrill-Palmer Quarterly, 37,* 59-82.

Fivush, R., Haden, C., & Reese, E. (1996). Autobiographical knowledge and autobiographical memories. In D. C. Rubin (Ed.), *Remembering our past: Studies in autobiographical memory* (pp. 341-359). New York: Cambridge University Press.

Forness, S. R., & Kavale, K. A. (1996). Treating social skills deficits in children with learning disabilities: A meta-analysis of the research. *Learning Disabilities Quarterly, 19,* 2-13.

Fox, N. (Ed.). (1994). The development of emotion regulation: Biological and behavioral considerations. *Monographs of the Society for Research in Child Development, 59*(2-3, Serial No. 240).

Fraiberg, S., Adelson, E., & Shapiro, V. (1975). Ghosts in the nursery: A psychoanalytic approach to the problems of impaired infant-mother relationships. *Journal of Child Psychiatry, 14,* 387-421.

Frankenburg, W. K., Dodds, J., & Archer, P. (1990). *Denver II.* Denver, CO: Denver Developmental Materials.

Freeman, N. (2000). Communication and representation: Why mentalistic reasoning is a lifelong endeavor. In P. Mitchell & K. J. Riggs (Eds.), *Children's reasoning and the mind* (pp. 349-366). East Sussex, UK: Psychology Press.

Fujiki, M., Brinton, B., Morgan, M., & Hart, C. H. (1999). Withdrawn and sociable behavior of children with language impairment. *Language, Speech, and Hearing Services in Schools, 30,* 183-195.

Fujiki, M., Brinton, B., & Todd, C. M. (1996). Social skills of children with specific language impairment. *Language, Speech, and Hearing Services in Schools, 27,* 195-202.

Furman, W., & Garvin, L. (1989). Peers' influence on adjustment and development. In T. Berndt & G. Ladd (Eds.), *Peer relationships in child development* (pp. 319-340). New York: John Wiley.

Gallagher, T. M. (1993). Language skill and the development of social competence in school-age children. *Language, Speech, and Hearing Services in the Schools, 24,* 199-205.

Gallagher, T. M. (1996). Social-interactional approaches to child language intervention. In J. H. Beitchman, N. J. Cohen, M. M. Konstantareas, & R. Tannock (Eds.), *Language, learning, and behavior disorders: Developmental, biological, and clinical perspectives* (pp. 418-435). New York: Cambridge University Press.

Gallagher, T. M. (1999). Interrelationships among children's language, behavior, and emotional problems. *Topics in Language Disorders, 19,* 1-14.

Gallagher, T. M., & Craig, H. K. (1984). Pragmatic assessment: Analysis of a highly frequent repeated utterance. *Journal of Speech and Hearing Disorders, 49,* 368-377.

Gascon, G., Johnson, R., & Burd, L. (1986). Central auditory processing and attention deficit disorders. *Journal of Child Neurology, 1,* 27-33.

Gardner, M. F. (2000). *Expressive One-Word Picture Vocabulary Test.* Novato, CA: Academic Therapy Publications.

Gathercole, S. E. (1998). The development of memory. *Journal of Child Psychology and Psychiatry, 39,* 3-27.

Gathercole, S. E., & Baddeley, A. (1990). Phonological memory deficits of language disordered children: Is there a causal connection? *Journal of Memory and Language, 29,* 336-369.

Ge, X., Conger, R. D., Cadoret, R. J., Neiderhiser, J. M., Yates, W., Troughton, E., & Stewart, M. A. (1996). The developmental interface between nature and nurture: A mutual influence model of child antisocial behavior and parenting. *Developmental Psychology, 32,* 574-589.

Gersten, M., Coster, W., Schneider-Rosen, K., Carlson, V., & Cicchetti, D. (1986). The socioemotional bases of communicative functioning: Quality of attachment, language development, and early maltreatment. In M. E. Lamb, A. L. Brown, & B. Rogoff (Eds.), *Advances in developmental psychology* (Vol. 4, pp. 105-151). Hillsdale, NJ: Lawrence Erlbaum.

Giddan, J. J., Bade, K. M., Rickenberg, D., & Ryley, A. T. (1995). Teaching the language of feelings to students with severe emotional and behavioral handicaps. *Language, Speech, and Hearing Services in Schools, 26,* 3-10.

Gillam, R. B., & Johnston, J. R. (1985). Development of print awareness in language disordered preschoolers. *Journal of Speech and Hearing Research, 28,* 521-526.

Girolametto, L., Pearce, P. S., & Weitzman, E. (1997). Effects of lexical intervention on the phonology of late talkers. *Journal of Speech, Language, and Hearing Research, 40,* 338-348.

Girolametto, L., Verbey, M., & Tannock, R. (1994). Improving joint engagement in parent-child interaction: An intervention study. *Journal of Early Intervention, 18,* 155-167.

Goldfried, M. R., & Wolfe, B. E. (1998). Toward a more clinically valid approach to therapy research. *Journal of Consulting and Clinical Psychology, 66,* 143-150.

Goldstein, H., & Gallagher, J. (1992). Strategies for promoting the social-communicative competence of young children with specific language impairment. In S. Odom, S. McConnell, & M. McEvoy (Eds.), *Social competence of young children with disabilities* (pp. 189-214). Baltimore, MD: Paul H. Brookes.

Goldstein, H., & Wickstrom, S. (1986). Peer intervention effects on communicative-interaction among handicapped and nonhandicapped preschoolers. *Journal of Applied Behavior Analysis, 19,* 209-214.

Goldstein, H., Wickstrom, S., Hoyson, M., Jamieson, B., & Odom, S. (1988). Effects of sociodramatic play training on social and communicative interaction. *Education and Treatment of Children, 11,* 97-117.

Gopnik, A., & Meltzoff, A. N. (1986). Relations between semantic and cognitive development in the one-word stage: The specificity hypothesis. *Child Development, 57,* 1040-1053.

Gough, P. B., & Wren, S. (1998). The decomposition of decoding. In C. Hulme & R. M. Joshi (Eds.), *Reading and spelling: Development and disorders* (pp. 19-32). Mahwah, NJ: Lawrence Erlbaum.

Graham, S., & Harris, K. R. (1999). Assessment and intervention in overcoming writing difficulties: An illustration from the self-regulated strategy developmental model. *Language, Speech, and Hearing Services in Schools, 30,* 255-264.

Green, R. J. (1989). "Learning to learn" and the family system: New perspectives on underachievement and learning disorders. *Journal of Marital and Family Therapy, 15,* 187-203.

Greenberg, M. T., Kusche, C. A., Cook, E. A., & Quamma, J. (1995). Promoting emotional competence in school-aged children: The effects of the PATHS curriculum. *Development and Psychopathology, 7,* 117-136.

Greenberg, M. T., Kusche, C. A., & Speltz, M. (1990). Emotional regulation, self control and psychopathology: The role of relationships in early childhood. In D. Cicchetti & S. Toth

(Eds.), *Rochester symposium on developmental psychopathology* (Vol. 2, pp. 21-55). New York: Cambridge University Press.

Greenspan, S. (1992). *Infancy and early childhood: The practice of clinical assessment and intervention with emotional and developmental challenges*. Madison, CT: International Universities Press.

Grice, J. P. (1975). Logic and conversation. In P. Cole & J. L. Morgan (Eds.), *Syntax and semantics* (pp. 41-58). New York: Academic Press.

Griffith, P. L., Rogers-Adkinson, D. L., & Cusick, G. M. (1997). Comparing language disorders in two groups of students with severe behavioral disorders. *Behavioral Disorders, 22,* 160-166.

Grigorenko, E. L., Wood, F. B., Meyer, M. S., Hart, L., A., Speed, W. C., Shuster, A., & Pauls, D. L. (1997). Susceptibility loci for distinct components of developmental dyslexia on chromosome 6 and 16. *American Journal of Human Genetics, 60,* 27-39.

Gualtieri, T., Koriath, U., Van Bourgondien, M., & Saleeby, N. (1983). Language disorders in children referred for psychiatric services. *Journal of the American Academy of Child and Adolescent Psychiatry, 22,* 165-171.

Guralnick, M. J. (1990). Social competence and early intervention. *Journal of Early Intervention, 14,* 3-14.

Hadley, P., & Rice, M. (1991). Conversational responsiveness of speech- and language-impaired preschoolers. *Journal of Speech and Hearing Research, 34,* 1308-1317.

Halliday, M. A. K., & Hasan, R. (1976). *Cohesion in English*. London: Longman.

Halperin, J. M., & McKay, K. (1998). Psychological testing for child and adolescent psychiatrists: A review of the past 10 years. *Journal of the American Academy of Child and Adolescent Psychiatry, 37,* 575-584.

Hammill, D. (1998). *Detroit Tests of Learning Aptitude–Fourth Edition*. Austin TX: Pro-Ed.

Hammill, D. D., Brown, V. L., Larsen, S. C., & Wiederholt, J. L. (1994). *Test of Adolescent and Adult Language–3*. San Antonio, TX: Psychological Corporation.

Happé, F., & Frith, L. (1996). Theory of mind and social impairment in children with conduct disorder. *British Journal of Developmental Psychology, 14,* 385-398.

Hart, B., & Risley, T. R. (1995). *Meaningful differences in the everyday experience of young American children*. Baltimore, MD: Paul H. Brookes.

Harter, S. (1999). *The construction of the self: A developmental perspective*. New York: Guilford.

Hay, D. F., Pawlby, S., Sharp, D., Mills, A., Asten, P., Allen, H., & Kumar, A. R. (2000, July). *Cognitive and behavioural problems in 11 year olds whose mothers had postpartum mood disorders*. Paper presented at the International Conference on Infant Studies, Brighton, UK.

Hayden, D. A., & Pukonen, M. (1996). Language intervention programming for preschool children with social and pragmatic disorder. In J. H. Beitchman, N. J. Cohen, M. M. Konstantareas, & R. Tannock (Eds.), *Language, learning, and behavior disorders: Developmental, biological, and clinical perspectives* (pp. 436-467). New York: Cambridge University Press.

Hembree-Kigin, J. L., & McNeil, C. B. (1995). *Parent-child interactional therapy*. New York: Plenum.

Hinshaw, S. (1992). Externalizing behavior problems and academic underachievement in childhood and adolescence: Causal relationships and underlying mechanisms. *Psychological Bulletin, 111,* 127-135.

Hinshaw, S. P., Lahey, B. B., & Hart, E. L. (1993). Issues of taxonomy and comorbidity in the development of conduct disorder. *Development and Psychopathology, 5,* 31-50.

Hoagwood, K., Jensen, P. J., Petti, T., & Burns, B. J. (1996). Outcomes of mental health care for children and adolescents: I. A comprehensive conceptual model. *Journal of the American Academy of Child and Adolescent Psychiatry, 35,* 1055-1063.

Hodges, K. (1991). *Child Assessment Schedule.* Lansing: Michigan State University.

Hohnen, B., & Stevenson, J. (1999). The structure of genetic influences on general cognitive, language, phonological, and reading abilities. *Developmental Psychology, 35,* 590-603.

Hossain, Z., Field, T., Gonzalez, J., Malphurs, J., & Del Valle, C. (1994). Infants of "depressed" mothers interact better with their nondepressed fathers. *Infant Mental Health Journal, 15,* 348-357.

Howlin, P., Mawhood, L., & Rutter, M. (2000). Autism and developmental receptive language disorder—a comparative follow-up in early adult life: II. Social, behavioural, and psychiatric outcomes. *Journal of Child Psychology and Psychiatry, 41,* 561-578.

Howlin, P., & Rutter, M. (1987). The consequences of language delay for other aspects of development. In W. Yule & M. Rutter (Eds.), *Language development and disorders* (pp. 271-294). Oxford, UK: Blackwell.

Hughes, C., Dunn, J., & White, A. (1998). Trick or treat? Uneven understanding of mind and emotion and executive dysfunction in "hard-to-manage" preschoolers. *Journal of Child Psychology and Psychiatry, 39,* 981-994.

Hummel, L. J., & Prizant, B. M. (1993). A socioemotional perspective for understanding social difficulties of school-age children with language disorders. *Language, Speech, and Hearing Services in the Schools, 24,* 216-224.

Huntington, D. D., & Bender, W. D. (1993). Adolescents with learning disabilities at risk? Emotional well-being, depression, suicide. *Journal of Learning Disabilities, 26,* 159-166.

Jensen, P. S., Brooks-Gunn, J., & Graber, J. A. (1999). Dimensional scales and diagnostic categories: Constructing crosswalks for child psychopathology assessment. *Journal of the American Academy of Child and Adolescent Psychiatry, 38,* 118-120.

Johnson, C. J., Beitchman, J. H., Young, A., Escobar, M., Atkinson, L., Wilson, B., Brownlie, E. B., Douglas, L., Taback, N., Lam, I., & Wang, M. (1999). Fourteen-year follow-up of children with and without speech/language: Stability and outcomes. *Journal of Speech, Language, and Hearing Research, 42,* 744-760.

Johnson, M. H. (2000). Functional brain development in infants: Elements of an interactive specialization framework. *Child Development, 71,* 75-81.

Johnston, J. K. (1988). Specific language disorders in the child. In N. J. Lass, L. V. McReynolds, J. Northern, & D. Yoder (Eds.), *Handbook of speech language pathology and audiology* (pp. 685-715) Toronto: B. C. Decker.

Jung, J. (1987). *Genetic syndromes in communication disorder.* London, ON: College-Hill Press.

Kagan, J. (1984). *The nature of the child.* New York: Basic Books.

Kail, R. (1984). *The development of memory in children* (2nd ed.). New York: Freeman.

Kaler, S. R., & Kopp, C. (1990). Compliance and comprehension in very young toddlers. *Child Development, 61,* 1997-2003.

Kamhi, A. G., & Catts, H. W. (1999). Reading development. In H. W. Catts & A. G. Kamhi (Eds.), *Language and reading disabilities* (pp. 25-50). Needham Heights, MA: Allyn & Bacon.

Kaplan, P. S., Bachorowski, J.-A., & Zarlengo-Strouse, P. (1999). Child-directed speech produced by mothers with symptoms of depression fails to promote associative learning in 4-month-old infants. *Child Development, 70,* 560-570.

Karlsen, B., & Gardner, E. F. (1995). *Standard Diagnostic Reading Test–4.* San Antonio, TX: Harcourt Brace.

Kaufman, A. S., & Kaufman, N. L. (1993). *Kaufman Assessment Battery for Children.* Circle Pines, MN: American Guidance Service.

Kazdin, A. (1995). Bridging child, adolescent, and adult psychotherapy: Directions for research. *Psychotherapy Research, 5,* 258-277.

Kazdin, A. E. (1997). A model for developing effective treatments: Progression and interplay of theory, research, and practice. *Journal of Clinical Child Psychology, 26,* 114-129.

Kazdin, A. E., Siegel, T., & Bass, D. (1992). Cognitive problem-solving skills training and parent management training in the treatment of antisocial behavior in children. *Journal of Consulting and Clinical Psychology, 60,* 733-747.

Kellam, S. G., Brown, C. H., Rubin, B. R., & Ensminger, M. E. (1983). Paths leading to teenage psychiatric symptoms and substance use: developmental, epidemiological studies in Woodlawn. In S. B. Guzo, F. J. Earls, & J. E. Barratt (Eds.), *Childhood psychopathology and development* (pp. 17-51). New York: Raven Press.

Kelly, J. F., Morisset, C. E., Barnard, K. E., Hammond, M. A., & Booth, C. L. (1996). The influence of early mother-child interaction on preschool cognitive/linguistic outcomes in a high-socio-risk group. *Infant Mental Health Journal, 17,* 310-324.

Kerns, K. A., Tomich, P. L., Aspelmeier, J. E., & Contreras, J. M. (2000). Attachment-based assessments of parent-child relationships in middle childhood. *Developmental Psychology, 36,* 614-626.

Klackenberg, G. (1980). What happens to children with retarded speech at 3? Longitudinal study of a sample of normal infants up to 20 years of age. *Acta Paediatrica Scandinavica, 69,* 681-685.

Klinnert, M. D., Campos, J. J., Sorce, J. F., Emde, R. N., & Svejda, M. (1983). Emotions as behavior regulators: Social referencing in infancy. In R. Plutchik & H. Kellerman (Eds.), *The emotions: Vol. 2. Emotions in early development* (pp. 57-86). New York: Academic Press.

Kopp, C. B. (1982). Antecedents of self regulation: A developmental perspective. *Developmental Psychology, 18,* 199-214.

Kopp, C. B. (1989). Regulation of distress and negative emotion: A developmental view. *Developmental Psychology, 25,* 343-354.

Korkman, M., Kirk, U., & Kemp, S. (1997). *NEPSY.* San Antonio, TX: Psychological Corporation.

Kotsopoulos, A., & Boodoosingh, L. (1987). Language and speech disorders in children attending a day psychiatric programme. *British Journal of Disorders of Communication, 22,* 227-236.

Kovacs, M. (1992). *Children's Depression Inventory.* Toronto: MultiHealth Systems.

Kristensen, H. (2000). Selective mutism and comorbidity with developmental disorder/delay, anxiety disorder, and elimination disorder. *Journal of the American Academy of Child and Adolescent Psychiatry, 39,* 249-256.

Kuhl, P. (1980). *Naming and necessity.* Cambridge, MA: Harvard University Press.

Kuvshinoff, B. E., & Creaghead, N. A. (1994). Literacy in elementary school: Getting started. In D. N. Ripich & N. A. Creaghead (Eds.), *School discourse problems* (pp. 29-62). San Diego, CA: Singular Press.

Ladd, G. W. (1990). Having friends, helping friends, making friends, and being liked by peers in the classroom: Predictors of children's early school adjustment? *Child Development, 61,* 1081-1100.

LaPlante, D. P., Zelazo, P. R., & Kearsley, R. B. (1991). The effect of a short-term parent implemented treatment program on the production of expressive language. *Society for Research in Child Development Abstracts, 8,* 336.

Leonard, L. (1997). *Children with specific language impairment.* Cambridge: MIT Press.

Levine, M. (1994). *Educational care: A system for understanding and helping children with learning problems at home and in school.* Cambridge, MA: Educators Publishing Service.

Lezak, M. D. (1995). *Neuropsychological assessment* (3rd ed.). New York: Oxford University Press.

Lieberman, A. F. (1993). *The emotional life of the toddler.* New York: Free Press.

Lieberman, A. F., Weston, D. R., & Pawl, J. H. (1991). Preventive intervention and outcome with anxiously attached dyads. *Child Development, 62,* 199-209.

Liles, B., Duffy, R. J., Merritt, D. D., & Purcell, S. L. (1995). Measurement of narrative discourse ability in children with language disorders. *Journal of Speech and Hearing Research, 38,* 415-425.

Liles, B. S. (1985a). Cohesion in the narratives of normal and language-disordered children. *Journal of Speech and Hearing Research, 28,* 123-133.

Liles, B. S. (1985b). Production and comprehension of narrative discourse in normal and language disordered children. *Journal of Communication Disorders, 18,* 409-427.

Linder, T. (1993). *Transdisciplinary play-based assessment: A functional approach to working with young children* (Rev. ed.). Baltimore, MD: Paul H. Brookes.

Lipsky, D. K. (1985). A parental perspective on stress and coping. *American Journal of Orthopsychiatry, 55,* 614-617.

Lively, P. (1987). *Moon tiger.* London: Penguin.

Lochman, J. E., & Dodge, K. A. (1994). Social-cognitive processes of severely violent, moderately aggressive, and nonaggressive boys. *Journal of Consulting and Clinical Psychology, 62,* 366-374.

Locke, J. L. (1993). *The child's path to spoken language.* Cambridge, MA: Harvard University Press.

Loeber, R., Wung, P., Keenan, K., Giroux, B., Stouthamer-Loeber, M., Van Kammen, W. B., & Maughan, B. (1993). Developmental pathways in disruptive child behavior. *Development and Psychopathology, 5,* 103-133.

Lord, C., & Pickles, A. (1996). Language level and nonverbal social-communicative behaviors in autistic and language-delayed children. *Journal of American Academy of Child and Adolescent Psychiatry, 35,* 1542-1550.

Love, A., & Thompson, M. G. G. (1988). Language disorders and attention deficit disorders in young children referred for psychiatric services. *American Journal of Orthopsychiatry, 58,* 52-63.

Luria, A. R. (1961). *The role of speech in the regulation of normal and abnormal behavior.* Oxford, UK: Pergamon.

Main, M. (1995). Recent studies in attachment. In S. Goldberg, R. Muir, & J. Kerr (Eds.), *Attachment theory: Social, developmental, and clinical perspectives* (pp. 437-473). Hillsdale, NJ: Analytic Press.

Main, M., Kaplan, N., & Cassidy, J. (1985). Security in infancy, childhood and adulthood: A move to the level of representation. In I. Bretherton & E. Waters (Eds.), Growing points of attachment theory and research. *Monographs of the Society for Research on Child Development, 50,* 66-106.

Main, M., & Solomon, J. (1986). Discovery of an insecure disorganized disoriented attachment pattern. In T. Brazelton & M. W. Yogman (Eds.), *Affective development in infancy* (pp. 95-124). Norwood, NJ: Ablex.

Manolson, A. (1985). *Hanen Early Language Parent Program.* Toronto: The Hanen Centre.

Manolson, A. (1992). *It takes two to talk* (2nd ed.). Toronto: Hanen Early Language Resource Centre.

Mariani, M. A., & Barkley, R. A. (1997). Neuropsychological and academic functioning in preschool boys with Attention Deficit Hyperactivity Disorder. *Developmental Neuropsychology, 13,* 111-129.

Maughan, B. (1995). Annotation: Long-term outcomes of developmental reading problems. *Journal of Child Psychology and Psychiatry, 36,* 357-371.

Mawhood, L., Howlin, P., & Rutter, M. (2000). Autism and developmental receptive language disorder—a comparative follow-up in early adult life: I. Cognitive and language outcomes. *Journal of Child Psychology and Psychiatry, 41,* 547-560.

McClellan, J. M., & Werry, J. S. (2000). Special section: Diagnostic interviews. *Journal of the American Academy of Child and Adolescent Psychiatry, 39,* 19-99.

McCune-Nicolich, L. (1977). Beyond sensorimotor intelligence: Assessment of symbolic maturity through analysis of pretend play. *Merrill-Palmer Quarterly, 23,* 89-99.

McCune-Nicolich, L. (1981). Toward symbolic functioning: Structure of early pretend games and potential parallels with language. *Child Development, 52,* 785-797.

McFadyen, R. G., & Kitson, W. J. H. (1996). Language comprehension and expression among adolescents who have experienced childhood physical abuse. *Journal of Child Psychology and Psychiatry, 37,* 551-562.

McGee, R., Share, D., Moffitt, T. E., Williams, S., & Silva, P. A. (1988). Reading disability, behaviour problems, and juvenile delinquency. In D. H. Saklofske & S. B. G. Eysenck (Eds.), *Individual differences in children and adolescents: International perspective* (pp. 158-172). London: Hodderd Stoughton.

McGee, R., Williams, S., Share, D. L., Anderson, J., & Silva, P. (1986). The relationship between specific reading retardation, general reading backwardness, and behavioural problems in a large sample of Dunedin boys: A longitudinal study from five to eleven years. *Journal of Child Psychology and Psychiatry, 27,* 597-610.

Mehler, J., Jusczyk, P., Lambert, G., Halsted, N., Bertoncini, J., & Amiel-Tison, C. (1988). A precursor of language acquisition in young infants. *Cognition, 29,* 143-178.

Meins, E. (1997). *Security of attachment and the social development of cognition.* Hove, UK: Psychology Press.

Meisels, S. J., & Fenichel, E. (Eds.). (1996). *New visions for the developmental assessment of infants and young children.* Landover, MD: Corporate Press.

Menna, R., & Cohen, N. J. (1997). Social perspective taking. In M. McCallum & W. E. Piper (Eds.), *Psychological mindedness: A contempory understanding* (pp. 189-210). Mahwah, NJ: Lawrence Erlbaum.

Miller, P. J., Mintz, J., Hoogstra, L., Fung, H., & Potts, R. (1992). The narrated self: Young children's construction of self in relation to others in conversational stories of personal experience. *Merrill-Palmer Quarterly, 38,* 45-67.

Moffitt, T. E. (1993). Neuropsychology of conduct disorders. *Development and Psychopathology, 5,* 135-151.

Montgomery, J. W. (1992). Easily overlooked language disabilities during childhood and adolescence. *Pediatric Clinics of North America, 39,* 513-524.

Morisset, C. E., Barnard, K. E., Greenberg, M. T., Booth, C. L., & Spieker, S. J. (1990). Environmental influences on early language development: The context of social risk. *Development and Psychopathology, 2,* 127-149.

Muir, E., Lojkasek, M., & Cohen, N. J. (1999). *Watch, Wait, and Wonder: A manual describing a
dyadic infant-led approach to problems in infancy and early childhood.* Toronto: Hincks-
Dellcrest Institute.

Mundy, P., & Gomes, A. (1998). Individual differences in joint attention skill development in the
second year. *Infant Behavior and Development, 21,* 469-482.

Mundy, P., Kasari, C., & Sigman, M. (1992). Nonverbal communication, affective sharing, and
intersubjectivity. *Infant Behavior and Development, 15,* 377-381.

Mundy, P., & Willoughby, J. (1998). Nonverbal communication, affect, and social-emotional
development. In A. M. Wetherby, S. F. Warren, & J. Reichle (Eds.), *Transitions in prelinguistic communication* (pp. 111-133). Baltimore, MD: Paul H. Brookes.

Murray, A. D., & Hornbaker, A. V. (1997). Maternal directive and facilitative interaction styles:
Associations with language and cognitive development of low risk and high risk toddlers.
Development and Psychopathology, 9, 507-516.

Murray, L. (1992). The impact of postnatal depression on infant development. *Journal of Child
Psychology and Psychiatry, 33,* 543-561.

Murray, L., Hipwell, A., Hooper, R., Stein, A., & Cooper, P. (1996). The cognitive development
of 5-year-old children of postnatally depressed mothers. *Journal of Child Psychology and
Psychiatry, 37,* 927-935.

Murray, L., Kempton, C., Woolgar, M., & Hooper, R. (1993). Depressed mothers' speech to their
infants and its relation to infant gender and cognitive development. *Journal of Child Psychology and Psychiatry, 7,* 1083-1101.

Myers, W. C., & Mutch, P. J. (1992). Language disorders in disruptive behavior disordered homi-
cidal youth. *Journal of Forensic Sciences, 37,* 919-922.

Nation, K., & Snowling, M. J. (1998). Individual differences in contextual facilitation: Evidence
from dyslexia and poor reading comprehension. *Child Development, 69,* 996-1011.

National Institute on Deafness and Other Communicative Disorders. (1995). *National strategic
research plan for language and language impairments, balance and balance disorders,
and voice disorders* (NIH Publication No. 97-3217). Bethesda, MD: Author.

Naylor, M. W., Staskowski, M., Kenney, M. C., & King, C. A. (1994). Language disorders and
learning disabilities in school-refusing adolescents. *Journal of the American of Academy
of Child and Adolescent Psychiatry, 33,* 1331-1337.

Nelson, K. (1973). Structure and strategy in learning to talk. *Monographs of the Society for
Research in Child Development, 38*(1-2, Serial No. 149).

Nelson, K. (1981). Social cognition in a script framework. In J. Flavell & L. Ross (Eds.), *Social
cognitive development* (pp. 97-118). New York: Cambridge University Press.

Nelson, K. (1986). *Event knowledge: Structure and function in development.* Hillsdale, NJ:
Lawrence Erlbaum.

Nelson, K. (1989). *Monologue as representation of real-life experience* (pp. 27-72). Cambridge,
MA: Harvard University Press.

Nelson, K. (1993). The psychological and social origins of autobiographical memory. *Psychological Science, 4,* 1-8.

Nelson, K. (1996). *Language in cognitive development: The emergence of the mediated mind.*
New York: Cambridge University Press.

Newcomer, D. D., & Hammill, P. L. (1997). *Test of Language Development–3 Intermediate.* Austin, TX: Pro-Ed.

Nicely, P., Tamis-LeMonda, C. S., & Bornstein, M. H. (2000). Mothers' attuned responses to infant affect expressivity promote earlier achievement of language milestones. *Infant Behavior and Development, 22,* 557-568.

NICHD Early Child Care Research Network. (1999). Chronicity of maternal depressive symptoms, maternal sensitivity, and child functioning at 36 months. *Developmental Psychology, 35,* 1297-1310.

Nowakowski, R. S., & Hayes, N. L. (1999). CNS development: An overview. *Development and Psychopathology, 11,* 395-417.

Nowicki, S., & Duke, M. P. (1994). Individual differences in the nonverbal communication of affect: The Diagnostic Analysis of Nonverbal Accuracy Scale. *Journal of Nonverbal Behavior, 18,* 9-35.

Offer, D., Ostrov, E., Howard, K. I., & Dolan, S. (1992). *Offer Self-Image Questionnaire–Revised.* Los Angeles: Western Psychological Services.

O'Connor, T., Bredenkamp, D., Rutter, M., & English and Romanian Adoption Group. (1999). Attachment disturbances and disorders in infants exposed to early severe deprivation. *Infant Mental Health Journal, 20,* 10-29.

Ostrosky, M. M., Kaiser, A. P., & Odom, S. L. (1993). Facilitating children's social-communicative interactions through the use of peer-predicted interventions. In A. P. Kaiser (Ed.), *Enhancing children's communication: Research foundation for intervention* (pp. 159-185). Baltimore, MD: Paul H. Brookes.

Papoûsek, H., & Papoûsek, M. (1986). Structure and dynamics of human communication at the beginning of life. *European Archives of Psychiatric and Neurologic Sciences, 236,* 21-25.

Parker, J. G., & Asher, S. R. (1987). Peer relations and later personal adjustment: Are low-accepted children at risk? *Psychological Bulletin, 102,* 357-389.

Patterson, G. R., DeBaryshe, B. D., & Ramsey, E. (1989). A developmental perspective on antisocial behavior. *American Psychologist, 44,* 329-335.

Patterson, J., & Westby, C. (1994). The development of play. In W. O. Haynes & B. B. Shulman (Eds.), *Communication development: Foundation processes and clinical application* (pp. 135-161). Englewood Cliffs, NJ: Prentice Hall.

Paul, R. (1993). Patterns of development in late talkers. *Journal of Childhood Communication Disorders, 15,* 7-14.

Paul, R. (1995). *Language disorders from infancy through adolescence: Assessment and intervention.* St. Louis, MO: C. V. Mosby.

Paul, R. (1996). Clinical implications of the natural history of slow expressive language development. *American Journal of Speech-Language Pathology, 5,* 5-18.

Paul, R., & Smith R. (1993). Narrative skills in four year olds with normal, impaired, and late developing language. *Journal of Speech and Hearing Research, 36,* 592-598.

Paul, R., Spangle-Looney, S. S., & Dahm, P. S. (1991). Communications and socialization skills at 2 and 3 in "late-talking" children. *Journal of Speech and Hearing Research, 34,* 858-865.

Pelaez-Nogueras, M., Field, T., Cigales, M., Gonzalez, A., & Clasky, S. (1994). Infants of depressed mothers show less depressed behavior with their nursery teachers. *Infant Mental Health Journal, 15,* 358-367

Pennington, B. L., Bennetto, L., McAleer, N., & Roberts, R. J. (1996). Executive functions and working memory: Theoretical and measurement issues. In G. R. Lyon & N. A. Krasnegor

(Eds.), *Attention, memory, and executive function* (pp. 322-348). Baltimore, MD: Paul H. Brookes.

Pennington, B. F., Groisser, D., & Welsh, M. C. (1993). Contrasting cognitive deficits in Attention Deficit Hyperactivity Disorder versus reading disability. *Developmental Psychology, 29,* 511-523.

Perry, B. D., Pollard, R. A., Blakley, T. L., Baker, W. L., & Vigilante, D. (1995). Childhood trauma, the neurobiology of adaptation and "use dependence" development of the brain: How "states" become "traits." *Infant Mental Health Journal, 16,* 271-289.

Piers, E. V., & Harris, D. B. (1984). *Piers-Harris Children's Self-Concept Scale–Revised.* Toronto: WPS.

Pine, F. (1985). *Developmental theory and clinical process.* New Haven, CT: Yale University Press.

Pollak, S., Cicchetti, D., Klorman, R., & Brumaghim, J. (1997). Cognitive brain event-related potential and emotion processing in maltreated children. *Child Development, 68,* 773-787.

Powell, R. P., & Bishop, D. V. M. (1992). Clumsiness and perceptual problems in children with specific language impairment. *Developmental Medicine and Child Neurology, 34,* 755-765.

Prizant, B. M. (1999). Early intervention: Young children with communication and emotional/behavioral problems. In D. L. Rogers-Adkinson & P. L. Griffith (Eds.), *Communication disorders and children with psychiatric and behavior disorders* (pp. 295-342). San Diego, CA: Singular Publishing.

Prutting, C. A. (1982). Pragmatics as social competence. *Journal of Speech and Hearing Disorders, 47,* 123-133.

Prutting, C. A., & Kirchner, D. M. (1987). A clinical appraisal of the pragmatic aspects of language. *Journal of Speech and Hearing Disorders, 52,* 105-119.

Puckering, C., & Rutter, M. (1987). Environmental influences on language development. In W. Yule & M. Rutter (Eds.), *Language development and disorders* (pp. 102-128). London: MacKeith.

Purvis, K. L., & Tannock, R. (1997). Language abilities in children with Attention Deficit Hyperactivity Disorder, reading disabilities, and normal controls. *Journal of Abnormal Child Psychology, 25,* 133-144.

Purvis, K. L., & Tannock, R. (2000). Phonological processing, not inhibitory control, differentiates ADHD and reading disability. *Journal of the American Academy of Child and Adolescent Psychiatry, 39,* 485-494.

Rapin, I. (1996). Practitioner review: Developmental language disorders: A clinical update. *Journal of Child Psychology and Psychiatry, 37,* 643-655.

Reich, C., Hambleton, D., & Houldin, B. (1977). The integration of hearing-impaired children in regular classrooms. *American Annals of the Deaf, 122,* 534-543.

Rescorla, L. (2000, July). *Early predictors of language and reading outcomes at age 13 for late talking toddlers.* Paper presented at the International Conference on Infant Studies, Brighton, UK.

Rescorla, L., & Schwartz, E. (1990). Outcomes of toddlers with specific expressive language delay. *Applied Psycholinguistics 11,* 393-407.

Reynell, J. (1985). *Reynell Developmental Language Scales* (2nd ed.). Windsor, UK: NFER-Nelson.

Reynolds, C., & Richmond, B. O. (1985). *Children's Manifest Anxiety Scale.* Los Angeles: Western Psychological Services.

Rice, M. L. (1993). "Don't talk to him; he's weird"; A social consequences account of language and social interaction. In A. P. Kaiser & D. B. Gray (Eds.), *Communication and language interventions series: Vol. 2. Enhancing children's communication: Research foundations for intervention* (pp. 139-158). Baltimore, MD: Paul H. Brookes.

Rice, M. L., Sells, M. A., & Hadley, P. A. (1991). Social interactions of speech and language impaired children. *Journal of Speech and Hearing Research, 34,* 1299-1307.

Richman, N., & Stevenson, J. (1977). Language delay in three-year olds. *Acta Pediatrica Belgica, 30,* 213-219.

Richman, N., Stevenson, J., & Graham, P. (1982). *Pre-school to school: A behavioural study.* New York: Academic Press.

Ripich, D. N., & Griffith, P. L. (1988). Narrative abilities of children with learning disabilities and nondisabled children: Story structure, cohesion, and proportions. *Journal of Learning Disabilities, 3,* 165-173.

Robertson, C., & Salter, W. (1997). *The Phonological Awareness Test.* East Moline, IL: LinguiSystems.

Robertson, S. B., & Weismer, S. E. (1999). Effects of treatment on linguistic and social skills in toddlers with delayed language development. *Journal of Speech, Language, and Hearing Research, 42,* 1234-1248.

Rock, E. E., Fessler, M. A., & Church, R. P. (1997). The concomitance of learning disabilities and emotional/behavioral disorder: A conceptual model. *Journal of Learning Disabilities, 30,* 245-263.

Rosner, J. (1975). *Test of Auditory Analysis Skills.* Novato, CA: Academic Therapy Publications.

Rossetti, L. (1990). *Infant-Toddler Language Scale.* East Moline, IL: LinguiSystems.

Roth, F. P. (1986). Oral narratives of learning disabled students. *Topics in Language Disorders, 7,* 21-30.

Rovee-Collier, C. K. (1990). The "memory system" of prelinguistic infants. In A. Diamond (Ed.), *The development and neural bases of higher cognitive functions* (pp. 517-542). New York: New York Academy of Sciences.

Rubin, K. H., Hymel, S., & Mills, R. (1989). Sociability and social withdrawal in childhood: Stability and outcomes. *Journal of Personality, 57,* 237-255.

Russ, S. W. (1998). Special section on developmentally based integrated psychotherapy with children: Emerging models. Introductory comments. *Journal of Clinical Child Psychology, 27,* 2-3.

Russell , R. L. (1998). Linguistic psychotherapy research: New directions and promising findings. *Journal of Clinical Child Psychology, 27,* 17-27.

Russell, R. L., Greenwald, S., & Shirk, S. R. (1991). Language change in child psychotherapy: A meta-analytic review. *Journal of Consulting and Clinical Psychology, 59,* 916-919.

Russell, R. L., van den Broek, P., Adams, S., Rosenberger, K., & Essig, T. (1993). Analyzing narratives in psychotherapy: A formal framework and empirical analyses. *Journal of Narrative and Life History, 3,* 337-360.

Rutter, M. (1979). Protective factors in children's responses to stress and disadvantage. In M. W. Kent & J. E. Rolf (Eds.), *Primary prevention of psychopathology: 3. Social competence in children* (pp. 49-74). Hanover, NH: University Press of New England.

Rutter, M. (1985). Resilience in the face of adversity: Protective factors and resistance to psychiatric disturbances. *British Journal of Psychiatry, 147,* 598-611.

Rutter, M. (1995). Clinical implications of attachment concepts: Retrospect and prospect. *Journal of Child Psychology and Psychiatry, 36,* 549-571.

Rutter, M., Dunn, J., Plomin, R., Simonoff, E., Pickles, A., Maughan, B., Ormel, J., Meyer, J., & Eaves, L. (1997). Integrating nature and nurture: Implications of person-environment correlations and interactions for developmental psychopathology. *Development and Psychopathology, 9,* 335-364.

Rutter M., & Giller, H. (1983). *Juvenile delinquency: Trends and perspectives.* Harmondsworth, UK: Penguin.

Rutter, M., & Mawhood, L. (1991). The long-term sequelae of specific developmental disorders of speech and language. In M. Rutter & P. Casaer (Eds.), *Biological risk factors in childhood and psychopathology* (pp. 233-259). Cambridge, UK: Cambridge University Press.

Sattler, J. (1992). *Assessment of children* (3rd ed.). San Diego, CA: Author.

Sattler, J. M., Feldman, J., & Bohanan, A. L. (1985). Parental estimates of children's receptive vocabulary. *Psychology in the Schools, 22,* 303-307.

Schuhmann, E. M., Foote, R. C., Eyberg, S. M., Boggs, S. R., & Algina, J. (1998). Efficacy of parent-child interaction therapy: Interim report of a randomized trial with short-term maintenance. *Journal of Clinical Child Psychology, 27,* 34-45.

Schultz, L. H., & Selman, R. L. (1989). Bridging the gap between interpersonal thought and action in adolescence: The role of psychodynamic processes. *Development and Psychopathology, 1,* 133-152.

Schultz, L. H., Yeates, K. O., & Selman, R. L. (1989). *The Interpersonal Negotiation Strategies (INS) Interview: A scoring manual.* Cambridge, MA: Harvard Graduate School of Education.

Seligman, M. E. P. (1995). The effectiveness of psychotherapy: The *Consumer Reports* study. *American Psychologist, 50,* 965-974.

Selman, R. L. (1980). *The growth of interpersonal understanding: Developmental and clinical analyses.* New York: Academic Press.

Selman, R. L., Beardslee, W., Schultz, L. H., Krupa, M., & Podorefsky, D. (1986). Assessing adolescent interpersonal negotiation strategies: Toward the integration of functional and structural models. *Developmental Psychology, 22,* 450-459.

Selman, R. L., & Schultz, L. H. (1988). Interpersonal thought and action in the case of a troubled early adolescent: Toward a developmental model of the gap. In S. R. Shirk (Ed.), *Cognitive development and child psychotherapy: Perspectives in developmental psychology* (pp. 207-246). New York: Plenum.

Selman, R. L., & Schultz, L. H. (1990). *Making a friend in youth: Developmental theory and pair theory.* Chicago: University of Chicago Press.

Selman, R. L., Watts, C. L., & Schultz, L. H. (1997). *Fostering friendships: Pair therapy for treatment and prevention.* New York: Aldine De Gruyter.

Semel, E., Wiig, E., & Secord, W. (1995). *Clinical Evaluation of Language Fundamentals–3.* San Antonio, TX: Psychological Corporation.

Semel, E., Wiig, E., & Secord, W. (1996a). *Clinical Evaluation of Language Fundamentals–3. Observational Rating Scales.* San Antonio, TX: Psychological Corporation.

Semel, E., Wiig, E., & Secord, W. (1996b). *Clinical Evaluation of Language Fundamentals–3. Screening Test.* San Antonio, TX: Psychological Corporation.

Sharp, D., Hay, D., Pawlby, S., Schmucker, G., Allen, H., & Kumar, R. (1995). The impact of postnatal depression on boys' intellectual development. *Journal of Child Psychology and Psychiatry, 36,* 1315-1336.

Shatz, M., Wellman, H. M., & Silber, S. (1983). The acquisition of mental verbs: A systematic investigation of the first reference to mental state. *Cognition, 14,* 301-321.

Shaywitz, S. E. (1996). Dyslexia. *Scientific American, 275,* 98-104.

Shedler, J., Mayman, M., & Manis, M. (1993). The illusion of mental health. *American Psychologist, 48,* 1117-1131.

Sheslow, D., & Adams, W. (1990). *Wide Range Assessment of Memory and Learning.* Wilmington, DE: Jastak Associates.

Shirk, S. R. (1998). Interpersonal schemata in child psychotherapy: A cognitive-interpersonal perspective. *Journal of Clinical Child Psychology, 27,* 4-16.

Shirk, S. R., & Russell, R. L. (1996). *Change processes in child psychotherapy.* New York: Guilford.

Shriberg, L. D., Friel-Patti, S., Flipsen, P., & Brown, R. L. (2000). Otitis media, fluctuant hearing loss, and speech-language outcomes: A preliminary structural equation model. *Journal of Speech, Language, and Hearing Research 43,* 100-120.

Shure, M. B., & Spivack, G. (1982). Interpersonal problem-solving in young children: A cognitive approach to prevention. *Medical Journal of Community Psychology, 10,* 341-356.

Siegel, L. S. (1982). Reproductive, perinatal, and environmental factors as predictors of the cognitive and language development of preterm and full-term infants. *Child Development, 53,* 963-973.

Siegel, L., Cooper, D. C., Fitzhardinge, P. M., & Ash, A. J., (1995). The use of the Mental Development Index of the Bayley Scale to diagnose language delay in 2-year-old high-risk infants. *Infant Behavior and Development, 18,* 483-486.

Siegler, R. S. (2000). The rebirth of children's learning. *Child Development, 71,* 26-35.

Silva, P. A. (1980). The prevalence, stability, and significance of developmental language delay in preschool children. *Developmental Medicine and Child Neurology, 22,* 768-777.

Silva, P. A., Justin, C., McGee, R., & Williams, S. M. (1984). Some developmental and behavioral characteristics of seven-year-old children with delayed speech development. *British Journal of Disorders of Communication, 19,* 147-154.

Silva, P. A., McGee, R. O., & Williams, S. M. (1983). Developmental language delay from three to seven years and its significance for low intelligence and reading difficulties at age seven. *Developmental Medicine and Child Neurology, 25,* 783-793.

Silva, P. A., Williams, S. M., & McGee, R. (1987). A longitudinal study of children with developmental language delay at age three: Later intelligence, reading, and behavior problems. *Developmental Medicine and Child Neurology, 25,* 783-793.

Simon, C. S. (1994). *Evaluating Communicative Competence–Revised.* Tempe, AZ: Communi-Cog Publications.

Skarakis-Doyle, E., & Prutting, C. (1988). Characteristics of symbolic play in language disordered children. *Human Communication Canada, 12,* 7-17.

Skuse, D. (1984). Extreme deprivation in early childhood: II. Theoretical issues and a comparative review. *Journal of Child Psychology and Psychiatry, 25,* 543-572.

Slomkowski, C. L., Nelson, K., Dunn, J., & Plomin, R. (1992). Temperament and language: Relations from toddlerhood to middle childhood. *Developmental Psychology, 28,* 1090-1095.

Snowling, M., Bishop, D. V. M., & Stothard, S. E. (2000). Is preschool language impairment a risk factor for dyslexia in adolescence? *Journal of Child Psychology and Psychiatry, 41,* 487-600.

Spivack, G., Platt, J., & Shure, M. (1976). *The problem-solving approach to adjustment.* San Francisco: Jossey-Bass.

Sroufe, L. A. (1997). Psychopathology as an outcome of development. *Development and Psychopathology, 9,* 251-268.

Sroufe, L. A., & Waters, E. (1977). Attachment as an organizational construct. *Child Development, 48,* 1184-1199.

Stacey, K. (1994). Language as an exclusive or inclusive concept: Reaching beyond the verbal. *Australia and New Zealand Journal of Family Therapy, 16,* 123-132.

Stanovich, K. E. (1986). Matthew effects in reading: Some consequences of individual differences in the acquisition of literacy. *Reading Research Quarterly, 21,* 360-397.

Stanovich, K. E. (1988). Explaining the difference between the dyslexic and garden-variety poor readers: The phonological-core variable-difference model. *Journal of Learning Disabilities, 21,* 590-603.

Stark, R. E., & Tallal, P. (1981). Selection of children with specific language deficits. *Journal of Speech and Hearing Disorders, 46,* 114-122.

Stattin, H., & Klackenberg-Larsson, J. (1993). Early language and intelligence development and their relationship to future criminal behaviour. *Journal of Abnormal Psychology, 102,* 369-378.

Staub, E., & Eisenberg, N. (1981). Social cognition, affect, and behavior: An essay [and review of Robert Selman's *The growth of interpersonal understanding: Developmental and clinical analysis.*] *Developmental Review, 1,* 385-402.

Steinberg, L., & Avenevoli, S. (2000). The role of context in the development of psychopathology: A conceptual framework and some speculative propositions. *Child Development, 71,* 66-74.

Steinhausen, H., & Juzi, C. (1996). Elective mutism: Analysis of 100 cases. *Journal of the American Academy of Child and Adolescent Psychiatry, 35,* 606-614.

Stern, D. N. (1985). *The interpersonal world of the infant: A view from psychoanalysis and developmental psychology.* New York: Basic Books.

Stevens, L. J., & Bliss, L. S. (1995). Conflict resolution abilities of children with specific language impairment and children with normal language. *Journal of Speech and Hearing Research, 38,* 599-611.

Stoel-Gammon, C. (1998). Role of babbling and phonology in early linguistic development. In A. M. Wetherby, S. F. Warren, & J. Reichle (Eds.), *Transitions in prelinguistic communication* (pp. 87-110). Baltimore, MD: Paul H. Brookes.

Stothard, S. E., Snowling, M. J., Bishop, D. V. M., Chipchase, B., & Kaplan, C. A. (1998). Language-impaired preschoolers: A follow-up into adolescence. *Journal of Speech, Language, and Hearing Research, 41,* 407-418.

Swanson, H. L. (1994). Short-term memory and working memory: Do both contribute to our understanding of academic achievement in children and adults with learning disabilities? *Journal of Learning Disabilities, 27,* 34-50.

Szatmari, P., Boyle, M., Offord, D., Siegel, L. S., Finlayson, M. A. J., & Tuff, L. (1990). The clinical significance of neurocognitive impairments among children with psychiatric disorders: Diagnosis and situational specificity. *Journal of Child Psychology and Psychiatry, 31,* 287-299.

Tager-Flusberg, H. (1999). Language development in atypical children. In M. Barrett (Ed.), *The development of language* (pp. 311-348). Hove, UK: Psychology Press.

Tallal, P., Sainburg, R., & Jernigan, T. (1991). Neuropathology of developmental dysphasia. *Reading and Writing, 4,* 65-79.

Tallal, P., Stark, R., Kallman, C., & Mellits, D. (1981). A re-examination of some nonverbal perceptual abilities of language-impaired and normal children as a function of age and sensory modality. *Journal of Speech and Hearing Research, 24,* 351-357.

Tannock, R. (1998). Attention deficit hyperactivity disorder: Advances in cognitive, neurological, and genetic research. *Journal of Child Psychology and Psychiatry, 39,* 65-99.

Tannock, R., Girolametto, L., & Siegel, L. S. (1992). Language intervention with children who have developmental delays: Effects of an interactive approach. *American Journal on Mental Retardation, 97,* 145-160.

Tannock, R., Purvis, K. L., & Schachar, R. J. (1993). Narrative abilities in children with Attention Deficit Hyperactivity Disorder and normal peers. *Journal of Abnormal Child Psychology, 21,* 103-117.

Tannock, R., & Schachar, R. (1996). Executive dysfunction as an underlying mechanism of behavior and language problems in Attention Deficit Hyperactivity Disorder. In J. H. Beitchman, N. J. Cohen, M. M. Konstantareas, & R. Tannock (Eds.), *Language, learning, and behavior disorders: Developmental, biological, and clinical perspectives* (pp. 128-155). New York: Cambridge University Press.

Tarter, R. E., Hegedus, A. M., Winsten, N. E., & Alterman, A. I. (1984). Neuropsychological, personality, and familial characteristics of physically abused delinquents. *Journal of the American Academy of Child and Adolescent Psychiatry, 23,* 668-674.

Terrell, B. Y. (1994). Emergent literacy: In the beginning there was reading and writing. In D. N. Ripich & N. A. Creaghead (Eds.), *School discourse problems* (pp. 9-27), San Diego, CA: Singular Publishing.

Thal, D., & Katich, J. (1996). Predicaments in early identification of specific language impairment: Does the early bird always catch the worm? In K. N. Cole, P. S. Dale, & D. J. Thal (Eds.), *Assessment of communication and language* (Vol. 6, pp. 1-28). Baltimore, MD: Paul H. Brookes.

Thal, D., Tobias, S., & Morrison, D. (1991). Language and gesture in late talkers: A 1-year follow-up. *Journal of Speech and Hearing Research, 34,* 604-612.

Thorndike, R., Hagen, E., & Sattler, J. (1986). *Stanford-Binet Intelligence Scale–4.* Chicago: Riverside.

Tomasello, M. (1995). Understanding the self as a social agent. In P. Rochat (Ed.), *The self in infancy: Theory and research* (pp. 449-460). Amsterdam: Elsevier.

Torgesen, J. K. (1994). Issues in the assessment of executive functions: An information processing perspective. In G. R. Lyon (Ed.), *Frames of reference for the assessment of learning disabilities: New views on measurement issues* (pp. 143-162). Baltimore, MD: Paul H. Brookes.

Torgesen, J. K., & Bryant, B. R. (1994). *Test of Phonological Awareness.* Austin, TX: Pro-Ed.

Trevarthen, C. (1979). Communication and cooperation in early infancy: A description of primary intersubjectivity. In M. Bullowa (Ed.), *Before speech: The beginning of interpersonal communication* (pp. 321-348), Cambridge, UK: Cambridge University Press.

Tronick, E. (1989). Emotions and emotional communication in infancy. *American Psychologist, 44,* 112-149.

U.S. Department of Education. (1998). *To assure the free appropriate public education of all Americans: Twentieth annual report to Congress on the implementation of the Individuals With Disabilities Education Act* (Publication No. 1998-716-372/93547). Washington, DC: Government Printing Office.

Vallance, D. D., & Cohen, N. J. (1998). [Development of the capacity to understand complex emotions in children with language impairment and normal controls]. Unpublished raw data.

Vallance, D. D., Im, N., & Cohen, N. J. (1999). Discourse deficits associated with psychiatric disorders and with language impairments in children. *Journal of Child Psychology and Psychiatry, 40,* 693-704.

Vallance, D. D., & Wintre, G. M. (1997). Discourse processes underlying social competence in children with language learning disabilities. *Development and Psychopathology, 9,* 95-108.

van den Broek, P. (1997). Discovering the cement of the universe: The development of event comprehension from childhood to adulthood. In P. W. van den Broek, P. J. Bauer, & T. Bourg (Eds.), *Developmental spans in event comprehension and representation* (pp. 321-342). Mahwah, NJ: Lawrence Erlbaum.

van IJzendoorn, M. H., Dijkstra, J., & Bus, A. G. (1995). Attachment, intelligence, and language: A meta-analysis. *Social Development, 4,* 115-128.

van IJzendoorn, M. H., Goldberg, S., Kroonenberg, P. M., & Frenkel, O. J. (1992). The relative effects of maternal and child problems on the quality of attachment: A meta-analysis of attachment in clinical samples. *Child Development, 73,* 840-858.

Vernberg, E. M. (1998). Developmentally based psychotherapies: Comments and observations. *Journal of Clinical Child Psychology, 27,* 46-48.

Vernberg, E., Routh, P., & Koocher, G. (1992). The future of psychotherapy with children. *Psychotherapy, 29,* 72-80.

Vygotsky, L. S. (1962). *Thought and language.* New York: John Wiley.

Vygotsky, L. S. (1978). *Mind in society: The development of higher psychological processes.* Cambridge, MA: Harvard University Press.

Wagner, C. O., Gray, L. L., & Potter, R. E. (1983). Communicative disorders in a group of adult female offenders. *Journal of Communication Disorders, 16,* 269-277.

Warr-Leeper, G., Wright, N. A., & Mack, A. (1994). Language disabilities of antisocial boys in residential treatment. *Behavioral Disorders, 19,* 159-169.

Waters, E., Merrick, S., Treboux, D., Crowell, J., & Albersheim, L. (2000). Attachment security and early adulthood: A twenty-year longitudinal study. *Child Development, 71,* 684-689.

Webster, D. D., Brown-Triolo, D., & Griffith, P. L. (1999). Linguistic factors affecting personality assessment of children and adolescents. In D. Rogers-Adkinson & P. Griffith (Eds.), *Communication disorders and children with psychiatric and behavioral disorders* (pp. 259-294). San Diego, CA: Singular Publishing.

Webster-Stratton, C. (1989). *Parents and children: A ten program videotape parent training series with manuals.* Eugene, OR: Catalia Press.

Wechsler, D. (1989). *Wechsler Preschool and Primary Scale of Intelligence–Revised: Manual.* San Antonio, TX: Psychological Corporation.

Wechsler, D. (1991). *Wechsler Intelligence Scale for Children–Third Revision.* San Antonio, TX: Psychological Corporation.

Wechsler, D. (1992). *Wechsler Individual Achievement Test.* San Antonio, TX: Psychological Corporation.

Wechsler, D. (1997). *Wechsler Adult Intelligence Scale–III.* San Antonio, TX: Psychological Corporation.

Weismer, S. E., Evans, J., & Hesketh, L. J. (1999). An examination of verbal working memory capacity in children with specific language impairment. *Journal of Speech, Language, and Hearing Research, 42,* 1249-1260.

Weisz, J. R., & Weiss, B. (1993). *Effects of psychotherapy with children and adolescents.* Newbury Park, CA: Sage.

Weitzman, E. (1992). *Learning language and loving it.* Toronto: The Hanen Centre.

Werker, J., & Pegg, J. (1992). Infant speech perception and phonological acquisition. In C. Ferguson, L. Menn, & C. Stoel-Gammon (Eds.), *Phonological development* (pp. 285-312). Timonium, MD: York Press.

Werner, E. (1989). High-risk children in young adulthood: A longitudinal study from birth to 32 years. *American Journal of Orthopsychiatry, 59,* 72-81.

Westby, C. (1999). Assessment of pragmatic competence in children with psychiatric disorders. In D. Rogers-Adkinson & P. Griffith (Eds.), *Communication disorders and children with psychiatric and behavioral disorders* (pp. 177-258). San Diego, CA: Singular Publishing.

Westby, C. E., & Cutler, S. K. (1994). Language and ADHD: Understanding the bases and treatment of self-regulatory deficits. *Topics in Language Disorders, 14,* 58-76.

Wetherby, A. M., & Prizant. B. M (1992). Profiling young children's communicative competence. In S. Warren & J. Reichle (Eds.), *Causes and effects in communication and language intervention* (pp. 217-253). Baltimore, MD: Paul H. Brookes.

Wetherby, A. M., & Prizant, B. M. (1993a). *Communication and Symbolic Behavior Scales.* Chicago: Riverside Publishing.

Wetherby, A. M., & Prizant, B. M. (1993b). Profiling communication and symbolic activities in young children. *Journal of Childhood Communicative Disorder, 15,* 23-32.

Wetherby, A. M., & Prizant, B. M. (1997). *CSBS Quick-Score.* Chicago: Applied Symbolix.

Wetherby, A. M., & Prizant, B. M. (1998). *Infant/Toddler Checklist for Communication and Language Development.* Chicago: Applied Symbolix.

Whitehurst, G. J. (1997). Language process in context. In L. B. Adamson & M. A. Romski (Eds.), *Communication and language acquisition: Discoveries from atypical development* (pp. 233-265). Baltimore, MD: Paul H. Brookes.

Whitehurst, G. J., & Fischel, J. E. (1994). Practitioner review: Early developmental language delay: What, if anything, should the clinician do about it? *Journal of Child Psychology and Psychiatry, 35,* 613-648.

Whitehurst, G. J., Fischel, J. E., Lonigan, C. J., Valdez-Menchaca, M. C., DeBaryshe, B. D., & Caulfield, M. B. (1988). Verbal interaction in families of normal and expressive language delayed children. *Developmental Psychology, 24,* 690-699.

Wickstrom-Kane, S., & Goldstein, H. (1999). Communication assessment and behavior in toddlers. *Topics in Language Disorders, 19,* 70-89.

Wiederholt, J. L., & Bryant, B. R. (1992). *Gray Oral Reading Test–3.* Austin, TX: Pro-Ed.

Wiig, E. (1984). Language disabilities in adolescents: A question of cognitive strategies. *Topics in Language Disorders, 4,* 41-58.

Wiig, E. H., & Secord, W. (1989). *Test of Language Competence–Expanded Edition.* San Antonio, TX: Psychological Corporation.

Wiig, E. H., Secord, W., & Semel, E. (1992). *Clinical Evaluation of Language Fundamentals– Preschool.* San Antonio, TX: Psychological Corporation.

Wiig, E., & Semel, E. (1973). Comprehension of linguistic concepts requiring logical operations by learning disabled children. *Journal of Speech and Hearing Research, 16,* 627-636.

Williams, K. T. (1997). *Expressive Vocabulary Test.* Circle Pines, MN: American Guidance Service.

Williams, S., & McGee, R. (1994). Reading attainment and juvenile delinquency. *Journal of Child Psychology and Psychiatry, 35,* 441-459.

Williams, S., & McGee, R. (1996). Reading in childhood and mental health in early adulthood. In J. H. Beitchman, N. J. Cohen, M. M. Konstantareas, & R. Tannock (Eds.), *Language, learning, and behavior disorders: Developmental, biological, and clinical perspectives* (pp. 530-554). New York: Cambridge University Press.

Willmer, S. K., & Crane, R. (1979). A parental dilemma: The child with marginal handicap. *Social Casework, 60,* 30-35.

Wimmer, H., & Perner, J. (1983). Beliefs about beliefs: Representation and the constraining function of wrong beliefs in young children's understanding of deception. *Cognition, 13,* 103-128.

Windsor, J. (1995). Language impairment and social competence. In M. E. Fey, J. Windsor, & S. F. Warren (Eds.), *Language intervention: Preschool through the elementary years* (Vol. 5, pp. 213-240). Baltimore, MD: Paul H. Brookes.

Wolraich, M. L., Felice, M. E., & Drotar, D. (1997). *The classification of child and adolescent mental diagnoses in primary care.* Elk Grove Village, IL: American Academy of Pediatrics.

Wood, M., & Valdez-Menchaca, M. (1996). The effect of a diagnostic label of language delay on adults' perception of preschool children. *Journal of Learning Disabilities, 29,* 582-588.

Woodcock, R. W., Johnson, M. B., Mather, N., McGrew, K. S., & Werder, J. K. (1991). *Woodcock-Johnson Psychoeducational Battery–Revised.* Allen, TX: DLM Teaching Resources.

World Health Organization. (1993). *The ICD-10 classification of mental and behavioural disorders.* Geneva: Author.

Yeates, K. O., & Selman, R. L. (1989). Social competence in the schools: Toward an integrative developmental model for intervention. *Developmental Review, 9,* 64-100.

Yeates, K. O., Schultz, L. H., & Selman, R. L. (1990). Bridging the gaps in child-clinical assessment: Toward the application of social-cognitive developmental theory. *Clinical Psychology Review, 10,* 567-588.

Yeates, K. O., Schultz, L. H., & Selman, R. L. (1991). The development of interpersonal negotiation strategies in thought and action: A social-cognitive link to behavioral adjustment and social status. *Merrill-Palmer Quarterly, 37,* 369-406.

Yoder, P. J., Warren, S. J., McCathren, R., & Leew, S. V. (1998). Does adult responsivity facilitate communication development? In A. M. Wetherby, S. F. Warren, & J. Reichle (Eds.), *Transactions in prelinguistic communication* (pp. 39-55). Baltimore, MD: Paul H. Brookes.

Young, A., Beitchman, J. H., Johnson, C. J., Atkinson, L., Escobar, M., Douglas, L., & Wilson, B. (2000). *Young adult academic outcomes in a longitudinal sample of speech/language impaired and control children.* Manuscript submitted for publication.

Zeanah, C. H. (1996). Beyond insecurity: A reconceptualization of clinical disorders of attachment. *Journal of Consulting and Clinical Psychology, 64,* 42-52.

Zeanah, C. H., Boris, N. W., & Scheeringa, M. S. (1997). Psychopathology in infancy. *Journal of Child Psychology and Psychiatry, 81,* 81-100.

Zentall, S. (1988). Production deficiencies in elicited language but not in the spontaneous verbalizations of hyperactive children. *Journal of Abnormal Child Psychology, 16,* 657-673.

Zero to Three/National Center for Clinical Infant Programs. (1994). *Diagnostic classification: 0-3. Diagnostic classification of mental health and developmental disorders of infancy and early childhood.* Arlington, VA: Author.

Zimmerman, I. L., Steiner, V., & Pond, R. (1992). *Preschool Language Scale–3.* San Antonio, TX: Psychological Corporation.

AUTHOR INDEX

SUBJECT INDEX

Abuse. *See* Child abuse/neglect
Adaptive functioning, 167
Adolescence:
  academic achievement, 90-91
  affect/behavior regulation, 93
  child abuse and language
    development, 57-58
  developmental tasks of, 87-89
  language/cognitive development,
    89-91
  language impairment and, 89, 90-91,
    93-96
  literacy skills and, 40
  mental health services and, 93-96
  problem solving in, 36, 90
  social-emotional development, 91-93
  thinking, conscious control of, 90
Affect-Extraversion measurement, 59, 60
Affect regulation, 29-30
  adolescents and, 93
  attachment figures and, 50
  conversation, prescriptive/self-
    directed, 49
  goal-corrected partnership and, 50-
    51, 66
  intersubjectivity and, 43
  joint attention interactions and, 49-50
  middle childhood and, 75-76
  misunderstandings and, 50-51
  preschoolers and, 68
  psychopathology and, 55-56
  sensitive/contingent responding and,
    45-46
  social referencing, 48
  trade-off model of expression, 48-49

verbal control and, 48-49, 50
Ages and Stages Questionnaire, 104
Ambivalent attachment, 31
American Speech-Language-Hearing
  Association (ASHA), 115
Anxiety disorders, 7, 17 (table), 20-21
Aphasia, 4
Articulation disorder, 6-7
Assessment, 3-4, 79
  achievement, 118-119
  caregiver-infant interaction, 128-129,
    129-130 (table)
  cognitive ability, 115-118
  communication competence, 107-115
  constitutional factors, 101-102
  developmental psychopathology,
    perspective of, 99-100
  dynamic assessment techniques, 106
  emotion recognition/understanding,
    119, 120-121 (table)
  environmental factors, 102-103
  executive functions, 117-118
  family history, 102
  feedback session, 133-135
  hearing screening/assessment, 103-
    104
  interviews, family, teachers, subject,
    100-103
  language impairment, 106-107, 114-
    115
  memory, 117
  mind, theory of, 120-121(table), 123
  narrative discourse skills, 109-113,
    111 (table)
  play, 124-128, 126-127 (table)

207

ABOUT THE AUTHOR

Nancy J. Cohen is Director of Research at the Hincks-Dellcrest Centre for Children's Mental Health and the Hincks-Dellcrest Institute. She is also Professor of Psychiatry at the University of Toronto and Adjunct Professor of Psychology at York University. Since receiving her doctorate in developmental psychopathology from McGill University in Montreal, she has published widely about the overlap of language impairment and psychopathology, infant mental health, and adoption. Currently, she has expanded her research to include community-based interventions for infants and preschoolers aimed at preventing language-based problems. She has served as a consultant to numerous projects and community agencies and has made presentations and conducted workshops on language impairment and psychopathology, postadoption services, and infant- and child-led interventions both nationally and internationally. She is coeditor of the book *Language Learning and Behavior Disorders* (Beitchman, Cohen, Konstantareas, and Tannock, 1996). She also is a consulting editor to the *Journal of Abnormal Child Psychology.* Along with her research, she has a private practice where she works primarily with children and their families.